Food and Culture in Contemporary American Fiction

Routledge Studies in Contemporary Literature

1. **Literature After 9/11**
   *Edited by Ann Keniston and
   Jeanne Follansbee Quinn*

2. **Reading Chuck Palahniuk**
   American Monsters and Literary
   Mayhem
   *Edited by Cynthia Kuhn
   and Lance Rubin*

3. **Beyond Cyberpunk**
   New Critical Perspectives
   *Edited by Graham J. Murphy
   and Sherryl Vint*

4. **Criticism, Crisis, and
   Contemporary Narrative**
   Textual Horizons in an
   Age of Global Risk
   Edited by Paul Crosthwaite

5. **Food and Culture in
   Contemporary American Fiction**
   Lorna Piatti-Farnell

Food and Culture in Contemporary American Fiction

Lorna Piatti-Farnell

Routledge
Taylor & Francis Group
LONDON AND NEW YORK

First published 2011 by Routledge

2 Park Square, Milton Park, Abingdon, Oxfordshire OX14 4RN
711 Third Avenue, New York, NY 10017

*Routledge is an imprint of the Taylor & Francis Group,
an informa business*

First issued in paperback 2018

Copyright © 2011 Taylor & Francis

Typeset in Sabon by IBT Global.

All rights reserved. No part of this book may be reprinted or reproduced or utilised in any form or by any electronic, mechanical, or other means, now known or hereafter invented, including photocopying and recording, or in any information storage or retrieval system, without permission in writing from the publishers.

Notice:
Product or corporate names may be trademarks or registered trademarks, and are used only for identification and explanation without intent to infringe.

Library of Congress Cataloging-in-Publication Data
Piatti-Farnell, Lorna, 1980-
　Food and culture in contemporary American fiction / by Lorna Piatti-Farnell.
　　p. cm.—(Routledge studies in contemporary literature ; 5)
　Includes bibliographical references and index.
　1. Food in literature. 2. American fiction—21st century—History and criticism. 3. American fiction—20th century—History and criticism. 4. Food habits in literature. 5. Cultural pluralism in literature. 6. Multiculturalism in literature. 7. Ethnicity in literature. I. Title.
　PS374.F63P53 2011
　813'.54093564—dc22
　2011008079

ISBN13: 978-0-415-88422-8 (hbk)
ISBN13: 978-1-138-54803-9 (pbk)

To Rob, who made it happen

Contents

	Acknowledgements	ix
	Introduction	1
1	Home and Away	18
2	Regionality	53
3	Race and History	76
4	Immigrant Identities	105
	Conclusion	149
	Notes	157
	Bibliography	177
	Index	187

Acknowledgements

I would like to thank my editor, Liz Levine, for her support throughout this project. Thanks also go to Erica Wetter, who accepted the book for publication in the first place.

I am grateful to all my University colleagues (old and new) who always showed enthusiasm and interest in my book. Thanks to Richard Canning, Claudia Capancioni and Claire Thomson at Bishop Grosseteste University College and Clare Hanson at University of Southampton. I am grateful to Brian Jarvis, my thesis supervisor at Loughborough University, for helping me to develop some of the ideas which later formed parts of this book. I am also grateful to the editors and publishers of *The Richard and Judy Book Club Reader* (Aldershot: Ashgate, 2011), as the chapter I wrote for their collection, 'The Delicious Side of the Story', inspired me to write short sections within this volume.

This book also wouldn't have happened without the support of my family and friends. Thanks to Gemma and Ian Gaskell, Jonathan and Maria Taylor, Andrew Dix, Marjory and David Farnell, Maria Beville and Jenna Pitchford. I am particularly indebted to Jenni Ramone, for her helpful advice and suggestions. Special thanks go to Fabrizio Rossi and Alessandra Mastrogiacomo, for their longstanding and sincere friendships.

A particular mention goes to my mamma and papá, Elena and Giorgio Piatti, who always believed in me and were only ever far in terms of geography.

Most of all, I would like to thank Rob Farnell . . . my bright star, my soul mate, my husband.

Introduction

> What we eat, where we get it, how it is prepared, when we eat and with whom, what it means to us—all these depend on social [and cultural] arrangements.
>
> —Marjorie DeVault, *Feeding the Family*[1]

According to the old adage, 'a day without bread is a long day indeed'. Food constitutes an inescapable necessity that all humans—like all living organisms—must access in order to survive. However, the significance of food for the species extends far beyond the essential nature of physical nourishment. Food intersects with all aspects of human existence: the material functions of food range from simple organic nourishment to being a symbolic agent in the development of socio-cultural politics. Although eating is a universal activity, food is constantly crossing boundaries and shifting registers—from biological to political, from economic to sexual. In a cultural framework, Wendy Leeds-Hurwitz argues, food serves 'as an indicator of social identity, from region to ethnicity, from class to age or gender'.[2] In response to this, my book addresses issues of food and culture in contemporary American fiction. My primary intention is to explore how multiple incarnations of the literary engage with essential connections between the preparation and consumption of food, and the formation of individual and cultural identity.

As a subject of study, food is not a new discovery. It is, however, a distinct prerogative. In a variety of disciplines—including sociology, cultural studies, gender studies, history, anthropology and literature—an interest in food has become increasingly evident. In recent years, seminal texts such as Stephen Mennell's *The Sociology of Food and Eating* (1983), Paul Fieldhouse's *Food and Nutrition* (1986) Deborah Lupton's *Food, the Body and the Self* (1996), Peter Atkins' *Food in Society: Economy, Culture, Geography* (2000) and George Ritzer's *The McDonaldization of Society* (2000) have contributed to the formation of an interdisciplinary field of research known collectively as 'food studies'.[3] These influential texts have drawn attention to how food interacts with different aspects of human life, focusing on important issues such as subjectivity and corporeality, economy, social organisation and globalisation. The increasingly wide-ranging academic interest should not come as a surprise. In itself, food is an interdisciplinary subject. Starting from the physical dimension of the body, food can move into political, social, cultural and economic relations. It is virtually impossible to pin down food to one aspect of life. Food is dynamic, malleable and subject to interpretation.

THE AMERICAN CULINARY

When it comes to food, history makes America an interesting continent. An overarching definition of 'the American culinary' appears split and dispersed into a multitude of different attitudes toward food and consumption. The development of America has been interlinked with immigration, a factor which has proved essential in the construction of a political and economic stability. Although populated by native populations for thousands of years, since it was allegedly 'discovered' by European explorers, the American continent has had the greatest influx of immigrants than any other land mass in the world. By the end of the nineteenth century, the famous metaphor of 'the melting pot' promoted the formation of an all-encompassing civilization which quickly came to be associated with the United States for many decades to come. Many saw America as the ideal embodiment of nations and cultures fusing together, all coexisting in the great nation that was hosting them.

Despite its strong stance not only in critical and historical texts, but also in the wider imaginary—a stance that is still, arguably, very prominent today—the metaphor of the melting pot features an array of conceptual problems. In principle, the idea of cultures melting together presupposes blending and synthesis (and therefore an extent of cultural erasure), promising the formation of a homogenous sense of nation and society. After 1970 the desirability of cultural assimilation—inherent to the idea of the melting pot—was openly challenged by vocal proponents of multiculturalism. The 'melting pot' image failed to satisfy in that it denied the possibility of cultural difference. Advocating the value of cultural resilience—and maintaining that different cultural belonging should be preserved—strands of sociology and cultural studies proposed the equally culinary-inspired alternative of the 'salad bowl', where separate cultures mix, and yet remain distinct.[4]

The current social status of the United States calls for expression of multiculturalism. The demographics of the country tell an important cultural tale; one in nine Americans is now 'foreign-born' and together with a very large number of 'ethnic group' members, they comprise over '30 percent' of the population.[5] With the country's history and current situation in mind, food becomes an inescapable cultural presence. As immigrants settled into the United States, they brought with them not only their language and their social structures, but also (and in particular) their food habits. The presence of different cuisines, however, does not stop with examples of individual homes or strict socio-cultural communities, where 'immigrant' or 'ethnic' food is consumed by selected members. One should only venture into any main street in any town or city in the United States to see an array of co-existing food joints which, more often than not bearing a certain level of ethnic affiliation, prove testimony to the level of multiculturalism and hybridisation which dominates the American culinary scene today.

Although this is not something which is only true of the Unites States, the country's prevalent history of immigration, assimilation and simultaneous cultural resistance draws attention to its variable and changeable gastronomic setting. If one is to believe that food habits, customs and cuisine are connected to a person's sense of identity, then it is not difficult to see how this high level of culinary multiculturalism questions the existence of a fully assimilated and homogenous American identity.

When it comes to highlighting the nature of food in an American context, however, both culinary metaphors—the melting pot and the salad bowl—appear to be inadequate. The age-old vision of the melting pot—promoting fusion, absorption and assimilation—seems to be at odds with today's realities of cultural mixture and exchange. In similar vein, the idea of envisioning identities as remaining completely separate does not answer the unavoidable demand for eclectic mainstream synthesis which incorporates different aspects from different cultures. Indeed, both metaphors deny the possibility that individuality and fusion can actually co-exist in a peculiar form of American culinary hybridisation. In a way, perhaps, it is necessary to rediscover 'the melting pot' of assimilation and consume it (as it were) together with a salad bowl of multiculturalism. This fundamental idea is what inspires my work.

This mixture of integration and confrontation lies at the heart of the American culinary paradox and must inform any analysis of food in the literary scene. A desire to explore multiple types of fiction is fuelled by a concrete awareness that, in literary terms, food cultures can emerge both as mainstream and marginal, central and subsidiary. It is perhaps necessary to find, as Tamar Jacoby suggests, a 'new definition' of assimilation, a way of considering the American dream of one nation which 'makes sense today', in an 'era of globalisation' and 'identity politics'.[6]

FOOD AND FICTION

Historically, there has been much interest in food and literature, particularly fiction.[7] The majority of critical works, however, are preoccupied with periods before that in which 'food studies' became prominent as an interdisciplinary field of research. As we get closer to fiction written during the time in which food studies became established, food/literary scholarship grows more scarce: Sarah Sceats' *Food, Consumption and the Body in Contemporary Women's Fiction* (2004) is a rare example of a major theoretically informed study of food in mid-to-late twentieth century literature.[8] In the context of such scholarly neglect, my contribution aims to offer a full-length study of food in contemporary American fiction. Although works of fiction, the novels provide a channel for expression which is interlinked with issues of social, cultural and ethnic affiliation. In its ability to be manipulated—both consciously and unconsciously by the author—literature allows us a very privileged view into eccentric and homely foodways, which are often moulded into specific story-telling threads and lead us into an exploration of character and society. In so doing, food, cooking and eating in contemporary American fiction cease to be simply themes, but—when looked at critically—develop into fully functional parts of the narrative which 'help define' the nature of 'the writing'.[9]

My selection of texts is not arbitrary. My choice is informed by the conviction that food is a collective necessity and there is a definite universality in eating practices that often transcends boundaries of geography. Simultaneously, however, I am aware of changing social attitudes to food and eating that can transform a basic activity into a specific cultural practice. Therefore, my decision to focus on writers from different times—primarily within a thirty year time-frame—and backgrounds in the American late twentieth and early twenty-first centuries is inspired by the dialogue between universality and individuality that is expressed by eating. As it has often been the case with analysis of fiction belonging to earlier historical periods, it is, as Doris Witt puts it, 'impossible to delineate in adequate detail the complex social circumstances from which these books have risen'.[10] As I am conscious of the multiple changes in context and circumstances which surround the writing of these texts, however, I strive to highlight how 'their heterogeneity' reflects 'the challenges' inherent to the conception of a stabilised American identity in the face of globalisation.[11]

Robert Lee asks an important question: 'How can America, or its literature, and from the puritans to the postmoderns, in any accurate sense ever have been thought other than multicultural?'[12] Lee's enquiry, although provocative in nature, does draw attention to the idea that while historically dominated by a Eurocentric sense of literary worth, America has not allowed diverse and multi-ethnic literary cultures to go unremarked. The main issue, of course, is to understand that diverse forms of fiction co-exist with mainstream white American writing, just like 'ethnic food' subsist with forms of what is understood by some as 'true American' food (with examples such as pancakes, hamburgers and apple pie featuring prevalently). Indeed, it is important to resist the temptation to marginalise immigrant texts or ethnic literature from 'canonical America' and define it as 'vernacular' or picturesque.[13]

As a result, it is not my intention to construct particular 'types' of fiction as mainstream or marginalise others. I do not intend to suggest some texts—say, for instance, African American—as completely detached from popular forms of what has become known as 'immigrant literature'—as in the case of Chinese or Italian American writers. Rather, I wish to analyse different shades of American literature that, far from being homogenised, are also not completely separate from one another. Indeed, these literary strands feed off each other, just like culinary traditions often blend and yet remain separate throughout America. In working within a wide range of American fiction—encapsulating thirty years of literary history—my approach takes after Lee's example and aims to map, compare and evaluate culinary visions in ethnic fiction, without excluding in any way that written by 'white-ethnic' American authors.[14]

However, in order to offer a level of analytical coherence to my book, I have divided my study into four separate, and yet inter-connected chapters. While this distinction is helpful in conceptual terms, it is important to remember that the shifting and malleable nature of food—touching on more than one aspect of life—will demand a level of flexibility between chapters and must allow for particular concepts (such as home and memory) to be present at different intersections. Chapter 1, 'Home and Away' focuses on depictions of eating inside and outside the home. Specifically, I analyse how contrasting concepts of 'home meals' and 'restaurant dining' intersect in works by Karen Stolz, Marylinne Robinson and Brett Easton Ellis. Employing primarily cultural materialist thinking, gender theory and anthropological perspectives, this chapter explores different kinds of food experiences among discordant classes of American eaters in contemporary fiction. On the one hand, I investigate Ellis' representations of fashionable restaurants, 'eating out' and chic food as cultural phenomena signalling the impact of advanced consumerism on American culinary identities. On the other, I map the presence of specific 'home' foods and drinks in Stolz and Robinson which show a particular cultural connection to American history. I also discuss how recognisable corporate signs and denominations (such as Coca-Cola) encourage a sense of cultural affiliation with an imagined 'American community'. In unveiling how slippery notions of 'public' and 'private' can be, I will reveal how eating allows the fiction to untangle racial, gender and economic politics. Chapter 2, 'Regionality', investigates how food can act as a social agent for local politics and construct a sense of regional pride in contemporary American fiction. Bearing in mind complicated notions of ethnocentrism and cultural alienation, I consider how concepts of reliability and authenticity question the validity of 'traditional foods' and encourage the idealised and compensatory formation of 'culinary groups'. Focusing specifically on examples of what is known as 'Southern literature' (the work of Fannie Flagg and Rebecca Wells in particular), I explore how the desire to maintain a connection to recognisable foods and methods of preparation remains present even in the face of momentous socio-historical changes. Attention will be given to the consumption of particular foods as examples of group affiliation, such as particular fish, meat and vegetables. This attachment to familiar, 'local' foods is shown as essential for the construction of individual and cultural identity, and simultaneously, as a deterrent in the establishment of a recognisable 'American cuisine'. The representation of food, consumption and cooking in contemporary African American fiction will be treated separately in Chapter 3, 'Race and History'; this reflects the particular social and historical formation of African American culinary identity and how it impacts on depictions of food in contemporary fiction. Concentrating on Ntozake Shange, Gloria Naylor, Toni Morrison and Edward P. Jones, the chapter contends that food imagery and culinary representations are used in African American fiction as a key trope in relation to racial stratification, typecasting and exploitation. I discuss how, particularly in the work of Shange, Jones and Morrison, elements such as 'hunger' (understood here as an emblematic symbol for racial oppression), sweetness and spirituality are skilfully satirised in connection to African American history of suffering and trauma. In similar vein, the chapter unveils how attachment to particular 'black foods' (or 'soul food') in Naylor and Shange is conveyed as an agent of resistance in the struggle against the colonisation of African American cultures by other cultural communities. In turn, Chapter 4, 'Immigrant Identities', focuses of what can be broadly be described as 'immigrant'—or 'hyphenated'—American fiction and concentrates on particular minority cultures. My discussion unravels how the concept of 'food preference' is influenced by specific socio-cultural factors, which are inevitably shaped by ethnic affiliation. Connecting patterns of food consumption in the work of Monique Truong and Amy Tan to notions of cultural and economic capital, my discussion investigates concepts of 'edible and 'inedible'—and, therefore, 'good' and 'bad'—food. Focusing particularly on representations of the family, domesticity, the exotic and the culinary experimental, the chapter explores different representations of culinary textures, looks and everyday eating habits. As cultural (and visceral) depictions of gastronomic likes, dislikes, assimilation and abjection are carefully scrutinised, the chapter establishes how cultural separations that mould food preferences inevitably affect the construction and existence of a homogenous American identity. I explore how the texts portray culinary preferences as interdependent upon both cultural knowledge and familiar experiences. I discuss how the idea of cuisine is inevitably related to the concept of 'tradition' within immigrant communities. As a result, my discussion gives attention to issues of culinary authenticity, questions the validity of 'traditional foods' and considers the idealised and compensatory formation of 'culinary groups'. Focusing on the work of Leslie Pietrzyk and Diana Abu-Jaber, Chapter 4 also investigates how, in examples from this specific sub-genre, representations of food habits and preferences are suffused by nostalgia, emotional attachment and public and personal narratives. Considering how food merges with issues of mourning, nationhood and recollection, I discuss how particular dishes encapsulate the impact of socio-cultural changes and allow the 'everyday' to be interpreted as 'history'. This selection aims to show the importance of food in a variety of literary forms, hoping to establish, as Terry Eagleton argues in 'Edible Écriture', that food 'makes up our bodies, just as words make up our mind,' and 'eating and speaking [. . .] continuously cross over in metaphorical exchange'.[15]

THEORETICAL APPROACHES

Following the protean and polysemic qualities of food itself, the nature of this volume necessitates a practical awareness of different methodologies. As a result, I will be synthesising critical frameworks from phenomenology, psychoanalysis, gender studies, socio-cultural anthropology and cultural materialism. An interdisciplinary approach to food and fiction must pay particular attention to both the embodied nature of consumption—in the form of hunger, gustation, and visceral response—and the everyday phenomena related to the experience of eating—including gender relations, advertising, cooking, food preferences, community bonding, memory and cuisine. In claiming such socio-cultural and political significance for eating, I follow Sarah Sceats' suggestion on how to approach food in a literary context: '[f]ood is not bound within any single discourse, but becomes impregnated with meanings from the many and various frameworks within which it figures'.[16]

In response to the inevitably multidisciplinary nature of my study, and the number of key conceptual frameworks which will work alongside discussions of American fiction, it is important not to ignore the possibility of tensions between some of the approaches mentioned above. A phenomenological reading of consumption, for instance, may seem at odds with a cultural materialist approach to food production and distribution. Nonetheless, my book promises to amalgamate theoretical approaches to food in the readings of literary texts and find a productive balance at the point of intersection between disciplines.

PHENOMENOLOGY, PSYCHOANALYSIS AND GENDER STUDIES

In her critical interpretation of corporeality, *Volatile Bodies*, Elizabeth Grosz argues that the body

> is defined by its relations with objects and in turn defines these objects as such [. . .] the body is [the subject's] being to the world and as such is the instrument by which all information and knowledge is received and meaning is generated.[17]

Food is so pivotal to the physical dimension of the body that it is virtually impossible not to imagine eating as a 'lived' experience. To understand the eating body in its fundamental corporeality is crucial if one wishes to explore the impact that food has on the construction of a bodily identity. In his inspirational and pioneering work, *Phenomenology of Perception* (1945), Maurice Merleau-Ponty built on the work of Edmund Husserl to illustrate the critical importance of the body and bodily activities in the development of perception. Merleau-Ponty argues: 'it is through my body that I understand others, just as it is through my body that I perceive things'.[18] The awareness of others, their bodies and surrounding objects constitutes an essential building block for the creation of the self. In *The Spell of the Sensuous*, David Abram extends this phenomenological claim on the body by saying that human experience 'always involves, at the most intimate level, the experience of an active interplay [. . .] between the perceiving body and that which it perceives'.[19] In phenomenological terms, the body incarnates the subject's existence in the spatial world and it is through the inseparable correlation between mind and body that information is received and, therefore, meaning is generated. As a result of this, the world of objects only exists by virtue of the body. Merleau-Ponty insists that not only does the body exist in perennial communion with the world, but also that the self—and, therefore, the mind—emerges through this communion. This last element inevitably binds up the mind with the body and everyday activities, such as eating.

In *The Visible and the Invisible* (1964), Merleau-Ponty points out that embodied activities represent an opening to the perceptual world, the connecting link between the body and the outside: embodied activities 'are not [. . .] vague and ephemeral deformations of the corporeal space, but the initiation to and opening upon [. . .] the world'.[20] A person's sensuous experiences form the foundation for any objectification of the world. Perceiving the world through our bodies cannot be interpreted as an inner representation of an inaccessible realm, but a 'relation of inhabiting the world'.[21] If one understands eating as an element of the 'outside world', then its function in the formation of individual and cultural identity becomes impossible to overlook. Especially seen as a communal activity, eating establishes a connection between 'embodied' entities.

Any study of the eating body as a 'lived-in' entity cannot afford to overlook the importance of the senses. In philosophical terms, 'taste'—as an actual bodily sensation—has traditionally occupied a lowly and humble position in the hierarchy of the senses. In *De Anima*, Aristotle proclaims 'sight' as the highest ranking of all senses.[22] Sight, in classical philosophy, is then followed, in descending order of importance, by hearing, smell, taste and touch.[23] Over the centuries, Western philosophy has continued, as Dabney Townsend and Carolyn Korsmeyer point out, to favour the 'distant' senses, such as sight and hearing; the more 'bodily' senses—including taste—have accordingly been demoted as 'lower' and less significant forms of perception.[24] It is my intention to re-vindicate the importance of taste and smell in everyday human existence. The smell and taste of specific foods are associated with mental images and consist of characteristics which almost transcend the physiological development of sensual stimuli themselves. The sensorial perception of food and drink—particularly in the form of taste and smell—is accompanied by a series of memories which constitutes not only a system of present recognition and recollection, but, also, a starting point for future perceptions, in which past and present become embodied through consumption. To put it simply, as one experiences food in the present, that experience is not only informed by past knowledge, but simultaneously becomes the basis for mnemonic activity in the future. Merleau-Ponty argues that 'to remember is not to bring into the focus of consciousness a self-subsistent picture of the past, it is to thrust deeply into the horizon of the past [. . .] until the experiences which it epitomises are as if relived in their temporal setting'.[25] In consuming a familiar food, the individual establishes a connection between the past and the present of experience. As a result, a person's unconscious ability to recognise 'resemblance' when eating becomes an essential part of sensory and social knowledge. In my study, I apply a phenomenological approach to eating, embodied experience and mnemonic activities in order to show how ingestion becomes central to the subject's connection with the world outside the body.

The acquisition of a corporeal identity is what enables the subject to develop a practical relation with objects in the world. The same practical relation generates what Grosz defines as a 'psychic attachment to our bodies and body parts'.[26] As a discipline, psychoanalysis recognises the critical importance of the body in the development of a psycho-social identity. Merleau-Ponty himself had a lifelong interest in psychoanalysis and, whilst being critical of aspects of the discipline, he remained deeply fascinated by its theories of the unconscious and insisted that utilising both psychoanalysis and phenomenology was the key to unlocking the secrets of perception. In *Phenomenology of Perception*, he specifically advocates an interdisciplinary approach by asserting that 'there is no thought that embraces all thought[s]'.[27]

Understanding eating in psychoanalytical terms inevitably leads to viewing food as a medium through which the body is first acknowledged as a separate entity. In 'The Ego and the Id', Freud notes that 'the ego is ultimately derived from bodily sensations, chiefly from those springing from the surface of the body'.[28] The ego is not only influenced by the presence of corporeal stimuli, but it is through the experience of bodily sensations that identity is created, shaped and expanded. From this concept derives the thought that all activities involving the body can be understood as essential elements for the formation of the psyche; as Freud argues, the ego is 'a mental projection of the surface of the body'.[29] However, considering eating as an essential activity for the construction of a 'body ego' raises the question of deciding how food is 'registered' in order to delineate the borders of the body and create the social subject. This consideration encourages Freudian psychoanalysis to understand the mouth as an essential component in the formation of subjectivity. According to Freud in *Three Essays on Sexuality*, the infant child associates satisfaction with oral stimuli—namely, sucking the mother's breast. In the 'oral phase', food—in the form of the breast-milk—consequently encapsulates the child's first sexual focus: 'the child sucking at his mother's breast [becomes] the prototype of every relation of love'.[30] In the infant's desire to incorporate the mother's breast, Freud finds strong cannibalistic undertones. As a result, he claims that healthy psychological progress into adulthood demands detachment from the pleasures of the oral/cannibalistic stage. Nonetheless, remnants of the infant's cannibalistic desires become evident in adult years through oral fixations—desires to incorporate people and objects orally which influence the constructions of the subject's models of pleasure. As adults, Freud argues, we sense that our relationship to the world is only 'a shrunken residue of a much more inclusive—indeed all-embracing—feeling which corresponded to the more intimate bond between the ego and the world'.[31]

Following Freud's interpretation of infantile pleasure, oral stimuli have been considered by later psychoanalysts as belonging to the field of 'semiotic' knowledge: a state of experience which precedes the entrance to the symbolic realm, which is marked by the development of linguistic abilities. The semiotic realm, described by Julia Kristeva in *Revolution in Poetic Language* as the *chora*, is associated with direct and unmediated sensorial experience. The infant moves, feeds and communicates only through stimuli regulated by primordial necessities. The semiotic, sensorial *chora*, Kristeva argues, 'is a modality of significance in which the linguistic sign is not yet articulated'.[32] The unmediated nature of sensorial experience is pre-linguistic and, therefore, a primitive form of experience. Gustation, as such, is inextricably attached to the oral organs of taste, the mouth and the tongue. The mouth is, of course, also related to the development of speech and, therefore, the primal site of vocal expression. Gustation is thus paradoxically connected to vocal representation through the sharing of an orifice. The dual nature of the mouth and taste—simultaneously expressing linguistic and pre-linguistic stimuli—is underlined by Grosz in *Volatile Bodies*: 'the mouth is especially privileged [. . .] it functions both introspectively and extroceptively. It is a primordial link [. . .] connecting perceptions from the inside to the outside'.[33] In my analysis, I employ this notion of oral stimuli as part of psycho-social development, in order to see how food functions as a marker of gender, class and socio-cultural identity.

The cultural association between women, gender and food has been a major focus of feminist scholarship. Feminist sociologists, anthropologists and cultural critics have drawn attention to the issues experienced by women in relation to food consumption and preparation. Research aims to show that food—ceasing to be a simple physiological necessity—is invested with great symbolic ambivalence in women's lives.

Having said that, it must be remembered that, especially during the Twentieth Century, men's affiliation with cooking has become great, so that in contemporary culture a substantial number of famous chefs are men. Yet, a substantial difference usually drives the imagery concerned; as Anne Murcott argues, 'women are cooks whereas men are chefs'.[36] When men cook, they usually do it as a profession, and it is, certainly, their own choice; in contrast, cooking can be considered as a woman's responsibility, almost inescapable. Despite the emancipation that the second part of the Twentieth Century brought to a large number of women—in and out of the household—cooking continues to figure as a practice that is a family prerogative of women. Nicky Charles and Melanie Kerr point out that gender division labour is seen 'as something which was historically and socially determined, it is not something that could be wished away merely by individual women exercising free choice'.[37] Simultaneously, however, we cannot vilify cooking as the ultimate activity which keeps contemporary women entrapped in routine; it is not my intention to suggest that if a mother cooks a meal for her children or husband, she is necessarily obeying the segregated regulations of gender division.

The treatment of food as a gendered substance has also encouraged some feminist sociologists who are keen to read men's consumption, especially of meat, as an act of patriarchal supremacy. In *The Sexual Politics of Meat*, Carol Adams argues that the 'mythology permeates all classes that meat is a masculine food and meat eating is a male activity'.[38] Jack Goody supports this claim by noting that 'men often play a part in the roasting' of meat and other foods, highlighting the 'barbecue' as part of a male realm of activities.[39] Women, on the other hand, are often associated with the consumption of 'lighter' foodstuffs, such as vegetables, grains and fruits—and, of course, sweet foods such as cakes and chocolate. Feminist anthropological research offers a simple explanation for associating men with the consumption of meat: in the hunter-gatherer society, men's role as hunters allowed their primary consumption of the prey. Mythologically, eating the flesh of strong animals is associated with the transmission of strength to the eater. The principal 'attributes of masculinity', as Adams argues, are ritually 'achieved through eating [. . .] masculine foods'.[40] Adams' idea utilises Freud's concept of ritualised introjection and the desire to 'become' that which is being eaten.[41]

SOCIO-CULTURAL ANTHROPOLOGY AND CULTURAL MATERIALISM

Over the years, anthropological research has drawn attention to food as a social matter, particularly in terms of ritual practices and group membership. In this context, cooking can be seen as a defining human activity. In 'Eating Virtue', Paul Atkinson argues that 'food is a liminal substance; it stands as a bridging substance between nature and culture, the human and the natural, the outside and the inside'.[42] Cooking methods draw attention to different ritual habits within social groups, since 'in any cuisine, nothing is simply cooked, but must be cooked in one fashion or another'.[43] Claude Lévi-Strauss argues that cooking is, along with language, 'a truly universal form of human activity: if there is no society without language, nor is there any which does not cook in some manner at least some of its food'.[44] Lévi-Strauss charts the differentiation of cooking methods through a triangular model, in which each point of the triangle corresponds to one specific category: the raw, the cooked and the rotted. In respect to modes of cooking, the raw represents an 'unmarked pole', an uncharted category which is not managed by human control.[45] Only a limited number of foods can be eaten raw and even then they must be appropriately selected, washed and cut. The cooked, as the exemplification of human control, is understood as a 'cultural transformation' of the raw. The rotted, on the other hand, is part of an environmental process which induces 'natural transformation' of the food.[46] Lévi-Strauss maintains that the triangular categorisation of food underlines a 'double opposition' between 'elaborated/unelaborated' and 'culture/nature'.[47]

Since cooking is a civilised practice, its application—and the different types of food to which it is applied—can become a marker of cultural belonging. Deborah Lupton argues that 'food is instrumental in marking differences between cultures, serving to strengthen group identity [. . .] sharing the act of eating brings people into the same community'.[48] Eating the same food becomes symbolically important for cultural identification; choosing to eat certain foods rather than others represents human beings' acknowledgement of their belonging—or wish to belong—to a particular cultural faction. The act of eating, therefore, serves as an important means through which social and ethnic exclusion or inclusion is perpetrated. Nick Fiddes reminds us that 'the foods we select reflect our thought, including our conception of our actual or desired way of life and our perceptions of the food choice of people with whom we wish to identify. We eat nothing but as part of our culture'.[49]

If it is true that human beings do not simply eat, but the practice is embedded with meaning, then foods themselves are not simply selected depending on their nutritional value.[50] In its function as a vector of cultural belonging, food can then be understood as a sign. In 'Towards a Psychology of Contemporary Food Consumption', Roland Barthes shows an interest in applying a semiotic model to consumption, arguing that 'food has a constant tendency to transform itself into situation'; he argues that food acts as a signifier in the metaphorical and metonymic construction of a signified social group.[51] Barthes proposes that we think of food as a system of communication, containing 'syntaxes ("menus"), and styles ("diets") [. . .] in a semantic way—in a way, that is, that will enable us to compare them to each other'.[52]

Extending Barthes's semiotic model to an anthropological context, Mary Douglas sets out the process of 'deciphering a meal'. Douglas starts from the premise that eating is always a ritual activity. Every meal is reliant on a strict structure. When something is eaten, how and where is decided by an unspoken set of social rules that relies on and reveals cultural affiliation. Applying a methodology borrowed from structural linguistics, and including terms such as 'taxonomy' and 'paradigm', Douglas argues that meals rely on a culturally established structure, creating order within any social system. This type of anthropological analysis discloses how food categories construct social boundaries, dictating rules of consumption that expose markers of class, gender and race. The meal, Douglas concludes, 'is a microcosm of wider social structures and definitions'.[53] In my study, I will employ this understanding of 'the meal' as ritual to show how food constructs the basis for a communal system which is dependent on hidden but essential cultural values, beliefs and regulations.

Following the perception of meal as 'ritual', it is important to remember that, when it is related to the socio-cultural experience of eating and drinking, the word 'taste' is employed to reflect the actual sensation that individuals feel when they put food into their mouths. In sociological scholarship, the use of the word 'taste' refers to, in Lupton's words, 'the broader understanding of style or fashion related to any commodity'.[54] This interpretation of taste appears inspired by philosophical theories—especially Kantian—which emerged in the eighteenth century and understood 'taste' in relation to art and 'pleasure'. However, one cannot avoid seeing 'good taste' as a standardised concept which is necessarily connected to cultural regulations. Taste, in both its physiological and idealised understanding, is applicable, as Lupton argues, 'to all members of a society', acting as an 'ideal that is socially communicable'.[55] The idea of 'good taste', therefore, can be interpreted as a tool for social distinction, acquired through long-lasting integration with a specific cultural system. Basing his discussion on class observation in French society, sociologist Pierre Bourdieu develops the analysis of acculturated 'taste' as a joined expression of individual preference and social disposition. The concept of 'habitus', Bourdieu argues in *Distinction*, encapsulates the methods by which social tastes are expressed. The habitus exemplifies how a person's 'taste' is communicated through several selections of commodity use. The habitus—especially affecting distinctions of class—expresses itself most clearly through embodied practice, where social choices are reproduced: 'the body is the most indisputable materialisation of class taste'.[56] In the class system, Bourdieu argues, expressions of 'taste' include the ability to choose the right commodities to 'consume', according to specific cultural rules. Expressions of class 'taste' are necessarily dependent on articulations of gender, race and age. Bourdieu is adamant that 'tastes' are expressed in embodied existence particularly through the idiom of food. He also maintains that consumption 'categorises' existence and ranks different social groups 'in different ways'.[57]

The favourite foods of each nation can become a key ingredient in the tangible expressions of a collective cultural memory. Food availability—influenced of course by geographical location—also becomes an essential component for the construction of a national cuisine. Eating can never be interpreted as an historically detached practice; every food communicates a social narrative which contributes towards the formation of a concept of mutual belonging. In *Tasting Food, Tasting Freedom*, social anthropologist Sydney Mintz reminds us that 'food is never simply eaten [. . .] [it] has histories associated with the pasts of those who eat' it.[58] Through the exploitation of culinary knowledge, conceptions of identity are inevitably reinforced, so that food recipes and their usage can come to represent a form of recognisable heritage for any social and ethnic group.

As food communicates history and belonging, the concept of 'tradition' becomes prominent. Alan Warde reminds us of the need to appreciate how 'the term "tradition" may serve as a rhetorical device for the legitimisation of a particular set of preferences'.[59] Faced with the possible breaking down of cultural boundaries, 'tradition' may be employed to 'valorise the foods and culinary habits of a nation or of any particular ethnic group'. The concept of 'tradition', however, is mutable and changes according to the cultural faction in question. There exists, therefore, the distinct possibility that the authenticity often associated with traditional foods is part of ethnocentric fiction.[60]

Warde also claims that, in Western societies, tradition is being 'invented anew'.[61] It could be suggested that, in an age 'dominated by technological advances' and increasing detachment from the 'everyday', the idea of traditional food offers a compensatory surrogate. The appeal of culinary 'traditions', however, does not stop at the authentication of familiar conduct. The justification of culinary 'tradition', Warde claims, is inspired by the 'commercial gains' that derive from 'enacting or displaying' familiar food practices.[62] The possible exploitation of culinary tradition has to be confronted if one wishes to explore the relationship between food, consumption, community and cultural groups.[63]

As food emerges as an essential socio-cultural marker, it is important to remember that, in cultural studies, the word 'consumption' is not only used to denote eating and drinking. Consumption is also understood, as Lupton puts it, as 'the uses people make of commodities or goods, including food but also those that are inedible'.[64] The 'consumption' of commodities, in sociological discourse, can also refer to clothes, television, radio and a variety of purchasable items which interact with each other in order to form 'consumer identity'. In *The World of Goods*, Mary Douglas and Baron Isherwood propose that the value of goods is constantly framed by a cultural context. Material goods do not only function as objects, but also have a broader meaning and significance for social relations. The use of goods exemplifies identities, so that it is through acquiring and sharing possessions that individuals construct a social identity. The choice of a consumable—whether food specifically or other commodities—creates distinction among sub-groups and expresses membership. As a result, the consumption of material goods becomes indivisible from their socio-cultural meaning. In simultaneously being material and symbolic objects, goods are 'endowed with value by agreement of fellow consumers' and act as 'the visible part of culture'.[65]

In line with Douglas and Isherwood's anthropology of consumption, Jean Baudrillard argues—in more historically specific terms—that the meaning of goods within modern capitalist society originates from external agencies, including advertising. Through representations in the media, goods are translated into 'signs' with an attributed value. The same value, Baudrillard argues, constructs and justifies commodity culture: objects 'tyrannically induce categories of persons [and] undertake the policing of social meanings'.[66] Baudrillard highlights the manner in which goods function as 'symbols in the sphere of consumption' and draws attention to commodities as 'regulating agents in the domain of culture'.[67]

Unlike Baudrillard—who decentres the social aspect of goods in favour of the *system* of objects themselves—in *Culture and Consumption* Grant McCracken discusses possessing goods in terms of performance. According to what McCracken labels as 'possession rituals'—the collecting, comparing and flaunting of objects—individuals are able to express their outlook on social life and experience.[68] Through these possession rituals, people 'personalise' goods and are thereby able to project an idea of 'personal self': 'the individual deploys possession rituals and manages to extract the meaningful properties that have been invested in the consumer good'.[69] In this framework, food plays a vital role in the performance of commodity culture. Lupton labels food as the 'ultimate consumable commodity'.[70] By the act of purchasing, preparing and consuming food, Lupton argues, cultural standards are transferred to the individual, so that consumables can 'reflect' how people 'perceive themselves, or would like to be perceived'.[71] Indeed, food uncovers how the physical dimension of eating is juxtaposed with the world of cultural commodities, epitomising the eating body as an entity affected by issues of class, race, ethnicity and gender. I believe that understanding food as a 'cultural commodity' is essential if one wishes to address eating as an activity expressing socio-political and economic relations.

Cultural materialists have also carried out research into food, consumerism and 'the everyday'. This field of study considers eating as an everyday practice which exposes a system of hidden socio-political, cultural and economic combinations. In *The Practice of Everyday Life* Michel de Certeau states that the purpose of studying food habits is 'to make explicit' the existing 'models of action' which continuously determine the choices of the consumer.[72] Within a system of everyday experience, food acts as the 'the representation of a society' and 'its mode of behaviour'.[73] De Certeau considers the study of everyday habits necessary if one aims to determine the socio-cultural forces acting upon groups or individuals. In capitalist societies, de Certeau argues, everyday life is regulated by systems of consumption which rely on hidden strategy—'the calculus of force-relationships': the selling of goods relies on marketing tactics which, according to de Certeau, 'must constantly manipulate events in order to turn them into opportunities'.[74] In my study of food and American fiction, therefore, I will start from the idea that analysing food habits can reveal the cultural and economic systems that regulate everyday life. I will concentrate particularly on how everyday life can be manipulated by cycles of production, distribution and consumption that turn the purchaser of food into a 'consumer'.

From this cultural materialist perspective, the experience of dining out, for a large number of people in Western cultures, is what Lupton calls 'the apotheosis of civilised eating'.[75] Formal, chic and fashionable restaurants—where food is expected to be of a superior quality—appeal not only to the tastebuds, but to people's desire to distinguish themselves and affirm a 'taste' for luxurious commodities. The elegant dining experience is 'privileged as the ultimate eating event'.[76] Fine foods and lavish surroundings are treated by many as the expression of a special occasion, a celebration, something that is, to put it simply, out of the ordinary. Expressing wealth and social status, the fine dining experience takes individuals out of the home and, removing them from the comfort of familiar eating, places them in a context of sophistication and social elevation. While the family meal—often prepared by a mother or a wife—is representative of comfortable surroundings, security and unadventurous reassurance, the restaurant meal is expected to conjure up feelings of pride and hedonistic pleasure, induced by a fine social experience as much as by the food itself. Dining out in Western culture, therefore, can be interpreted as an important practice of the self. The choice of restaurant, the foods and wine ordered, and the final economic value of the experience, add to the idea of a group's cultural capital and transform the dishes at restaurants into, in Lupton's words, 'markers of identity'.[77]

One must bear in mind that food preferences and practices can be mutable according to the socio-cultural group in question. The value of restaurant dining as a practice of the self, therefore, is not universally accepted, even in Western cultures. In *Dining Out*, Joanne Filkenstein points out that eating in restaurants is in fact a very 'artificial exercise in manners'.[78] Affected by the pressure of social identification, people who eat in restaurants tend to imitate others and thereby suffocate their own desire for individual experience. The social setting of the restaurant, according to Finkelstein, actually limits the 'choice of self' available to the individual.[79] In this social context, restaurant dining merges corporeal experiences into a system of cultural communication. Finkelstein's position, however, seems excessively fixated on the idea of an 'authentic self' struggling to get out in an oppressive eating environment. One should consider the possibility that the self is actually *constructed by* the dining experience and that construction is, in Lupton's words, 'highly contextual upon the setting in time and space'.[80]

Having briefly sketched the key sociological, physiological, anthropological, historical and psychological approaches to eating and cooking rituals in people's lives, it is important to remember that, while food does not intrinsically symbolise, human interaction has invested it with potent symbolic functions, so that food, to borrow Deborah Lupton's words, has assumed 'the symbolic meaning par excellence'.[81]

1 Home and Away

> Ice cream, ice cream, ice cream . . . He scanned the swamp-fire prose of the menu, and through the caloric waves he spotted a single ice-cream dish: hand-Churned Vanilla Ice Cream Topped with Walnut Chili Chutney. *Chili*? Well, he would scrape the topping to one side and stick to the ice cream. He didn't have the nerve to ask the trendy waitress with all the honey curls to leave the topping off. He didn't want to look like an unadventurous wimp.
>
> —Tom Wolfe, *The Bonfire of the Vanities*[1]

The contrast between eating in and eating out has attracted considerable literary attention in recent years. The separation between 'in' and 'out'—or home and away—is deemed extreme and unchangeable by many. Home is meant to signify comfort, relaxation and close relationships, while the restaurant—or any other public place of consumption—is routinely associated with detachment, social expectations and distant acquaintances. It is difficult to overlook the sardonic descriptions and cynical commentaries of restaurants and diners offered by Tom Wolfe in *The Bonfire of the Vanities* (1987). Wolfe's satirically keen eye does not miss an opportunity to expose the often ludicrous nature of restaurant obsession in the emergent yuppie New York, as endless cycles of dining out are accompanied by episodes of sexual prowess, thievery and even physical illness (in the form of very aptly chosen heart attacks and choking on food). In similar fashion, one cannot forget the cathartic nature of food in Jonathan Franzen's *The Corrections* (2001), as the long-awaited 'one-last' Christmas dinner at home promises to bring together a family that is on the verge of destruction. The fact that the family dinner—with its forceful ability to gather members of the family—allows the characters to assess their flaws and begin to make 'corrections' in their lives highlights the power that the dinner at home holds over the collective imaginary. The role of food practices, it would seem, has a fundamental value in 'producing and reproducing' the concept of 'home'.[2]

Nonetheless, despite the hold exercised over Western social organisation by almost stereotyped visions of consumption, in and outside the home, it is my intention to show that these conceptions are not so easily accepted in contemporary American fiction. While scenes of lavish dinners and quite home meals unfold, the division between 'home' and 'away' become less radical, as the line that separates the private from the public grows increasingly thinner.

HOME SYMBOLS, AMERICAN ICONS

As a routine activity—which often revolves around issues of timing, measuring and location—cooking contributes to the identification of social roles in any given setting. The interdependence among cooking, specific food and social regulation (especially in terms of gender) is explored by Marilynne Robinson in *Home* (2008). The novel, which won several awards—including the Orange Prize for Fiction in 2009—chronicles the life of Reverend Robert Boughton and the complicated return of his adult children, Jack and Glory, to their family home in Gilead, Iowa. Avid readers of Robinson's work would recognise the location and the characters from her previous, Pulitzer Prize winning novel, *Gilead* (2004). Indeed, *Home* works as a fictional companion to *Gilead*, whose events are meant to be unfolding during the same time and with intersecting characters.

Whilst *Home* does not quite achieve the political and psychological depth of *Gilead*, its thematic and narrative trajectories do offer a more 'personal' account of home life for the Boughton family which is regrettably overlooked in *Gilead*. However, just as the novel feels like a more personal and individualised evaluation of home life, it also unravels a number of issues which surround everyday family life and its mixture of love and politics. *Home* has a touch of the confessional, as it mischievously allows the reader to enter a family domain which is usually kept (literally) 'behind closed doors'. As the story explores feelings of guilt, inadequacy and conflicted affection, food figures prominently in the lives of characters. It is through food that emotions are unveiled, in ways that words fail to achieve. Although this is not surprising, considering the 'home' setting of the novel and its conceptual expectations regarding home-made food, Robinson does invest eating and cooking with powerful, semi-incriminating qualities.

Beef, in particular, is granted place of honour in Robinson's politicised re-elaboration of food metaphors. The cooking of beef—and the conceptual affinity it bears with daughter Glory—is placed in particular focus. As Glory returns home to the paternal residence, it becomes clear that one of her principal roles is to cook for her father and brother. Reverend Boughton, in turn, does not refrain from asking what he wishes for on a regular basis. Beef towers on top of the list of favourites, as the Reverend declares his culinary desires as an order for his daughter to follow: 'I'd like roast beef for Sunday dinner. I want the whole house to smell like roast beef'.[3] The Reverend's demands here are important on a number of levels. Firstly, the desire for beef on a special occasion—for which the Reverend declares he will even 'put on a necktie' and light 'the candles' (164)—testifies to the socially privileged role continuously occupied by meat in the culinary scale. Julia Twigg points out that 'meat is the most highly prized of food. It is the centre around which a meal is arranged. It stands in a sense for the very idea of food itself'.[4] In the Boughton household, the beef is a symbol of prestige and brings promises of a great culinary experience. Secondly, if one accepts the conceptual association between men, eating meat and strength, then the Reverend's desire symbolises his wish to ascertain his position of power in the house. The idea of 'smelling beef' here can be interpreted as a symbolic appropriation of manhood, recalling the long-standing linguistic propensity of referring to men as 'beef'.

Simultaneously, one could argue that the Reverend's desire to smell and consume beef expresses a need to feel part of a family, a wish which is conceptually encapsulated in the meat dinner. Charles and Kerr remind us that 'the shared experience of family meals' has the power to unite 'families ideologically and culturally'. Meat, in particular, has traditionally played 'a central part' in 'family occasions' (from which take place often to those that only happen annually) and always makes the gathering 'special and memorable'.[5] Within the beef—the centrepiece of the Sunday family dinner—lies a nostalgic longing for a stable home unity, something which was broken when the Reverend's children left home but now has an opportunity to be reinstated since Glory and Jack have returned.

The beef takes on a dual meaning in the novel, as Robinson shifts its representation to offer a close perspective on gender politics in the American home. Glory's wishes to meet her father's expectations—as an embodiment of society's approval—are mirrored in the constant efforts she puts into her cooking. As the Reverend's demands for culinary excellence are put forward, Glory dedicates a lot of attention not only to preparing the beef, but also to ensure that the whole dining experience is worthy of her father's praise:

> The dining room table was set for three, lace tablecloth, good china, silver candlesticks [. . .] She had the grocery store deliver a beef roast, two pounds of new potatoes, and a quart of ice cream [. . .] And the day passed quickly, with those sweet flavours rising. (40)

The description of the beef dinner as 'sweet' is put in contrast with the dining room which, in spite of its aesthetic beauty, is described as 'oppressive' (41), signalling issues of gender stratification which relegate women to preparing and serving food. The contradicting feelings displayed by Glory towards the beef dinner could be symptomatic of an identity-related condition that Brett Silverstein defines as 'gender ambivalence'.[6] According to Silverstein, gender ambivalence represents 'the conflict over femininity' triggered by anxiety in the home environment.[7] As Glory strives to gastronomically please her father, she is also subjected to continuous doubts about her value within the family unity. In a way, one could also see the beef as a multiple extension of Glory herself, providing a form of bovine acquiesce, as she symbolically serves herself to social imperatives which regulate the home dynamics within the Boughton household. This approach to beef politics shows affinity with Peter Blos' contention that, as family politics are scrutinised, gender 'ambivalence denotes contradictory emotional attitudes toward the same object, either arising alternatively, or existing side by side'.[8]

Glory, however, shows clear awareness towards her father's invested desires—especially when it come to Sunday dinners—as she recognises the social value of beef within their home:

> 'Whatever part of her father's hopes for the evening could be satisfied [. . .] by food consecrated to the rituals of Boughton celebration, the part at least had been seen to. The roast beef was tender, the glazed beets were pungent'. (192)

Glory's evaluation of the beef dinner here is extremely revelatory. In channelling the daughter's anxieties, Robinson indicates uncertainties towards the curative powers of the beef. Alert to the meat's cultural significance for white-ethnic groups, Robinson registers a sense of disillusionment in the projected unity of the American family and challenges—in an openly provocative manner—the vision of union built into an all-American conceptualisation of home. In subverting the traditionally embedded function of the 'family beef' Robinson signals the problematic state of the 'family' as a social construction. The mythology of meat joins the idea of 'home' in highlighting the possible disintegration of the perfect family unity which, Robinson seems to be suggesting, might be nothing more than an imagined social construction.

In the majority of family economies—at least in Western cultures—feeding is still generally understood as 'woman's work'. It is through cooking and feeding the family that women, Marjorie DeVault argues, actually 'do gender'.[9] Cooking and nurturing remain associated with the woman in her capacities as wife and mother, so that food itself becomes an important component in the distinction of gender roles. This particular dynamic is crystallised by Karen Stolz in *World of Pies* (2000). The story, set in the Sixties and running through to the Nineties, narrates the life of protagonist Roxanne, a young teenager who lives with her parents in the small town of Annette, Texas. While Stolz details the days in this coming-of-age story, food and eating come to be an important presence in Roxanne's life, as her complex relationships with her family are dissected.

A lot of attention in the novel is dedicated to Roxanne's parents (Carl and Christine) and how, within the home, they wish to project a proper image of wholesomeness and reliability. Meal times, in particular, are viewed as the pinnacle of family life, with Roxanne's mother Christine taking the lead in delivering a perfectly executed meal on every occasion. As a result, the dinner table proves an important site for social interaction. On a particular night in the household when there is tension between Roxanne's parents, eating together becomes a revealing activity: 'At dinner that night, I realised my parents weren't speaking to each other, but it was funny how long it took me to see this'.[10]

It is important to see how Roxanne notices an argument between her parents only once at the dinner table. This clearly suggests the social importance that dining together has for the family. The dinner table is not simply a place to consume food, but a social medium through which the integrity of the family can remain intact. While social interaction could be avoided between two members of the family in other areas of the home, the dinner table virtually demands some form of contact. This is of course not only in virtue of the table's logistical organisation—where people are sitting next or in front of each other—but also of its function as a family-bonding element. David Bell and Gill Valentine point out that in sociological research the dinner table 'has been identified as an important site for the socialisation' of the family. As the host of the family meal, the dinner table allows members of the family to converse, share experiences and catch up. Once all household members sit at the table, a moment of social communion is created through the act of eating, which brings not only physical nourishment to the family, but allows it to 'come together'.[11] In *World of Pies*, the fact that Roxanne's parents are not speaking creates a social split into the act of eating and sharing a common experience at the table. As the usual table dynamics are interrupted, the unity of the family is jeopardised. The eating routine is interrupted by the lack of conversation which is interpreted almost as synonymous with the dinner table.

Another important element emerges from the awkward dinner situation in the household. The lack of conversation is clearly not the only detail that troubles Roxanne and communicates a rupture between her parents. As she is about to consume her food, Roxanne notices that 'the pots and pan' are 'on the table', where 'typically' her mom serves 'from china bowls' (6). It is made very clear that the careless presence of the pans is clearly 'unheard of', as her parents are 'usually formal at the table' (6). In addition, her mother's appearance is also seen as far too casual; she is wearing a 'housecoat', even though she is aware that her dad likes 'to see her in pretty dresses' (6).

In traditional families—where cooking duties fall on the mother–'domestic routines usually centre around men'.[12] In this sense, women's role as the formidable cook and the provider of prepared food is also a symbolic, as well as a material task. Preparing food for the husband and the children becomes a way to not only express love, but also to assert one's position as the loving mother within the family. A cooked dinner is the perfect medium through which a mother—through a series of culinary routines and domestic habits—shows her attention to detail and love for the husband. Bell and Valentine argue that in traditional families 'women can derive both pleasure and identity from providing cooked dinners and meals'[13] The dinner table, therefore, can be seen as the perfect arena in which domestic performance takes place; the demonstration of ability on the mother's part is not only focused on the food cooked, but extends to a number of important details about the dinner experience which conforms to the husband's idea of perfection. In purposely disrupting the dinner table routine—and wearing clothes which she knows will not please her husband—Christina employs the tightly-constructed balance of the dinner table to show her disagreement. As Stolz portrays Christina's refusal to provide domestic 'pleasure' for her husband, she not only unveils the values of gendered domestic routines within the household, but also exposes the role of the dinner table in the creation of family roles. As a result, Christina's subsequent efforts to meet her husband's culinary desires, mirror the coveted re-stabilisation of the family unit within the story: 'Mom was lifting a spice cake from the oven, redolent of cloves and allspice. Daddy's favourite: a sure sign they'd made up' (68).

Food in Stolz's novel functions as the fundamental part of family life; food occasions are often the centre of attention, from those which occur on a daily basis (kitchen dinners and lunches), to those which take place annually or on special and memorable occasions (like in the case of Cousin Tommy's homecoming family dinner). DeVault argues that 'food is important to the social reproduction of the family in both its nuclear and extended forms'.[14] In *World of Pies*, food practices are instrumental in maintaining a coherent social ideology and reinforcing the idea of the family even in moments of struggle. Christina's cooked dinners are at the centre of Roxanne's memories of home and family. She is often portrayed experimenting in the kitchen, attempting to produce good meals for her daughter and husband. Food, it would seem, is not only a vital component of family life, but specifically, an important agent in the construction of Christina's identity as wife and mother.

DeVault reminds us that in traditional Western families, 'an important aspect of women's role within the family is to provide proper meals' on a daily basis.[15] Christina is extremely committed to cooking 'proper' and nutritious meals for the family, believing that a 'hot lunch' is 'good for you, even if it were a hundred degrees outside' (28). The cooked meal is treated by Christina as simultaneously the expression of her ability to perform as a mother and wife and a clear communicator of a healthy familiar ethic. A hot meal implies that the family will sit down and eat together, as it necessitates cutlery and plates—in opposition to an 'on the go' snack, which, in spite of being often provided by the mother, does not carry an ideological attachment to the family unity. The 'home cooked' meal is clearly interpreted by Christina as imbued with affection and warmth; within the household politics of the home, those qualities are viewed as essential indicators of the private sphere and in strict opposition to convenience foods which are the product of 'a public, industrialised and anonymous system of food production'.[16] The shared experience of the cooked, 'hot' family meal bonds members of the family on both a physical and an ideological level, highlighting the successful role of the mother as nurturer, carer and provider.

However, in spite of its ability to bond members of the family, food practices within the novel also manage to reinforce social and gender divisions.

Whilst she covers her role as wife and mother, Christina is expected to remain at home and look after the members of the family; she does not work and is somewhat tied to her husband and daughter in a state of dependence. Christina spends her time 'polishing silver and thumbing wildly though recipe books' (26), desperately trying to produce a pleasant dinner for the family which is not only tasty, but also looks as beautiful as the pictures she gathers inspiration from. Through Christina's seemingly loving act, one can uncover a kitchen philosophy of the Sixties that *World of Pies* is obviously keen to recall and resurrect. Here we see a portrayal of the Sixties eager housewife, whose world of domestic resourcefulness made her the perfect social product. However, in spite of Stolz's best efforts, the subliminal quality of the perfect food picture dictates a regime of domestic subordination, saying that a meal 'should' look as good as it appears in the magazines. The process of food preparation—although inspired by love and family devotion—is unveiled as laborious and time-consuming. Rosalind Coward reminds us that 'cooking food and presenting it beautifully' can be 'an act of servitude'.[17] Although I am not implying here that a mother looking after her loved ones is acting as a servant, the social and gender politics connected to food in *World of Pies* suggest that her role as the cook keeps her tied to the house in boredom and dissatisfaction. Assuming that, within the family, a mother's kitchen work is simply done out of love would insensitively ignore the fact that 'female domestic labour *is* labour'.[18] Christina is the constant producer of consumables which nourish her husband and daughter. In the private sphere of the household, whilst food practices produce and reproduce what is seen as a stable idea of the home, one can see complex negotiations of both place–particularly the kitchen—and social custom.

It is also clear that within the family dynamic there is great expectation surrounding not only Christine's daily cooking duties, but also the specific dishes she cooks as well. On several occasions throughout the novel, Roxanne and her father give a suggestion of the ideal of the 'proper meal' that resembles the standard working-class food combination of 'meat (sometimes fish) potatoes and vegetables'.[19] However, Christina's attempts to cook 'exotic' dishes, which challenge her creativity, are not well received by her husband. When she decides to prepare a dish of 'salmon and wild rice' (26), Roxanne is sure that her father will 'hate it' (26). We are also told that when Christina attempts bake a 'peculiar thing out of eggplants' (28), her husband refuses to be 'home for lunch' (28), 'afraid of this weird new food' that his wife 'had been cooking' (28).

Christina's experimentations with home cooking are also not well received by Roxanne: 'She [Christina] tried making foreign foods, like fried cookies and flat breads. She gave these to me and my friends for snacks, and I was mortified that she no longer served them normal things like Oreos or potato chips' (28). The emphasis here is placed on the fact that Christina's new foods are seen as 'foreign'—or not American enough—while manufactured snacks like Oreos are perceived as 'normal' and appropriate. One can see here how the family perceives the mother's cooking as something that should be recognisable, a subtle example of local, American identities. This particular function of home cooking seems to validate Bob Ashley's contention that consuming home-cooked food 'is a practice through which [. . .] we recognise ourselves as belonging to a culture'.[20]

The reaction to the 'new foods' is revelatory on several levels. Firstly, it exposes the demands that are placed on Christine the mother as the home cook; she must provide foods which please the other members of the family, especially the husband. A mother's cooking is often associated with notion of 'goodness', so that the food itself can be interpreted as the epitome and embodiment of a woman's love for her family. Cooking and feeding contribute to the formation of a gendered idea of family performance, a process of identifying, in DeVault's words, 'adequate women [. . .] through concerted activities'.[21] It goes without saying, of course, that layers of prejudice and social expectation surround the gendered interpretation of cooking, so that women who decide not to adhere to the proper model are often regarded as 'bad' wives and mothers.

Secondly, the desire to consume recognisable 'American' foods—even if they are not technically cooked by the mother—is a strong demonstration of group affiliation and ideological claims regarding the role of the family. Bell and Valentine suggest that consuming home-cooked food always constitutes 'a important social event' which 'plays a role' in representing 'the 'collective identity of the household'.[22] The food consumed by the family must be part of the culture they belong to, in order to be understood as 'proper'. Simultaneously, we get an idea of how the core of family's identity relies on established consumption patterns which must be recognisable, reliable and (especially) socially acceptable.

Issues about cooking (and what is being cooked) extend beyond gender politics in *World of Pies*. The novel begins with an insight into America's culinary affair with pies. The town of Annette is to hold a 'pie fair'—originally Roxanne's father's idea—with the intent of promoting 'community spirit' (2). It is made clear that much attention goes into the preparations for the fair, which is to be held (in all-American style) during the Fourth of July weekend: 'Everything would be pie-related: hand-made aprons, tablecloths, pottery pie plates. Children would make pot holders and there would be a Miss Cherry Pie and a King Key Lime' (2). The fact that the pie is chosen as a representation of community spirit should not come as a surprise. Even in contemporary America the pie maintains an attachment to the collective imaginary as a symbol of the country itself, a culinary transubstantiation of the American spirit. Barbara Sewell industriously sums up the evocative appeal of home-made pie to Americans: 'Pie is slow food in a too-fast world. Pie is a loving gesture. Good pie is sitting in front of the porch glider having a lively conversation with family and friends'. Pie, Sewell ceremoniously concludes, 'is home'.[23]

This romanticised attachment to pie, although not unforeseen, comes to us with a dose of irony, since the pie, of course, is not an American invention. Examples of early and rudimentary 'pies' are documented in Neolithic Egypt in 9000BC. Dishes comprising of a filling (more often than not meat) and a cereal, flour-based case have remained popular throughout history—early examples exist ranging from Roman cuisine to Medieval recipes. This form of consuming meat and refined cereal was often a core staple for travellers and working peoples in the European countries, with regional variations based on both the locally available meats and farmed cereal crops. Written references to 'pyes' appeared in England as early as the twelfth century. Nonetheless, pie historian Janet Clarkson believes it to be probable that it was the northern Italians of the Renaissance 'who redefined and developed pastry' into the incarnation of pie which is still recognised and appreciated today.[24]

The concept of pie as a staple food reached American shores, as one could probably expect, through the migrations of Puritans and Pilgrims. The new immigrants adapted the Old England recipe and, on occasions, exchanged wheat with the more widely available Native American ingredients. This proved to be a very efficient way to preserve food for long periods of time and allowed the early settlers to face the harsh American winters in their journey to the West. Apples, plentiful and wide-spread in the new continent, were considered a standard provision and began to be used in pies on a regular basis—no doubt firstly inspiring the saying 'as American as apple pie'. Pie, in this way, became one of the most highly-consumed pilgrim foods; wheat continued to be used in 'traditional' American pies, but the Americans quickly learned that a small amount 'goes further if it is used to make pies rather than bread'. By the time the 'West was won', pie had become a favourite American food; resisting the test of time, the pie reached the twentieth century with countless fillings, ranging from fruit to custard and meat, and maintained its popularity into the twenty-first. Pies, therefore, are particularly embedded in the history of America, preserving associations, in Clarkson's words, 'with the old country, the new country and the pioneering spirit', perennially identified with the American 'sense of nationhood and patriotism'.[25]

Perhaps feeding into this persistent American pioneering spirit, Roxanne's mother Christine, who is on the pie fair organisational committee, has the task or determining the rules for the contest. After publicising that 'all pies' are 'to be made completely from scratch', Christina also draws everybody's attention to the principal rule of the contest: 'no collaboration' (3). A printed flyer is circulated among perspective pie-makers (invariably female) in order to ensure that this particularly rule is observed: 'Your sister-in-law's crusts are divine but her fillings are watery, and your crusts are like sawdust but your fillings are a dream? Too bad, you do it all yourself' (3). This attention to pie-making detail, and the effort that must be put by any single baker in making the pie nostalgically recalls a 'simpler-time' in American history, when an 'American's woman's worth was inextricably connected to her ability to turn out a dandy homemade pie with a flaky crust'.[26]

The seemingly charming nature of the contest, which might truly inspire a sense of wistfulness and heart-warming desires in the reader, is quickly challenged by Stolz as the pie fair transforms into a statement on racial politics in the American, pre-integration Sixties:

> 'It had come out that the sweet potato pie Emma Reed intended to enter in the contest would be baked by Mary Willis, a black woman who did her cooking and ironing; it was Mrs. Willis's own recipe. Mrs Reed had meant to slip it into the contest as her own'. (4)

Roxanne's mother contests the possibility that the pie should be in someone else's name, following the rules that every baker should make her own. Christina finds herself fighting with the organisational committee in Annette, as she maintains that 'Mary Willis makes that pie and her name should be 'sitting in front of that pie when the contest rolls around'. (7) The issue emerging from this episode, however, does not stop at baking skills and extends, as Stolz herself puts it, to being ' a lot bigger than a pie' (8). The sweet potato pie incident poignantly draws attention to the stereotype of the black woman as a silent domestic. In insisting that African Americans should be allowed to bake for themselves, Stolz raises the problematic issues surrounding de-meriting the black cook for her culinary efforts, a widespread condition in the US up until the Sixties. The racial typecasting that results from the pie quarrel—including Roxanne being called 'Nigger lover' (8)—expressively mirrors the atmosphere of struggle which ruled America in the early Sixties.

The result of the pie debate also echoes the outcome of the historical struggle of the Civil Rights Movement. As Christina wins her battle with the town of Annette, Mary Willis is allowed to enter the pie contest and her image features in the official picture, standing proudly 'in the corner, with her sweet potato pies a blaze of orange' (11). The pie here acts not only as a clear metaphorical representation of white-ethnic America itself, but also as a symbol of social emancipation and racial freedom. In being lawfully appropriated by Mary Willis—as a culinary right which encapsulates the principles of social and racial equality—the pie becomes a tool through which the black woman is able to establish herself not as a subsidiary presence to her employers, but as an individual entity in society.

Pie, however, is not the only prominent politicised American culinary icon in *World of Pies*. A much-loved commodity of the United States—ice cream—seems to be a constant presence in Stolz's novel. It is eaten in a variety of different ways and in different locations. The ice cream parlour, Jerry's Dairy King—together with the local diner and burger joint, Doreen's—functions as the heart and soul of the town of Annette, as most occurrences are either related to the establishment or happen closely around it. Stolz doesn't not miss a chance to tempt with an array 'chocolate-dipped cones' (67) and 'big bowls of butter brickle ice cream' (81); every time ice cream is eaten, the story develops into an important event in the life of the protagonist, from the birth of her little sister Joan to the return of her cousin Tommy from Vietnam. This particularly characteristic is not difficult to perceive in the novel; Stolz, for her part, clearly establishes the culturally inscribed presence of ice cream in the story: 'Mom sent Daddy to the drugstore for calamine lotion, some colouring books, penny candy, and a few pints of Lady Borden ice cream' (63).

A few elements can be noticed about the way ice cream, treated almost as a living entity, interacts with people and events. First, in recalling the presence of Lady Borden as the favourite brand of ice cream, Stolz instils—once again—a sense of nostalgia about the American culinary. Indeed, Border Inc. was a successful American food producer which was founded in 1857; as a principal ice cream producer in the United States, the company was not only an integral part of the American economic revolution, but also responsible for the expansion of the ice cream business over two centuries. Furthermore, Borden has promoted the consumption of its ice cream tubs—branded Lady Borden—as a solid American activity; the slogan 'The most family pleasing ice cream around', coined in 1947, was used for over thirty years to advertise the product. It could be suggested, then, that in connecting Lady Borden ice cream to a sense of familiar unity Stolz is evoking a set of values which she sees as connected to America as a nation, putting together ice cream—historically one of the staple food of the nation—and 'Mom and Dad'. It is ironic that, in actual fact, Borden Inc. met its final demise in 2005—five years after *World of Pies* was initially published—as the last vestiges of the company were finally sold off and one of commercial empires that had been the cornerstone of American life for over 150 years disintegrated.

However, the most fundamental function of ice cream as a solid American culinary icon is revealed by Stolz as her discussions of ice cream unfold: in the novel, Roxanne claims that her family 'believed ice cream cured anything' (63). Although the almost curative properties of ice cream could just be attributed to a sense of sugar-coated nostalgia, a closer look could reveal a very specific dynamic connecting America as a nation to the historical uses of the frozen dessert. In order to grasp this, one needs to consider the part played by ice cream during World War II. By that time, techniques of mechanical refrigeration had developed sufficiently to make the transportation and storage of ice cream a feasible option. Wherever American troops were stationed in Europe, 'ice cream was in demand as a palate-pleaser and morale booster'.[27] The value of ice cream was supported by dieticians and psychologists alike who believed the dessert could 'relive the monotony of field rations' and stimulate 'the appetites of soldiers who were losing weight because food had lost its appeal'. While the troops' morale was boosted overseas, the almost patriotic value of ice cream became known on the home front as well. Anne Funderburg argues that 'as the scope of the war expanded', the function of 'ice cream, as a food and as a symbol, became widely recognised'.[28] As rations prevented the constant consumption of cream and sugar, low-fat, cheaper varieties of ice creams were made widely available to the public. Traditional ice cream—as it was transformed into a much longed-for commodity—became associated with the war effort, assisting American soldiers abroad and maintaining the American spirit alive in the face of danger. Since the end of World War II, one might then say, a close connection between ice cream, patriotism and warfare has existed in the larger American imaginary. Roxanne's claim about the curative power of ice cream highlights a system of belief which places faith not only in ice cream as staple symbolic of the American nation, but in the sense of American loyalty which emerges from its consumption.

There seems to be a general consent in America that ice cream is actually a quintessentially American food. Whilst this may be true in terms of cultural construction and social imagination, the origins of the foodstuff place outside of the American continent. Alan Davidson gives us a historical recounting of how ice cream became part of the great American cookbooks:

> The first ice creams, in the sense of an iced and flavoured confection made from full milk or cream, are thought to have been made in Italy and then in France in the 17th century, and to have been diffused from the French court to other European countries . . . The first recorded English use of the term ice cream (also given as iced cream) was by Ashmore (1672), recording among dishes served at the Feast of St. George at Windsor in May 1671 One Plate of Ice Cream. The first published English recipe was by Mrs. Mary Eales (1718) . . . Mrs. Eales was a pioneer with few followers; ice cream recipes remained something of a rarity in English-language cookery books . . . As for America, Stallings observes that ice cream is recorded to have been served as early as 1744 (by the lady of Governor Blandon of Maryland, nee Barbara Jannsen, daughter of Lord Baltimore), but it does not appear to have been generally adopted until much later in the century.[29]

The question remains of how it came to be that ice cream was treated by Americans as a true culinary exemplification of the United States, so much that ice cream has actually earned itself a spot on the altar of properly American products, joining unquestioned examples such as apple pie. The answer, perhaps, lies in not in the geographical origins of ice cream itself, but the way in which the product was developed and economically exploited in the United States. Indeed, a look into the history of ice cream in America allows us to reveal and reflect on 'changes in social customs, diet and nutrition, class distinctions, leisure activities, gender stereotypes and entrepreneurialism'.[30]

Although ice cream reached America from European shores, its encounter with the new society allowed it to not only evolve, but to redefine itself as a culinary product. In France and England, ice cream had been a special treat reserved for the upper classes. The expensive nature of cream, milk and sugar bestowed an aura of aristocratic indulgence upon the many varieties of iced fruit and dairy desserts which were enjoyed by the privileged. However, once ice cream landed in the New Continent, things dramatically changed. By the time Jefferson brought ice cream back from France—as an openly favoured product—in 1784, the dessert had taken on a completely new, revolutionary flavour. Although its adoption then owed much to French contacts in the period following the American Revolution, one must remember that early Americans still 'shared 18th century England's tastes [. . .] for ice creams [. . .] and proceeded enthusiastically to make ice cream a national dish'.[31]

However, as the treat grew in popularity in the United Sates, 'Americans rejected the idea of ice cream as an aristocratic treat and made it a democratic dish for all classes'.[32] This is perhaps the most important change in the history of American ice cream and, one of the reasons why it is thought of as an American product. The boom in economic development that defining the nineteenth century in the United States encouraged the production of new and exciting foodstuffs; the development of new technologies of refrigeration allowed food to be produced in greater quantities. As a result, prices of what had once been seen as a treat for the elite began to lower, placing a number of exciting foodstuffs (such as ice cream) within the reach of the common man. At the same time, the economic prosperity allowed small-time food entrepreneurs to develop their businesses into established companies, expanding the conceptual visualisation of America as the land of dreams. Indeed, the defining quality of American ice cream was its initiation as an everyday food; its consumption spread from the economically privileged to the masses, establishing ice cream in America 'as a symbol of growth and innovation'.[33]

The written history of American ice cream is not only connected to issues of class. The popularity of the dessert may have also been connected to issues of race. The suggestion that the Philadelphia style ice cream—a type of ice cream made without eggs, therefore separate from the custard-based French variety—may have been invented by an African American man also helped to establish ice cream's position as a foodstuff able to break social, racial and ethnic boundaries. Indeed, one may even suggest that the popularity of ice cream may have been employed—or even exploited—in a bid to promote America's newly-established sense of equality after the Civil War. According to ice cream folklore, the elusive Augustus Jackson is in fact credited with the invention of the defining American style ice cream. However, he does not appear in any reference books about scientists, inventors, black Americans or White House cooks. Nor is he referenced in the Library of Congress or U.S. Patent Office records. In historical terms, this should not come as a surprise; The Negro Alaman claims that during the nineteenth century many 'black inventions were not patented for various reasons, as was the case with ice cream, invented by Augustus Jackson of Philadelphia in 1832'.[34]

The only records of Jackson's dessert entrepreneurship come from local newspapers of the early twentieth century: *The Philadelphia Tribune*, for instance, announced that 'Ice cream, a more universally distinctive American dish than many others which through of earlier introduction are sectional in character, was invented by Augustus Jackson, a Negro confectioner, who was prominent here during the latter half of the nineteenth century'.[35] This rather mysterious explanation is also supported by *The Pittsburgh Courier*, which claimed that 'Augustus Jackson, a Philadelphia Negro, was the first to make America's favourite frozen confection—ice cream—according to the records in the possession of citizens living in the City of Brotherly Love. In 1832 there were five Negro confectioners in Philadelphia'.[36]

The desire to attribute the development of American ice cream to a 'negro' was perhaps inspired by a need to re-order the balance between races in the post-bellum period, adding an aura of nostalgia to the process. As the new Nation was unified and reborn, the choice of Philadelphia as the birth-place of American ice cream—and the establishment of its creator as an African American—renewed the patriotic feeling of national pride which was necessary to keep the country together. Even this contention, however, is simply a hypothesis and does not offer clarity into the dessert's ascent into the American culinary heaven. So, even in the written history of the United States, the development of ice cream as part of the national culinary corollary remains shadowed in doubt, story-telling and second-guessing. Nonetheless, the marketing of ice cream and its impact on the national economic remains unquestioned. By the twentieth century, ice cream's position as a favourite America food was unchallenged. Having gained accessibility for the masses–in spite of its social, racial or cultural background—ice cream became a culinary symbol of the United States, a 'national food' which did not suffer from the social prejudice of other strictly 'regional dishes'.[37]

The function of ice cream as the exemplification of American living does not become more explicit in the novel than when Tommy returns from Vietnam. Ice cream jumps into the scene, once again, as a peculiarly living presence, able to provide refuge and sacker. Upon his return home, Tommy displays signs of alienation which are regarded as typical in war veterans as a result of trauma. Permanently portrayed as smoking—something which is silently frowned upon by his family, almost signifying a level of social degradation—Tommy also displays a 'scarred face' (86), whilst he continues to tug 'at the corner of his lip' (87). His general appearance confirms his 'nervous' disposition (87), as he looks uneasy in what was once a known and familiar environment. As Tommy reacquaints himself with his family—especially Roxanne—he reluctantly gives them details of when he was 'over there' (88); his stories are particularly focused on the food he was forced to consumed, which was often full of 'bugs' (88). The memories of life 'over there' in Vietnam are met with the warm reality back in Annette; however, Tommy does not indulge in descriptions of life back in America, nor does he display happiness about having returned to his family's home. Tommy's admiration for his home country—and his family—is carefully orchestrated by Stolz through his tearful appreciation of home food. Specifically, he displays an attachment to his mother's 'hot fudge' sauce (88), which he proceeds to consume with 'three bowls of ice cream' (88).

In this episode, Stolz makes even clearer the connection between ice cream and American warfare. As Tommy consumes the ice cream, he seems to find a momentary sense of peace, as he proclaims the ice cream itself to be 'the best thing' he 'ever ate' (88). Embodying the figure of the American soldier who has returned home, Tommy also gives shape to the very American conceptual connections which establish the healing power of ice cream in traumatic times. Funderburg reminds us that, even during the times of the Vietnam War, 'military doctors routinely prescribed ice cream to help soldiers recover from combat fatigue'.[38] Field researchers reported that 'ice cream was the only food' that soldiers 'could eat after returning from missions'. The wartime connection between ice cream and the American forces that began in the Forties clearly continued to remain alive even during the years of Vietnam. In using ice cream to provide consolation to Tommy, however, Stolz takes that seemingly physiological connection a little bit further. Ice cream here is taken to embody not only the comfort of home and everyday life, but also of the American way of living. Ice cream, with its history of American entrepreneurship and associations with family unity, communicates a sense of belonging that Tommy—even if only for a few brief moments—can actually relate to. The dessert is the symbol of all that is American and its consumption in large quantities feeds the attachment to 'good times' and 'the American dream'.[39]

And yet, as nostalgic and reassuring as this interpretation may be, it does not completely satisfy. One particular element reveals the almost poisoned relationship connecting Tommy to his enjoyment of ice cream. After his return home—and even after his consumption of the best ice cream he has ever tasted—Tommy is unable to reintegrate himself in the life he used to lead. He is unable to find a stable job and he succumbs to heavy consumption of alcohol, marijuana and speed. The inability to reintegrate into everyday life, however, is not the remarkable element of Tommy's experience as a war veteran in the story. His lowest moments in the story—as he steals money from Roxanne or disappears for days without leaving trace—are accompanied by the consumption of ice cream. He often sneaks 'a bit of ice cream' (131), as he has moments of lucidity from the 'fabrications and evasions' (130) created in this mind by his severe drug use. Although one may be tempted to see Tommy's consumption if ice cream as a desire to become reacquainted with a sense of 'Americaness', another side of his relationship with the dessert is present. As a clear symbol of America—or, perhaps, of the cultural construction that is treated as the perfect American nation—ice cream paradoxically appears as a signifier of Tommy's alienation from his own country and his inability to lead a 'respectable' American life. As his distress generated from a wartime experience, the presence of ice cream does not simply remind the reader of the American spirit, but also introduces the possible disintegration of American values, founded on warfare and trauma. It would be a bit risky to suggest that Stolz was actually intending to offer this particular connection between ice cream and shattered American dreams when writing *World of Pies*. And yet, in its desire to push positive symbols of American cultural heritage into the wider imaginary, the book also draws attention not only the forcefully positive, but also the problematic side of American culture and history. The desire to portray ice cream as 'quintessentially American' exemplifies the conceptual power exercised by food in exposing the issues surrounding a stable concept of belonging and national pride.

The function served by what is interpreted as iconic 'American food' is even more evident in the novel when a barbecue is organised in honour of Tommy's return:

> Aunt Ruthie and Uncle Frank went without us to pick Tommy up at the airport. "We don't want to wear him out; he's still recovering" Aunt Ruthie said. We went over later for hamburgers. (86)

It should not be unexpected that Stolz chooses hamburgers as the other culinary agent to signify a return home to the Unites States. The history of the hamburger itself in inextricably tangled with the economic and cultural rise of modern America. The burger has its own history, 'a thick narrative line' which highlights the social ups and downs of a whole country.[40] Although the sandwich itself is said to have been invented in the Unites States in the nineteenth century—when it was 'gobbled by a rising class of urban factory workers'—the chronicle of the rise of the burger joins discussions of consumerism in the twentieth century. The popularity of the burger—and the velocity with which it spread throughout the food outlets of the country—was instrumental in producing the consumer (and corporate) culture which we are able to recognise as the driving force of contemporary American economic and cultural politics. By the time McDonalds' Restaurants were founded in the Forties in San Bernardino, California, the burger had established its presence in the American wider imaginary as part of the American diet, incorporating its status as 'the American beef meal par excellence'.[41]

In the Sixties, the burger became the gastronomic agent of Cold War propaganda. A famous promotional movie produced and distributed by Union Pacific railroad—and aptly entitled *Beef Rings the Bell*—proclaims that 'juicy, broiled hamburgers with just the right touch of charcoal taste from the fire have become an American institution'. The film, released in 1960, assumes that the audience—the American audience, of course—absolutely adores beef and consumes it on a regular basis. Consumption, however, is not the only concern of the narrator in *Beef Rings the Bell*; indeed, he goes on to identify the social value of the hamburger, announcing that 'even the process of broiling hamburgers is fun, and promotes friendships and good fellowship'.[42] The iconic status of the hamburger is used by Union Pacific to encourage a sense of family unity and 'golden age' American togetherness that—although it may have never actually existed—was still at the height of the utopian wishes for the American dream. Clearly, the narrator's openly hollow praise of the beef burger embodies everything that was conformist and predictable about Cold War politics. And yet, with its 'paternal pomposity' and 'tossed-off nostrums about the American way of Life', the narrator of *Beef Rings the Bell* draws attention to the status achieved by the humble hamburger. The product, it would seem, is more than just a sandwich, a consumable necessity of life. Even back in the Sixties *Beef Rings the Bell* was able to identify the hamburger as a 'social nexus', a political status which it still retains today. Josh Odersky points out that 'even before the hamburger became a universal signifier' for American imperialism, it had a special 'semiotic power'. The burger's ability to 'signify' a whole cultural system in itself unique and it is not shared even by other American iconic foods, such as the hot dog or the fried chicken. In spite of the likes and dislikes—together with various political musings—that may surround the food itself, one thing cannot be denied: 'nothing says America like the hamburger'.[43]

It is precisely this iconic status of the burger which is put forward in *World of Pies*. The burger seems to be on everyone's mind as Tommy's return home is announced. Roxanne and her mother prepare a 'hamburger casserole' (83) in his honour, to accompany the planned feast of grilled burgers which will take place at his parents' house. As Tommy returns from Vietnam—the foreign, 'un-American' land—the burger is there to welcome him home. The burger here can be taken to signify America itself, a whole system of belief and cultural affiliation which finds its perfect embodiment in the ubiquitous beef patty. Almost echoing the propaganda publicised by *Beef Rings the Bell*—a film that was well-known during by the early Seventies, the time of Tommy's return—the burgers embody a sense of family and kinship; the family's pride in their son and their country is communicated through the hamburger, so that the quintessence of American social unity can be transmitted by way of meat.

And yet, the status of the hamburger as an icon of American pride is not completely unchallenged in *World of Pies*. Like she does with ice cream, Stolz uses the hamburger—the quintessential American sandwich—to critique American war politics. This clearly emerges when one looks at Tommy's actual interaction with the burgers: 'When Uncle Frank went into the house to freshen our drinks, Tommy went over to flip the burgers. He made a show of flipping them with one hand, but one flipped onto the grass' (87). The flipping of the burgers—an activity which in itself communicates family fun and community bonding—could be seen as Tommy's attempt to reintegrate into the American way of life; the burger is his way into regaining a sense of 'good fellowship' with his country and his sense of being an American at home. However, Tommy has returned from Vietnam without an arm, the loss of a limb being a common war-time injury for soldiers. His inability to flip the burger—a consequence of his disability—calls into question his actual ability to reintegrate. Nonetheless, the fallen burger does much more for the socio-cultural politics of the novel. As Tommy drops the hamburger, attention is drawn to his absent arm, a clear sign of the impact of American war politics. As the burger falls, so does the legacy which comes with it; the sense of American fellowship collapses and the notion of American social supremacy and pride are questioned—in an ironic manner—by the very symbol which represents them. The social and cultural dislocation experienced by Tommy is emphasised even as he attempt to eat the burgers: he remains 'quiet during dinner' and he carefully squirts 'ketchup onto his hamburger (88). His inability to communicate reveals a sense of sadness and perhaps disillusionment, as the 'perfect' American hamburger is seasoned and consumed. Stolz, it would seem, does not fully commit to the burger's undisputed role as an icon of American freedom, which may prove popular with agents of political and nationalist propaganda. In the final years of the pre-9/11 age, the value of the American political burger had already become problematic. While the touch of food nostalgia that pervades the pages of the novel perhaps wishes to make the reader believe in the greater American good, its hidden gastronomic politics insist on telling otherwise.

As ice cream and hamburgers intersect in *World of Pies*, their presence reveals politicised representations of American history and social regulations. Nonetheless, there is another popular culinary icon in the text which unveils how depictions of food and drink can be connected to wishful constructions of the Unites States and American identities in the wider popular imaginary. Coca-Cola appears as a constant presence throughout the novel. It witnesses Roxanne's development from a baseball-loving child to a happily married mother. While growing up in the small town of Annette, Roxanne and her friend make a date of going 'over to Doreen's to get a Coke' (12); the bottles emerge 'beaded and steaming from the case' (16), almost beaming with a self-accomplished sense of glory. The beverage is often drank 'on the back porch' (36) and everybody manages to get 'enough money for Coke' (37). Coke accompanies Roxanne as she enjoys the bliss of summer evenings, and is there to comfort her in her moments of of sadness. While Roxanne's dad is constantly stocking 'the refrigerator with Coke' (69), her mother Christina turns a Coke into an unmissable staple presence to be served with food, as the drink is combined and consumed with a variety of foodstuffs, from 'sandwiches' (113), to 'grilled cheese and fries' (86) and 'potato chips, pickles and Cokes' (114). On different moments in the story, Coca-Cola appears in a lot of its different incarnations, from common coke bottles to 'lemon Cokes' (43) and 'cherry Cokes' (86). From yearly Fourth of July celebrations to moments of reckoning with adolescence and death, Coca-Cola never abandons its place as the drink of choice. The history of Roxanne's family is imbricated with Coca-Cola; no matter what the occasion at hand is, the characters of Stolz's novel are always 'drinking a Coke' (37).

It could be argued that, in presenting itself as a constant chronological and cultural coordinate which organises lives and occasions in the story, Coca-Cola also provides a sense of history to the novel. It is connected to the past, to the most beloved memories carried by Roxanne and it brings a comforting dimension of stability as situation becomes unbearable. Coca-Cola is a known entity, a reliable focus, a consumable piece of history. This association between a sense of past and identity and Coca-Cola does not come as a surprise. The drink's ability surpass chronological differences is solidified by the history of the company itself, which was made famous over the years and has now become a commonly known part of American cultural and economic history. As a product and a brand, Coca-Cola is fond of recalling its origins and its expansion reads as a 'microcosm of American history'.[44] All one needs to do to see this is visit the Coca-Cola museum in Atlanta—the birth place of the beverage—where high-tech props are used to 'indoctrinate' the millions of tourists who visit daily into the company's version of its glorious past. The most interesting part of the company's attachment to history is that the 'official' creation story promoted by Coca-Cola 'has all the earmarks of the classic American success myth'.[45] As Coca-Cola tells the tale of its providential and unexpected chemical birth, its creator—John Permberton—is portrayed as a humble doctor who had the great fortune of assembling the formula for the drink in 1886. Although the creation story promoted by Coca-Cola has very little historical truth in it, its impact on the general American public remains unquestioned. Offering the proof that the American dream can actually come true—where young workers from humble origins can obtain great wealth through 'perseverance', 'hard work' and 'good luck'–Coca-Cola enjoys its privileged position as a distinctly American brand. The Coca-Cola sign is almost universally recognised in America and the world; in its emblematic role as a fortunate and 'persevering' drink, Coca-Cola is ubiquitously understood, in Mark Pendergrast's words' as 'the sublimated essence of America'.[46]

Using Coca-Cola also adds a dimension 'of the past' to the story. It openly communicates that the novel wishes to re-evoke the past, praise it and honour it. This sense of past importance in intrinsic to Coca-Cola as a brand. Not only is it a brand that has existed in America for over 150 years—developing almost in synchronised amicability with the Post-Bellum United States, as we know them today—but it also is one of the old brands in the country, becoming synonymous with its history. Also, Coca-Cola—unlike other brands in the U.S. and the world—has remained virtually unchanged. Its logo remains the same as it was in 1886 and also the usage of the affectionate 'Coke'—instead of the full brand name—testifies to a different approach to the drink over the years.

However, the function of Coca-Cola may not stop simply at its value as a symbol of the American past; its further—and much more proactive value—may be hidden not only in the fabricated history of its creation, but its specific purpose as well. Indeed, in spite of the company's desire to commercialise its history as a truly American example of the 'underdog to stardom' story, its historically accurate origins shed a rather different not only on the product, but on any use of its name that may be made. First, it must be sad, Coca-Cola as a beverage was not Pemberton's lucky and unexpected invention; it was created—purposefully—right at the end of the Civil War, a turning point of American history. In the midst of turmoil and cultural confusion, the drink found its perfect living condition; taking advantage of the desire for stability and clam that swept across the country, Coca-Cola was marketed as a 'brain tonic' that promised to heal headaches with its miraculously sweet tasting formula.[47] From the day of its creation Coca-Cola has had a sort of healing function for the United States as a country. After the first years of existence, spent gaining a stable reputation as an 'antidote cloaked in innocence',[48] Coca-Cola expanded into advertising campaigns and vigorous marketing strategies to expand its uncontested dominion through the United States. Although no longer marketed as a tonic, its mythological 'healing' function clearly appealed to the general American consumer. Coke provided the pleasure of a moment—'brief, carbonated, affordable' interruptions against the dullness of everyday life.[49] The implementation of new transport infrastructures allowed Coke's popularity to reach every corner of the country and established 'a distinctively American brand of capitalism', one which exalted the idea of pleasure and idealised the experience of the individual.[50] By the time the mid-twentieth century came, World War II had given the company another chance to engage in vigorous marketing campaigns and promote themselves as a patriotic, compassionate and all-rounded curative drink for nation and troops alike. After the war effort ended, Coca-Cola remained covered in sparkle, stars and stripes—the liquid saviour of a whole nation—and, with its distinct flavour of hope and success, it became 'as American as baseball'.[51]

This side of Coca-Cola as a product instigates questions about the collective use of its image. If the drink is tacitly associated by the whole American culture with a sense of healing and gratification, then perhaps its employment of the drink in *World of Pies*—to define particular moments within the story—is not simply iconic, but verges on the metaphysical. Not only does Coca-Cola always appear within the story to lift the spirits when things go bad, but its therapeutic function could go beyond the limits of the storytelling itself. If one assembles together Coke's attributes as icon of the American past, symbol of freedom and happiness and cultural remedy, we could see how the novel could be engaging with a form of capitalist spiritualism. The mere invocation o the name 'Coca-Cola' could be a way to show devotion towards an ideal, as the universally recognisable 'curvaceous image' of the drinks pops into people's minds and beckons 'toward the American way'.[52] Perhaps, Coke is meant to be doing for the idea of small town America within Stolz' novel what it did for the whole country upon its creation. Its remedial purpose functions against the loss of sense of what is American in the year 2000, when the novel was written. Coca-Cola does for the novel what it was originally marketed for upon its invention: it is an antidote for nerves, a calming essence of America, a glue that can hold together—albeit only symbolically—the belief in the country, its customs and its past. Perhaps, then, that is what the whole book is trying to do for the reader: it squeezes together the tastes and flavours of nostalgia, to promote an increasingly threatened sense of small-town American existence. The novel makes a virtue of promoting a version of American small-town living which is perhaps as fabricated and socially constructed as the history of Coca-Cola itself, with which it is constantly associated.

Recalling the image of Coca-Cola as an all-American remedy, the drink is promoted as a 'necessity' in the novel: 'Penny said she would die if she didn't have Coca-Cola in the next fifteen minutes' (16). The declaration that Penny absolutely 'needs' a bottle of Coca-Cola is interesting on several levels. Constance Hays reminds us that Coca-Cola has been one of the only brands—in American and worldwide—to have 'crossed the line between consumer product and object of desire'.[53] Indeed, Coca-Cola has made a virtue throughout its history of its famous and much loved advertising campaigns. Particularly, in the Sixties—interestingly, the period when *World of Pies* begins and Penny is said to absolutely require a Coca-Cola—the company's focus was turned on the idea of refreshment and pleasure more than ever before. From 1960 onwards, a succession of adverts—in the form of billboards, signs and magazines—praised the drink's ability to provide an experience which was truly impossible to miss. In 1961, the drink was advertised with the slogan "Coke refreshes you best!' In 1962, it was claimed by the adverts that 'Only Coke gives you that refreshing feeling'. By 1963, the need for Coke became almost imperative and the adverts incited the consumers to 'Have a Coke now'.[54] Strategically chosen words such as 'best', 'only' and 'now' were associated with the brand and mixed together to form a potent advertising mantra which made the drink incredibly desirable.

In cultural materialist studies, the consumer dream is a product of contemporary capitalist society, in which the individual imagines future pleasures to be obtained through using a specific product. Such a dream, however, is never entirely fulfilled by the commodity itself; the consumer, therefore, perpetually longs for satisfaction and continues to purchase. As Colin Campbell argues, 'many of the cultural products offered for sale in modern societies are in fact consumed because they serve as aids to the construction of day-dreams'.[55] While the economic expansion continued in Sixties America, eating and drinking became the epicentre of a utopian ideal in advertising discourses. The promotion of food and drink was a principal interest in the consumer world. As part of a strategy to satisfy the consumers' domestic desires, advertising was also increasingly influenced by psychoanalytical research.[56] Writing in 1957, Vance Packard was aware that 'the use of mass psychoanalysis to guide campaigns of persuasion' had become 'the basis of a multimillion-dollar industry'.[57] With the commercial excitement of the Fifties still going strong, Sixties consumerism embraced the idea of cheerful optimism and desire that would define advertising campaigns throughout the whole decade. The food industry, in particular, embraced the idea of 'persuasion' through psychoanalytical manipulation. The Freudian approach not only affected, but truly revolutionised the way in which food was sold to consumers. Considering food advertising in context, this does not come as a surprise. The Fifties and Sixties were the golden age of the supermarket, when local shops were rapidly replaced by the retail chains which spread across America. The foods themselves were changing: the idea of 'fresh' was being replaced by technologically advanced frozen, powdered and packaged foods.[58]

In the early Fifties, David Potter argued that psychoanalytical advertising became an institution that touched on every aspect of everyday life, and aimed to 'enforce already existing attitudes, to diminish the range and variety of choices' and 'to exalt the materialistic virtues of consumption'.[59] Advertising strategies were coordinated as a system of external stimuli—literally making the purchaser 'desire' the product—which aimed to promote consumption whilst reinforcing the identity of the brand as indispensable. As a result of its heavy advertising campaigns in the Sixties, Coca-Cola was promoted as a truly 'essential' drink, which people could literally not live without. And this is truly the image of the drink which is given in *World of Pies*. Stolz does not mention Coca-Cola adverts in the novel, nor does she discuss their marketing strategies. And yet, she does not need to. The Coca-Cola brand of American philosophy is draped over every page of *World of Pies*.

The feeling of nostalgia and childhood memories that emerges from drinking Coca-Cola in Stolz's novel is actually unveiled as the product of commercial enterprise. It is worth recalling here that, already in the early Sixties, Sylvia Plath affirmed that food advertising in magazines provided her with 'an Americaness' she felt 'a need to dip into'.[60] Plath recognised the power of advertising in promoting a sense of American identity. It is difficult to assert whether Stolz is aware of her feeding into the capitalist pot; the tendency would probably be to say that she is just trying to evoke the warmth of the past and add a touch of melancholy by recalling brands that in her mind epitomise the American experience in the early Sixties. That experience, however, is not without mediation. Indeed, what Stolz tries to promote as a wonderful sense of nostalgic attachment to history actually translates into a walking advert for Coca-Cola as a company. Memory of the American past is made commercial; even something that might look as an innocent a figure of speech is influenced by advertising.

The commercialisation of culinary politics, inside and outside of the home, is not a concern which is only evident in Stolz. Brett Easton Ellis' *American Psycho* (1991) draws our attention to how the power of capitalist enterprise, brand calling and advertising have an effect on every aspect of life, including eating. The novel, which displays numerous qualities of postmodern literature, narrates a few months in the life of Patrick Bateman, a wealthy and self-obsessed Manhattan broker. Bateman, who also serves as the unreliable narrator, shows signs of psychological disturbances, as his disgust for the current state of yuppie society develops into homicidal, torturous and even cannibalistic manias. Given its setting in the early Eighties, it is not unexpected to see that the novel focuses on long descriptions and evaluations of expensive commodities; food, in particular, features as a telling extension of fashionable trends and psychotic fixations in Bateman's New York society.

Dinner at home in *American Psycho*, however, is a rather different experience from what is put forward in *World of Pies*. Separated from Stolz's notions of home cooking by an array of complicated dishes and expensive dinner paraphernalia, eating with friends is a matter of display. The dinner held at Evelyn's house is a clear example of this. Bateman describes the whole event in detail, paying particular attention to how it is 'set up'. Flaunting an impressive knowledge of stores and products, Bateman surveys the dinner room carefully, pondering on how costly the items on the table are and, especially, where they were purchased. The dinner table, we are told, proudly shows 'beeswax candles from Zona lit in their sterling silver candleholders from Fortunoff'.[61] There is no idea of 'relaxation' communicated by eating at Evelyn's; every element of the event under inspection and enquiry.

The food to be served—consisting of various examples of sushi—receives the same treatment. Evelyn, the host, is portrayed as trying to 'spell' initials, 'the P in yellowtail, the B in tuna' (9). She then proceeds to place 'strips of pale ginger delicately in a pile next to small porcelain dish filled with soy sauce' (10). The whole endeavour, for both Evelyn and the guests, is described by Bateman as 'harassed' and is perceived with 'darkly' emotions (10). Dinner at Evelyn's, it would seem, challenges all conceptions of 'comfort' that are supposedly associated with the home dinner in Stolz's work. When Bateman's attention is focused on the food itself, it is only in order to describe its visual qualities. He considers how the tuna, yellowtail, mackerel, shrimp' all seem 'so fresh', with 'piles of wasabi and clumps of ginger placed strategically around the Wilton platter' (12). The emphasis on the term 'strategically' here draws attention to how the beautiful food is acting not only as display, but as advertising for a very specific set of ideas. One can see here how, in the home dinner, Evelyn gains an opportunity to distinguish herself from the group. Lupton suggests that, in the home dinner, 'the things that people do for each other are considered acts of love', rather than being based on 'monetary or utilitarian terms'.⁶² This conception, however, is willingly destroyed in Ellis' novel. Through the carefully displayed sushi, Evelyn inscribes upon herself a valuable status in front of her guests. Far from wanting to please her guests for reasons of love or affection, Evelyn turns the sushi into a performance of social image, encapsulating 'the endless producing and reproducing of desire, of the body in the world's image and the world in the body's image'.⁶³

The watchful descriptions of lavish dining 'in the home' also recall Barthes' conception that all cooking might involve a degree of display. When looking at the home dinner in *American Psycho*, Barthes' interrogation of display cuisine seems to be instructive in order to grasp how Ellis constructs food and its function as a cultural commodity. In 'Ornamental Cookery'—an essay in *Mythologies*—Barthes specifically considers food as a commodity and how cooking has evolved into a consumerist practice. Looking at examples of food photography from French magazines as a point of departure, Barthes describes cooking in consumerist contexts as evidently 'based on coatings and alibis' and the 'persistence of glazing'. The highly decorative quality of food presentation in *haute cuisine*, Barthes argues, aims 'to disguise the primary nature of foodstuffs, the brutality of meat or the abruptness of sea-food'.⁶⁴

As Bateman observes the sushi, he briefly wonders where Evelyn obtained the fish. However, this questioning state does not last long. He quickly admits not only to not knowing where the food came from, but also to his fundamental indifference to the matter: 'I like the idea that I *don't know*, will *never know* and will never *ask* where it came from and that the sushi will sit there in the middle of the glass table from Zona (. . .) like some mysterious apparition from the Orient' (12). Bateman's disinterest in the provenance of the fish–how it was caught, killed and ultimately sold—is consistent with what Barthes sees as a definitive quality of contemporary culinary commercialisation. Barthes claims that in obscuring the origins of products from the consumer—who is only presented with idealised pictures of finished dishes—food on display then becomes 'openly dream-like' and 'totally magical'.⁶⁵ With this concept in mind, Bateman's almost hypnotic description of the fish as a 'mysterious apparition' feeds into the food's quality as commercial exhibition, constructing a consumer-orientated fantasy of ungraspable, yet coveted beauty. The fact that Bateman's fish commodification happens within the home—a site commonly associated in the wider collective imagery with 'genuine' experiences—only highlights the possibility that, in the economic landscape of late capitalist cultures, the 'division between public and private is over-stated' and, as Bell and Valentine put it, 'difficult to draw' in the midst of 'shared activities' such as eating.⁶⁶

Indeed, food is treated as the ultimate commodity in *American Psycho*. Home food stands here, almost paradoxically, for 'prestige, status and wealth' and acts as 'a means of communication and personal relations'.[67] Separated both visually and conceptually from the humble family dinner, dining at home for Bateman and friends is not only an activity based on presentation, but also a medium for the economically privileged to parade their wealth. The combination of the dishes on the table becomes, as Lupton puts it, a very 'public demonstration of an individuals' possession of both economic and cultural capital, phrased as their sense of taste'.[68] Eating is part of an extended commercial enterprise that continues in the home what might be happening on the outside. Bateman keeps the guests under constant scrutiny, meticulously noting even what clothes they are displaying: 'Price is wearing a sic-button wool and silk suit by Ermenegildo Zegna, a cotton shirt with French cuffs by Ike Behar, a Ralph Lauren silk tie and leather wing tips by Fratelli Rossetti' (5); 'Courtney opens the door and she is wearing a Krizia cream silk blouse, a Krizia rust tweed skirt and silk-satin d'Orsay pumps from Manolo Blahnik' (8). Bateman's interest in the clothes brands feeds into the cycle of commercial consumption in which eating is placed. Ellis' treatment of the dining experience with friends openly disputes the idea of the home as 'a place where people are offstage (. . .) in control of their immediate environment'.[69]

DINING OUT

Although one may have expectations regarding the home meal, in *American Psycho* Ellis refuses to adhere to ordinary notions of comfort and relaxation. The dinner at Evelyn's is just as much an activity of display as would be dining in a restaurant. Nonetheless, issues of display, surveillance and 'image', become even more evident when Bateman's attention turns to restaurants and 'dining out'. It is in meals 'away from home' that *American Psycho* offers its most acute critique of Eighties social and cultural politics. The restaurant experiences described by Bateman in the novel have become legendary. If one wanted to be provocative, it would be possible to describe Bateman as the ultimate literary 'foodie', as his interests in eating and consumption lie more in the exhibitive qualities of the food, rather than its function as palatable enjoyment.

The restaurant is not simply portrayed as a site of food consumption. Although the food does make a sizeable appearance and it is carefully scrutinised, it is also made clear that the location is the centre of the attention. Choosing a restaurant is not just a matter of taste—or, at least, not in the gustatory sense. If there is any sense of taste involved in Bateman's ruminations about which restaurant to choose or which table to sit at, it definitely contains a high degree of performance. Posed in clear opposition with a quite meal at home presented by Stolz , away from the buzz and lights of the city, the restaurant experience is identified by Ellis as almost a reflection of self. What is 'on display' is not simply the food, or not even just the individual amongst others, but a whole set of social rules and codes that define a particular cultural setting as such. The interaction between Bateman, the food and the other diners gives us an insight in the normative regulations which control and shape society in *American Psycho*.

What is being promoted and coveted by Bateman and his acquaintances is the 'total consumption package'.[70] Food and drink are associated with people—who must, of course, be of an acceptable social standard—clothes and outfits, theatre shows and magazine reviews. Eating at a particularly famous and fashionable restaurant becomes a social statement of distinction, a way to establish presence and standing. The restaurant—with its ideal setting for mingling and exchange—provides all the coordinates to achieve not only gustatory satisfaction, but an overall titillation for the social and sociable self. Restaurants in *American Psycho* are not just sites of food and drink; they open the diners to a 'whole experience'. It is that 'experience' which is sought after and paradoxically despised by Bateman.

As the 'dining experience' takes on a whole new meaning, Ellis presents the restaurant as a carefully managed environment. Bateman is aware of every single detail within the site, from the position of the table, to the waitressing staff and, finally, the food. Bell and Valentine remind us that as a particular place of financial exchange, the restaurant might have certain characteristics which is 'suitable for consumption', with an 'atmosphere' that will be appreciated by diners.[71] Although this position seems to validate Bateman's approach to the restaurant, in reality it highlights his failure to appreciate the restaurant as site for pleasure and enjoyment. Bateman's restaurant experiences are never deemed as enjoyable. A fixation with being 'seen' and 'evaluated' goes hand in hand with Bateman's obsession with having a reservation at a good restaurant. Bateman's feelings upon entering restaurant are often surrounded by an aura of despair, as his desire to be seen in a prominent location surpasses all desires to eat or enjoy himself: "I'm on the verge of tears by the time we arrive at Pastels since I'm positive we won't get seated' (39). Not having a reservation, it would seem, is seen as embarrassing: 'We need to make a reservation. I'm not standing at some fucking bar' (36). 'Standing at the bar' here is understood as negative display, proof that one is not worthy, not part of the elite group. Whenever a table is not booked, it is cause of annoyance and surprise for Bateman: 'I'm sitting in DuPlex, the new tony McManus restaurant in Tribeca, with Christopher Armstrong (. . .) We, *inexplicably*, could not get reservations at Subjects' (137). This desire to have a reservation recalls Alan Beardsworth and Teresa Keil's contention that 'eating in the public domain becomes a mode of demonstrating one's standing'.[72]

It is indeed this obsession with 'demonstrating' that motivates Bateman's actions. Possessed by a sense of self-worth that is confirmed by obtaining a good table in a fashionable restaurant, Bateman engages with acts of culinary exhibitionism, as he creates a way of flaunting his own social distinction by 'associating' himself with the 'ready-made ambience of the restaurant itself'.[73] Far from being plagued by the idea of constantly being 'watched', Bateman desires a good table, where he can not only be seen by others, but also observe others in his own right. Bateman is constantly putting himself on display, inviting offers of surveillance and scrutiny as an essential part of the restaurant experience.

The customers of each restaurant are placed, effectively, 'under surveillance'. Throughout his critical analyses of power, Foucault returned to the determining significance of 'knowledge' and 'surveillance'.[74] In *Discipline and Punish*, he claims that 'there is no power relationship without the correlative constitution of a field of knowledge, nor any knowledge that does not presuppose, and constitutes at the same time, power relations'.[75] The panopticon in particular was, according to Foucault's reading, an especially effective technology for rendering subjects knowable and docile through surveillance: 'a mechanism of power reduced to its ideal form'.[76] While Foucault does not specifically address links between the rise of capitalism and the emergence of panoptic techniques of surveillance, the model he provides has been extended by others in critical analyses of consumer society.[77] David Lyon also observes in *Surveillance Society*, that the capitalist market has witnessed 'a massive expansion of efforts to use surveillance technologies to manage customers'.[78] Capitalism is dependent on the gathering and processing of information in order to ensure the most efficient extraction of value from production and consumption.

In *American Psycho*, the panoptic nature of the restaurant exercises constant examination on the diners 'as a mechanism of disciplinary power without any physical instrument'.[79] One could argue, therefore, that as he inspects his fellow diners and the food, Bateman himself is 'under surveillance' all the time. It must be said, however, that the feeling of oppression that derives from being 'surveyed' is, to some extent, self-inflicted; Bateman is constantly exercising self-surveillance and self-discipline, ranging from the clothes he wears and where he lives to what he consumes, even when alone. His self-scrutiny reaches uncontrollable levels, both in public and in private:

> 'At the island in the kitchen I eat kiwifruit and a slices Japanese pear (they cost for dollars each at Gristede's) out of aluminium storage boxes that were designed in West Germany. I take a bran muffin, a decaffeinated herbal tea bag and a box of oat-bran cereal from one of the large glass-front cabinets that make up most of an entire wall in the kitchen; complete with stainless-steel shelves and sandblasted wire glass, it is framed in metallic dark-grey blue'. (28)

Outside of the home, the restaurant is a site of observation on a number of levels. Everything the characters eat—or, on a number of occasions, what they do not eat—is on constant display. Ellis dedicates pages and pages to description of food choices and particular dishes. Bateman does not miss an opportunity to careful scrutinise what appears on his friends' plates; his watchful eyes describes the food and how it is presented in detail:

> 'Our appetizers are removed and at the same time our entrées arrive [. . .] she [Evelyn] ordered quail stuffed into blue corn tortillas garnished with oysters in potato skins. I have the free-range rabbit with Oregon morels and herbed French fries'. (123)

Food is never simply eaten: it is continuously surveyed, evaluated and judged. Every dish is accompanied by a journalistic review, which is recalled in Bateman's head as a testament to its presumed superiority. The quality of the food is not tested through tastebuds, bit is placed in the hands of food critics on a regular basis. When faced with a dish of 'peach butter soup with smoked duck and mashed squash' (77), for instance, Bateman believes that the ensemble 'sounds strange' (77); however, when he quickly recounts how the soup was described as 'playfully mysterious'(77) by the *New York Times*, his opinions subside and he praises the dish as 'actually quite good' (77). Bateman's watchful eye and his continuous recanting of food reviews—placing the food is a unremitting state of inspection—highlight the restaurant experience as a state of 'continual surveillance'.[80]

One might be tempted here to suspect that in the mists of all this vacant obsession with tables, appearance, setting and decor, the food itself may actually be overlooked, a floating presence which only acts as a means to an end. In fact, it is not. The food which arrives at the table receives a severe amount of attention, every single detail—from presentation, of course, to price—is meticulously scrutinised; Bateman surveys a never-ending array of 'venison with yoghurt sauce and fiddlehead ferns with mango slices' (40), 'pilot fish with tulips and cinnamon' (263) and 'chocolate-covered almonds' and 'gazpacho with raw chicken in it' (364). Nonetheless, the attention given to the food is not what one might expect; Bateman does not often indulge in descriptions of taste, neither does he revel in evocative recollections of dishes and recipes. His interest in the food is, almost entirely, of a very socio-economic nature. He also ponders over the price of each ingredient and compares its 'visual' qualities with dishes he has had before at other restaurants:

> Evelyn is talking but I'm not listening. Her dialogue overlaps her own dialogue. Her mouth is moving, but I'm not hearing anything and I can't listen, I can't really concentrate, since my rabbit has been cut to look . . . just . . . like . . . a . . . star! Shoestring french fries surround it and chunky red salsa has been smeared across the top of the plate—which is white and porcelain and two feet wide—to give the appearance of a sunset, but it looks like one big gunshot wound to me and shaking my head slowly in disbelief I press my finger into the meal. (123)

The first thing to notice here is that the idea of turning elegant food into an iconic sunset is reminiscent Wolfe's equally fanciful dinners in *The Bonfire of the Vanities*, written at the height of the Eighties:

> The first course arrived. Fallow had ordered a vegetable pâté. The pâté was a small pinkish semicircle with stalks of rhubarb arranged around it like rays. It was perched in the upper-left hand quadrant of a large plate. The plate seemed to be glazed with an Art Nouveau painting of a Spanish galleon on a reddish sea sailing towards the . . . sunset . . . but the setting sun was, in fact, the pâté, with its rhubarb rays, and the Spanish galleon was not done in glaze at all but in different colours of sauce.[81]

Although Wolfe's lump of pâté is substituted with a cut of rabbit, the metaphor of the sunset as a romanticised symbol of over-elaborate culinary design in the Eighties continues to shine for Ellis in his early Nineties reflection on the previous decade's obsessions, desires and frustrations.

Bateman's interaction with the rabbit, however, is revelatory. Not only do we get a reminder of his no-longer latent psychopathology—exemplified in his envisioning of gunshot wounds–but we also get Ellis' insight into the state of food as decorative commodity in the Eighties and its effects on conceptions of 'reality'. The food experience, it is made clear, is not an unmediated experience. As Bateman touches the rabbit to ensure that it does not have signs of a gunshot, he also does so—one could argue—in order to see if it actually 'exists'. The idea of 'touching' with one's finger is rendered here as a common and recognisable sign of anyone wanting to ascertain the presence of an object.

It should not come as a surprise that Ellis chooses meat in order to discuss the possibly 'unreal' qualities of the food. Looking at the metaphorics of carnivorous consumption, Adams points out that 'meat is seen as a vehicle of meaning and not as inherently meaningful'.[82] In spite of Adams' suggestion, one must remember that meat itself, as a concept, relies on obscuring one the nature of the dead animal, in order to offer it as a consumable. The consumption of animals implies the supremacy of the human species. The concept of 'meat' is inevitably connected to the demise and destruction of other species. In the process of producing meat, animals become what Adams calls 'absent referents': dead bodies replace the living animals, so that creatures themselves can be transformed into 'food'.[83] Furthermore, animals can be interpreted as absent referents because of their literal consumption or through linguistic expression (when 'animal' is suddenly turned into 'meat').

As the unfortunate rabbit is transformed into a romanticised sunset image in *American Psycho*, Ellis exposes the potentially constructed nature of the restaurant. Indeed, we witness here a potentially politicised sensitivity to the way in which the reality of food itself is consumed by images which belong to the representational regimes of social identity. As Roger

Haden insists, commercial enterprise exploits the fact that food, especially of animal origin, has 'the capacity to take on a plethora of meanings [that] pushes it beyond its role [. . .] into [. . .] being a language'.[84] The rabbit, therefore, 'becomes' not only a sunset, but also a representation of a higher social value.

For Bateman, however, the rabbit-sunset also speaks another language: the language of the unreal and the disturbing absurd—embodied in the gunshot fantasies. The rabbit brings back the idea that display cuisine tries to remove the reality—the death of a live animal, a reminder of finality—so that it could be turned into food. In the light of the dubious descriptions given by Bateman, one might venture that the food he observes is *more than* 'unreal' and in fact belong to the realm of the 'hyper-real'. Jean Baudrillard's critique in *The Consumer Society* (1970) proposes that visual media were supplanting material reality with inauthentic images, creating a world of pseudo-existence: 'the world of the pseudo-event, of pseudo-history, and of pseudo-culture [. . .] [is] produced [. . .] as artefacts from the technical manipulation of the medium and its coded elements [. . .] it is this and nothing else, which defies all signification whatsoever as consumable'.[85]

Baudrillard's critique is broadly consonant with that offered by Guy Debord. In his seminal study of *Society of the Spectacle* (1967), Debord proposes that Marx's prophecy—'all that is solid melts into air'—has come to pass in contemporary consumer society: 'all that was once directly lived has become mere representation'.[86] The explosive proliferation of images and representations of commodities produces 'moments of fervent exaltation' similar to 'convulsionary' and 'miraculous cures' of the 'old religious fetishism'.[87] This process is also described, in Baudrillardean terms, by Haden: 'consumer understanding and appetites are continually exposed to recursive forms of mediation which undermine any[thing] real'.[88] Bateman's sense of the 'unreal' quality of the rabbit—which necessitates touching to see that it actually exists—reveals, in a nascent form, a consciousness of the extent to which images of food are deployed in consumer society as a tool of artifice in the manufacture of lifestyle. Ellis proclaims the restaurant in *American Psycho* as the domain of the culinary hyper-real. The food represents a social standard, a belonging to a particular privileged group. The reservation anticipates the entrance to the group and in so doing, the concept of booking a table itself becomes 'representation'.

Food evaluations, discussions and appreciation in *American Psycho* go hand in hand with the world of technology establishing eating as part of a simulated reality. Bateman is continuously reflecting on contemporary music—including Whitney Houston, Genesis, Huey Lewis and the News and 'American Music Awards' (252)—magazines, like *Billboard* and *Rolling Stone* (253), *Time* (163) and *USA Today* (28). Relentlessly bombarded by images of the popular show *Les Misérables*, Bateman regularly worries about the quality of his 'huge' Sony television (139) and the workings of his CD player, focusing on methods of improvement like 'laser lens cleaner'

(28). He obsesses over monitors and video player models, meticulously comparing brands such as Pioneer and Panasonic (307). He even goes as far as 'imagining' himself 'on television, in a commercial for a new product', speculating that it would be a 'wine cooler' or 'sugar-free gum' (372). Life for Bateman is constantly mediated by instances of information sharing and technologies, which figuratively transform life into a pseudo-event. It is almost as if Bateman is given constant glimpses into this hyper-reality, which becomes particularly clear to him when he is eating. Eating is meant to fuel the body, it is meant to be 'real' experience. Doubting the uncertain value of food poses further doubts about the reliability of life. The restaurant is not just a geographical site; it seems to even transcend culture as Ellis uses the idea of the public place of consumption as a portal into critiquing the state of society as a slowly disintegrating entity.

The mixture of self-scrutiny, self-surveillance and 'unreal' culinary experiences is the source, arguably, of Bateman's violent crimes. He 'loses control' when not in public; his blood lust and cannibalistic tendencies could be seen as an internalised sublimation of his forced self-control in sites of consumption. His dissatisfaction with consumerist existence takes on a sadistic form, a paradoxical manifestation of his desire to feel 'alive'. Lewis Hyde introduces an interesting concept connecting consumption and forms of lust. He argues: 'The desire to consume is a kind of lust. We long to have the world flow through us like air or food. We are thirsty and hungry for something which can only be carried inside bodies'.[89] As Bateman's killings grow in number, he also begins to lose control in restaurants, the place where he maintained the most restrain. Angered and 'red-faced' (46) by the poor quality of a pizza he is served, he erupts in a loud complaint, his hatred rushing through his words, hungry for more:

> 'No one wants the fucking red snapper pizza! A pizza should be yeasty and slightly bready and have a cheesy crust! The pizzas here are too fucking thin because the shithead chef who works here overbakes everything! The pizza is dried out and brittle!' (46).

Indeed, as the novel progresses, Bateman's dislike for the commodified nature of consumption in the late Eighties becomes explicit. His disgust for the state of society emerges no longer in the form of a sublimated, deplorable blood lust, but as an open, conscious derision of consumerism. It is not a suprise, of course, that Bateman's scorn of commercialism should manifest through food. In an episode which has now become notorious, Bateman invites Evelyn to dinner in a famous restaurant and presents her with a Godiva chocolate box, containing a used urinal cake made to look like the popular and much-coveted confectionary. Bateman adorns the box with an irresistible 'silk bow' and has the waiter place the it under a 'silver dome' (336). Evelyn's reaction pleases Bateman immensely; excited about receiving what looks like Godiva chocolates, Evelyn proceeds to consume the urinal cake, declaring she 'adores' Godiva:

> She takes the first bite, chewing dutifully, immediately and obviously disgusted, the swallows. She shudders, then makes a grimace but tries to smile as she take another tentative bite [. . .] her face, twisted with displeasure, manages to blanch again as if she were gagging. (337)

The piercing irony here derives from Evelyn's inability to admit that the 'chocolate' disgusts her. Her complete consumerist faith in Godiva as a brand—which is popular and expensive, and therefore must be exceptional—overcomes her reservations about the product. Despite her disgust, she forces herself to take 'two bites', declaring that the 'chocolate' tastes 'minty' (337).

Chocolate here functions as the ideal embodiment of consumerist and commercial drive. In order to grasp this, we need to remind ourselves of the historical function of the cocoa bean, which places it in the midst of economic enterprise. Historically, the cocoa bean was known by the Maya for thousands of years before the European conquest. The bean's function as a sacred object within Mayan society remains undisputed. As Rowan Jacobsen points out, the cocoa bean 'was involved in many of [the Mayan] rituals [. . .] it was especially closely associated with blood and sometimes played that role in their ceremonies'.[90] It is also known, however, that the Maya established a well-developed network of trading systems which stretched across Mesoamerica. Many products were involved in the trade, but the exchange of cocoa beans remained the most symbolically and economically significant activity. The cocoa bean became so important that, as Jacobsen points out, it 'came to be used as currency'.[91] This element, in particular, confirms the economic value of the cocoa bean in Mayan society and its overall important function in early Mesoamerican trade.

By the time the Spaniards reached Central America, the Aztecs had conquered many of the local populations, including the Maya. It is precisely from the Maya that the Aztecs inherited a penchant for the cocoa bean. Indeed, by the time the Aztecs came to deal with the cocoa bean, its value had increased even further. Jacobsen remarks that, on several occasions, 'vast supplies of beans were shipped in tribute to the Aztecs from the conquered people of the South'.[92] This function of the cocoa bean as 'tribute' and 'currency' shifted its position from the realm of sacred artefact into the secular sphere of financial accumulation. At its height, the Spanish conquest signified not only the appropriation of riches and foodstuffs (such as chocolate) for Europe but, most importantly, the annihilation of the Aztec civilization. Spanish colonialism caused the destruction of the native Mesoamerican way of life. The Spanish occupation, Crystal Bartolovich proposes, tended 'in its mercantile and colonial forms toward limitlessness'.[93]

In this context, the European acquisition of chocolate can be seen as a symbol of early proto-capitalist hunger.

As the contents of Evelyn's chocolate box reveal a repulsive surprise, so does the association between the cocoa bean and financial gain. Chocolate here functions as tainted goods, a sugar-coated philosophy of pleasure hiding a hard (materialist) centre. It is also significant that Bateman serves the urinal cake to Evelyn in a restaurant, continuing to build a connection between food display and surveillance. In what can be viewed as the most poignant critique of commercial brands in the whole of *American Pyscho*, Ellis bestows on the chocolate a highly satirical function which recognises the economic history of this commodity. Bateman's personal mockery of consumerism dissects Godiva as an exemplary brand which rules public consumption—both economic and physical—in virtue of its commercial status.

Bob Ashley has remarked that, in contemporary Western societies, 'the distinction between public and private spheres often rests on the assumption that the public sphere is the realm of production and the private sphere that of consumption'.[94] This conception, of course, denies the reality of production taking place in the home and consumption happening in public spaces. We have seen how *American Psycho* draws attention to the fact that, far from being a time for relaxation and family time, the home meal involves 'spectacle', transporting the happiness and satisfaction that arises from restaurant dining into the private sphere. Nonetheless, Ellis' attention on cycles of production-consumption—which are as valid in the public eaterie as they are in the home—offers a vision of eating as part of greater consumption systems. *American Pyscho* places food within sequences of commercialised existence which leave little space for notions of pleasure or individuality to emerge and owe a lot to that feeling of social disillusionment which was arguably caused the Eighties, a commercially-driven decade that introduced a whole new aspect of the word 'consumption'.

However, if Ellis' vision of public consumption (as a soulless activity encouraging only greed and emotional degradation) seems too bleak, it must be said that this interpretation of the restaurant as a site of utilitarian spectacle decisively grew weaker with time. By the time Stolz was writing *World of Pies* in the late Nineties, the feeling towards the public space appeared to have changed. Refusing to stigmatise the public eating place in Ellis' manner, Stolz describes the local diner and drug store, Doreen's, as a site of friendship, family and enjoyment. Indeed, the novel shows forms of nostalgic attachment to Doreen's and goes as far as considering it an expression of 'home'. Roxanne's recollections of eating at Doreen's during childhood are entangled with emotional memories of her father, who died when she was still a teenager. Roxanne remembers fondly when she and Carl would go to the diner and consume their favourite dish—frozen fruit salad—mischievously keeping the event a secret from Christine and enjoying the experience as a special time together. As Roxanne grows older,

Doreen's becomes synonymous, in her mind, with her father. The emotional investment bestowed upon the food salad should not come as a surprise, since, as June Crawford points out, 'the fact that people recall the emotions they feel around food events suggests the importance of the experience'.[95]

In Stolz's novel, the popular sociological conception that home food has the exclusive power to communicate love and affection becomes redundant. Although the fruit salad is a 'purchased' culinary commodity, it bears the same emotional characteristic of home-made food. As Carl purchases the salad for Roxanne, he forms a mnemonic and social connection between himself and his daughter, embedding the food with an emotional significance which transcends any monetary value. Alan Warde and Lydia Martens contend that 'the circumstances in which people eat—their surroundings, their companions and their schedules—serve to create distinctive experiences'. Context, they argue, is 'all-important', especially 'when eating out' (16). The fruit salad has family value for Roxanne because it is provided for her by her father and, in so doing, it displays similar social characteristic to the home-cooked meal.

The family value of publically-consumed food reached it apogee in *World of Pies* as the adult Roxanne, who had lived in Austin for many years, decides to move back to Annette. As she becomes reacquainted with her home town, Doreen's is one of Roxanne's first destinations. As her husband jokingly calls her 'Doreen-aholic' (146), Roxanne's mind is fixed on consuming the frozen fruit salad of her memories:

> I had to have some, and I had to have it straight away. Doreen's niece bertie placed the coffee saucer in front of me. It nearly overflowed with smooth, shivery frozen salad. I took my fork and speared a maraschino cherry. In my mouth it was a freezy cold sphere of heaven. (146)

Roxanne's urgency testifies to the fact that the fruit salad is intended to be much more that mere physical nourishment. Indeed, it functions as an emblematic representation of the relationship with her father, her town and herself. The reference to a 'frozen heaven' here establishes the connection between Roxanne's father and the salad, an imagistic reminder that, whilst Carl is not sitting next to Roxanne, his emotional presence in the diner is uncontested. Stepping into the 'cold sphere of heaven' inhabited by her father (and being recognised as Carl's daughter by Doreen's staff), Roxanne finds herself announcing that she is finally 'home' (147). The episode, which also concludes the novel, establishes the presence of the restaurant as a site of family interaction and places it at great distance from the 'soulless' restaurant dishes described in *American Psycho*. Untouched by claims of commercialisation and capitalist enterprise—and perhaps a touch of nostalgic, semi-utopian longing on Stolz' part—Doreen's provides the ideal location for memories to be re-enacted and cherished. The fruit salad, although inherently commodified in nature, acts as an identity catalyst for Roxanne.

Her 'return home' is symbolised by the foods connected to her family and her sense of self. Comfort for Roxanne does not come from consuming home-cooked food, but from enjoying a dish which figuratively signifies home. Stolz's symbolic representation of the fruit salad transcends time and, in maintaining familiar links alive, confirms that family food, whether consumed at home or away, can symbolically eradicate the generally utilitarian and socially conceived distinction 'between need and luxury'.[96]

Literary negotiations of food in *Home*, *World of Pies* and *American Psycho* allow us access to evolving food psychologies regarding dining over periods of time. In *Home*, Robinson is sensitive to the gender politics associated with the practice of eating—and the socio-political issues connecting a sense of American identity to food—as a disillusioned projection of the current state of the American family unit. In 2008, it would seem, an aura of confessional cynicism surrounds Robinson's interpretation of American culinary trends. Texts from previous chronological times, however, show more assured perspectives on eating, in and out of the home. *World of Pies* and *American Psycho* pivot around very similar issues: eating in, eating out, the self and the world. However, their conceptual perspectives are very different. This is an indication of the time when the texts were written. An acerbic account of Yuppie culture, *American Psycho* offers food as part of a system of economic and commercial consumption, a reflection of the vacant morality which—as portrayed by Ellis—ruled wealthy life in the Eighties. In *World of Pies*, Stolz offers a different perspective; visibly touched by the wave of organic glory which invaded the food world in the late Nineties—inspiring feelings of nostalgia and a desire for rural, home-cooked goodness—food is proclaimed as the ruler of the home, the link between family members and a projection of love. And yet, even Stolz's account is not completely untouched by a sense of dissatisfaction, as the iconic American foods—eaten both at home and in restaurants—reveal the transforming presence of cultural and economic conflicts.

2 Regionality

> Nothing rekindles my spirits, gives comfort to my heart and mind, more than a visit to Mississippi . . . and to be regaled as I often have been, with a platter of fried chicken, field peas, collard greens, fresh corn on the cob, sliced tomatoes with French dressing . . . and to top it all off with a wedge of freshly baked pecan pie.
>
> —Craig Claiborne, *Southern Cooking*[1]

When it comes to food, the concept of 'region' is a complicated one. In the previous chapter, we saw how both Stolz and Ellis draw attention to food customs, habits and practices which, within the texts, are closely associated with living in specific geographical areas (Texas for Stolz, and New York City for Ellis). Region, however, is not the same as geographical position. In discussions of 'regionality' many elements come into play that go beyond the placing of a particular area on the map. Region finds its existence in the fusion between people's ways and topographical layout which, as I will discuss in this chapter, can be ideally articulated through food as a cultural vector.

The first element to demand attention is of course an issue of geography. The conformation of the soil and the physical position of the land become important factors in the creation of a regional cuisine. What can be produced, in terms of ingredients, will naturally be part of the typical cookbook of a geographical area. Examples that spring to mind here include the famous New England lobster, the Texan Chili and, of course, the Louisiana crayfish. Indeed, it is perhaps necessary to address representations of regional cuisine through what Bell and Valentine call specific 'regional geographies'. Those geographies, which become apparent through culinary practice, lie at the core of what is often referred to as 'regional pride' or 'local patriotism'.[2]

Ecology is also at the centre of systems of production and consumption. Variation is influenced by availability, manufacturing techniques and preservation. However, this mixed definition of culinary region, in itself, seems oddly unsatisfying. Landscape—as the only definitive factor in the construction of cuisine—fails to recognise human interaction. One cannot help but think of culinary regionality as an inherently human characteristic, one that is influenced not only by cultural preference, by a series of daily customs and habits which construct the culinary system in which a dish is produced. It is perhaps more productive to look at a region as a 'human-centred ecological system', in which food consumption is articulated into cycles of everyday practice which define life for a given group, in a given geographical area. The cuisine of the United States, one could suggest, is 'associated very strongly with a series of reasonably distinct regions where different physical conditions combine with localised histories to produce a rich map of food custom, habit and practice'.[3]

As one approaches the portrayal of culinary regionality in fiction, it is important to draw attention to some tensions and challenges which are posed by the concept itself. It has been a strong contention that the idea of region itself owes its existence to the workings of popular imagination. Fed by a desire for cultural belonging and a need to feel affiliated with a particular set of practices, regionality exposes how everyday habits can construct a sense of identity for a given group. As the attention turns to cuisine, regionality becomes an important socio-historical component, positioned in the observance of routine food preparation and consumption. Phil Crang has suggested that 'regional cuisines are invented traditions'.[4] Although Crang's comment is provocative in nature, the possibility that regional food practices continue to be maintained through a dose of imagination cannot be ignored. In virtue of the place they occupy in people's lives, culinary habits are a potent socio-cultural force. As it makes the change from individual to regional property, a culinary ritual is 'invested and reinvested with meanings', which are—more often than not—conjoined with a natural dose of vehement nationalism.[5] Food itself—and its preparation methods—is therefore endowed with layers of potent symbolism which, as they mix with memory and cultural politics, give birth to the idea of regional cuisine in people's minds. In this sense, the region allows culinary practices to inhabit a local space, an area composed of both emotion and geography, often intended to be set against the threat of globalised homogeneity.

Needless to say, if one accepts the possibility that the concept of region has a part to play in maintaining local pride, then it becomes difficult not to see how that concept can be heavily romanticised. R.J. Johnston points out that 'the creation of regions is a social act'. Regional cuisines, Johnston continues, 'differ because people have made them so'. Although in many cases geographical position—and subsequent natural food availability—have an impact on the creation of local culinary variations, personal preference, social interactions and human interactions have drawn different 'patterns' in very similar 'milieux'.[6] Nonetheless, as tempting as it may be to trivialise the idea of region as a simple social construct, it is important not to lose sight of the significance that food habits and cuisines play in the construction of the everyday. Through the maintenance of familiar modes of preparation over time, Bell and Valentine argue, food 'serves to structure our lives'.[7] In that structure, issues of social division, racial control and cultural assimilation are essential components for the construction of group identity. Regional foods, with their strong sociability, can be used to set apart local members of a particular faction from strangers. Paul Fieldhouse points out that 'shared food habits provide a sense of belonging; they are an affirmation of cultural identity and as such they are not easily given up'.[8] Expanding the interdependence of geographical attachment, personal knowledge and culinary experience, regional cuisines provide a site for community bonding and affiliation.

IN MAMMY'S CARE

This function of regional cuisine as bonding agent and source of belonging for the community is strongly exposed in Fannie Flagg's *Fried Green Tomatoes at the Whistle Stop Cafe* (1987).[9] Echoing the sense of local pride which Stolz bestows on the pie-making context in *World of Pies*, Flagg forms a connection between location, food and the idea of community. The novel is a recognisable example of 'Southern literature'; the genre is delineated by very specific characteristics, in which food figures as a constant presence. Southern literature is also exemplified through themes that are usually central to the narrative, such as the importance of the family, exploration of the past, sense of community, and use of a Southern voice of dialect. In *Fried Green Tomatoes*, an attachment to familiar foods is part of the role eating plays in the construction of individual and cultural identity. Evelyn Couch, a depressed, overweight, middle-aged housewife, meets 86-year-old Mrs. Ninny Threadgoode at the Rose Terrace Nursing Home in Birmingham, Alabama. Evelyn listens as Ninny narrates stories about her life experience, concentrating on her friends Idgie Threadgoode and Ruth Jamison. Ninny recalls events and people in Whistle Stop, a little village in Depression era Alabama, where the two women used to run a café. Story-telling plays a vital role in the novel, as Ninny's culinary stories create a connection between the present of the 1980s and Idgie and Ruth's lives at the end of the Twenties and through the Thirties. Flagg's novel underlines Joanne Hawks and Sheila Skemp's claim that Southern literature is characterised by the importance of food and family, a sense of community and a 'formidable understanding of the past'.[10] Food is the connective thread interweaving group identity, Southern history and racial mythology. Flagg proposes eating as an essential 'community maker'. Cuisine and its modes of preparation come to signify not only familial affiliation, but an entire social system. Flagg's sense of community transforms the café into a social haven, untouched by economic hardship and racial prejudice. I intend to show, however, that although the café signifies communal bonding for white people in both the Depression era and the novel's present, the café's economy is still marked by a disquieting racial division of labour.

In *Fried Green Tomatoes* food not only appears as an everyday necessity but also plays an important symbolic role in regard to locality and heritage. Food and eating practices create a connection between the characters' lives that supersedes generational differences. At the Rose Terrace

Nursing Home, memories of Whistle Stop, the Threadgoode family and the café are triggered in Ninny's mind by food: 'Eating a cup of vanilla ice cream with a wooden spoon, Mrs. Threadgoode was reminiscing to Evelyn about the Depression';[11] and again, 'they were busy eating Cracker Jack and talking. Or at least Mrs. Threadgoode was' (143). It is through culinary memories that Mrs. Threadgoode constructs a picture of the Depression years, which is characterised overall by food scarcity. Ninny stresses that the Depression in Alabama really 'hit hard' and 'a lot people died' of starvation (123). The Great Depression, as Alice Deck reminds us, 'put millions of American[s] [. . .] out of work'.[12] The Southern states, including Alabama, were particularly hit by unemployment and food scarcity, so that the whole South was 'panicked by economic disaster'.[13]

However, despite the devastation wrought by the Depression in the Thirties, Ruth and Idgie's café seems a safe place, a sanctuary untouched by economic hardship: 'Idgie and Ruth bought the cafe in 1929, right at the height of the Depression [. . .] it's odd, here the whole world was suffering so, but at the cafe, those Depression years come back to me as happy times' (248). Flagg's café possesses unreal and even idyllic qualities. Ninny claims that all members of the community would 'sit around up at the cafe' and enjoy each other's company (248). It might perhaps be argued that Flagg's representation of the café aims to show that social gathering around a meal, especially in times of hardship, can alleviate even the deepest pain. It is this sense of community that transforms the Depression days in Ninny's memories into unlikely 'happy times' (248). Flagg's depiction of culinary bonding seems to validate Jessamyn Neuhaus's claim that in difficult times familiar food can be 'served in part as an escape'.[14] Through the simple act of eating—whether small or large quantities of food—most of the inhabitants of Whistle Stop are brought together as a community and to share life experiences. This idea appears to also confirm Lupton's claim that 'the incorporation of food includes [the] individual into a culinary system and therefore a social group'.[15] The sense of community is what is most evidently attached to the memory of the café and what inspires the sense of happiness in Ninny's food recollections.

Whilst bringing the village community together at the café, Flagg attempts to reconstruct, through food, a working relationship between white and black ethnic groups. It becomes obvious that Idgie and Ruth's café was not an ordinary catering business. In a familiar atmosphere, the two women established a culturally symbolic relationship with the food they serve. Despite the disagreement that arises in the white community, especially with the members of the Ku Klux Klan, Idgie and Ruth persevere in serving food to black workers at the back of the café: 'Now, you ought not to be selling those niggers food, you know better than that. And there's some boys in this town that's not happy about it. Nobody wants to eat in the same place that niggers come' (53). Ninny recalls Idgie claiming that 'nobody was gonna tell her what she could and could not do' and when the need arose she 'stood right up to the Ku Klux Klan all by herself' (51). Ruth and Idgie's café both partially compensates for and implicitly challenges the inequalities and racist practices elsewhere in the community. Food at the café acts as a symbol of human interaction and, in Nicki Charles and Marion Kerr's words, 'has a part to play in cementing and reinforcing relations'.[16] The act of feeding African American workers, it would seem, challenges the racial division that is present in the community. The café in itself becomes an idealised place in which two white Southern women might confront racial and social prejudices.

We are repeatedly told by Flagg throughout the novel that, before getting to know Ninny (and her café stories of the brave Ruth and Idgie), Evelyn had become accustomed to eating 'foreign brands', such as Taco Bell and Baskin-Robbins. It is impossible to ignore here that the brand names testify to the virtual monopolisation of food production and consumption by corporate capital. On several occasions, Flagg gestures towards the idea that the consumer brands are 'tasteless'. Unlike the 'genuine' Southern dishes recalled in Ninny's memories, there is no past attributed to the corporate foods and, especially, no cognate memory that Evelyn can recall when eating them. Flagg appears to be hinting at the fact that the traditional Southern food—like the eponymous fried green tomatoes—is able to communicate emotions to the eater, while the branded foods limit themselves to providing empty disappointment and a lack of personal involvement. It is also made clear by Flagg that whenever Evelyn eats the corporate foods, she is often 'staring at the table' (40), feeling 'worthless' (233). There seems to be a suggestion here that Evelyn's depression and introversion generate from encountering these uncommunicative brands, which are perhaps representative of a whole consumer society which leave her senses unchallenged by history and memory. The corporate food brand is presented in the novel as selling a name as much as a product.

Elizabeth Hallam and Jenny Hockey claim that 'acts of forgetting stand as central issues in twentieth-century social relations' and that the development of commodity culture has been 'a major contributory factor in memory loss within Western societies'.[17] Amnesia is endemic within the system of Western commodity production. Advertising and packaging are geared towards erasing the material reality of labour. At the same time, commodification extends to individual sensations as part of a system of codified stimuli. Marx claimed that 'the forming of the five senses' in an individual person is 'a labour of the entire history of the world'.[18] He does not assume that the senses are 'natural' biological functions so much as forms of embodied experience determined by multiple historical factors. Following Marx's contention, Susan Stuart points out that for a person to 'rediscover' the senses, the body must be separated from 'the alienating effects of private property'.[19] In *Fried Green Tomatoes*, Evelyn's separation from the world of property—embodied in the corporate, 'capitalist' foods—and entrance into a regional culinary system signifies her reconnection with a sense of identity that she had forgotten. The experience of a 'genuine' regional product not only re-joins Evelyn with the land she comes from, but also steers her experience away from commercialised sensations. The consumption of properly prepared Southern recipes, after a long period of social alienation and culinary disappointment, rouses something in Evelyn that seems to go beyond the limits of everyday sensory perception. Evelyn's relationship with herself radically changes as her knowledge of old Whistle Stop people increases. She slowly starts to feel more confident and more resentful towards those who treated her unfairly in the past, including her husband Ed: "Evelyn even made up a secret code name for herself . . . Towanda the Avenger! [. . .] And so, when Ed yelled from the den for another beer, somehow, before Evelyn could stop her, Towanda yelled back, 'SCREW YOU ED!'"(240). In Evelyn's Southern epiphany, past, present and future are embodied and imbricated through a culinary act which permits the possibility of decommodified consumption.

In spite of the novel's portrayal of the Ruth and Idgie's café as a curative culinary presence across time—it is truly impressive, if oddly unbelievable, how only its memory can bestow confidence on the disheartened Evelyn— one cannot help but wonder how Flagg's catering business intersects with actual historical claims of social and racial equality. One may offer a critique that, against the grain, exposes the possible sentimental re-elaboration of food in Southern literature. Indeed, while in Flagg's novel the relationship between the café and its customers appears to challenge the limitations of racial boundaries in Alabama, this effort is not completely pursued in every aspects of the café's economy. Behind closed doors, the division of labour in the café's kitchen still shows signs of racial stratification. We learn this on the novel's opening page: 'Idgie says that for people who know her not to worry about getting poisoned, she is not cooking. All the cooking is being done by two coloured women, Sipsey and Onzell, and the barbecue is being cooked by Big George, who is Onzell's husband' (3). Carrying out her cooking duties, Sipsey plays a particularly important role in the novel in unveiling white Southern assumptions about African American women. Sipsey, as an older black woman in a 'white' environment, is still described by Ninny as a caring figure, devoted to the Threadgoode family for whom she works: 'She helped raise all the Threadgoode children' (48). Later in the story, when Idgie and Ruth open the café, Sipsey is there to cook obediently for their customers. While working as a kitchen servant, Sipsey's talent as a cook is not open to discussion: 'there wasn't a better cook in the state of Alabama [. . .] That's the reason most people came, because of her cooking' (48–50).

Flagg's description of Sipsey as the loyal black cook, who is completely devoted to her white family, is strongly reminiscent of the antebellum mammy archetype. As a figure belonging to the pre-Civil war South, the mammy represents the ideal representation of a different way of life in America. Deck describes the mammy as a 'black woman known for her associations with food preparation, with feeding other characters, and with emotional nurturing'.[20] With her cheerful nature and undying loyalty, the hard-working mammy wants nothing more than to look after her white masters. Her principal occupation is to cook wholesome meals that sustain the family physically, while offering constant moral support to each if its members. Her culinary knowledge is undisputed and her food is considered, as Deck points out, the 'tangible symbol' of her presence.[21] The image of the antebellum mammy—popularised as the quintessential housekeeper by Aunt Chloe in Harriet Beecher Stowe's *Uncle Tom's Cabin* (1852)—remains an iconographic presence in representations of the Old South. The stereotypical association between African American women and 'good food' is just as conspicuous in the collective American imaginary. The representation of the mammy as the cook is often employed to promote culinary products. The seminal example here would be Aunt Jemima: the archetypal mammy who promotes the sales of self-raising pancakes. Aunt Jemima was created as a 'product' and marketed just like her pancake flour. In 1893, the David Milling Company hired Nancy Green, a black cook, to travel across America and promote their self-rising pancakes. She played the part of 'Aunt Jemima' and enchanted white audiences and customers with, as Patricia Turner reminds us, 'wholesome stories of the old South'.[22] Since then, Aunt Jemima has been a symbol of 'wholesome' Southern cuisine in America for over a century, a symbol that has sustained—at least in terms of visual mythology—the racist fantasy of black women happily providing food for white families. Historical records in fact reveal the presence of the 'real' mammy as fictional as her literary and cultural representations. According to Catherine Clinton, there is no evidence to confirm the constant presence of black women in the plantation household. Clinton proposes that the idea of the mammy 'is not merely a stereotype', but indeed 'a figment' of the 'romantic imaginations' of the 'Southern ideologue'.[23] The mammy was used by Southern writers in the postbellum period to 'redeem' the Old South. The nurturing, cheerful black cook was created in response to antislavery attacks during the antebellum age and, in Clinton's words, 'to embellish it with nostalgia in the postbellum period'.[24]

Recalling the antebellum mammy, Sipsey is constantly viewed through a white American cultural frame—which attributes to her character innate instincts for the role of cook and nurturer. As Ninny's stories of Sipsey's food unfold, they have a strong impact on Evelyn. A compulsive overeater, Evelyn finds in food a source of consolation for everyday monotony and dissatisfaction: 'Evelyn Couch had locked herself in her sewing room and was eating a second pint of Baskin-Robbins chocolate chip ice cream (40). Evelyn treats food an escapist diversion through which to forget her personal dilemmas. In this context, it is worth noting Sally Cline's contention that 'in our culture women have a complex emotional and symbolic relationship with food'.[25] However, Evelyn's engagement with food and eating is crucially altered as her interest in Ninny's anecdotes grows stronger.

Before dying, Ninny leaves Sipsey's food recipes to Evelyn. At the end of the novel, the recipes are transcribed in detail, 'compliments of Evelyn Couch' (396). Examples range from 'Chicken and dumplings' that 'should float off the fork' (398), to 'Snap beans [. . .] happy beans [. . .] fun to eat' (340). Sipsey's food is passed on not simply to the white community, but particularly to the white woman. Flagg makes it clear that the recipes are meant to be treated as a memorial for the African American woman and her incredible cooking talents. Nonetheless, the cultural politics that connect Evelyn to Sipsey herself reveal a different function for the inheritance of cooking techniques. Indeed, the recipes can be seen as representative of a racialised division of kitchen labour in popular images in America.

The idea of the black woman 'teaching' the white woman how to cook is widely acknowledged in American popular culture. As we have noted previously, figures like Aunt Jemima established the black woman's presence and ability in the kitchen. In several advertisements in American magazines and newspapers—particularly during the first half of the twentieth century—the loyal black woman is pictured 'teaching' the white housewife how to prepare delicious dishes. As most consumers could not actually afford a live-in cook, the image of the black woman—inspired by the loyal mammy—could be purchased instead, suggesting, as Deck points out, that 'she would be going home with the consumer as a spiritual guide during the cooking process'.[26] Inheriting Sipsey's recipes, Evelyn can exploit their cultural value in order to become a 'better person' and renew her interest in a food tradition that she had forgotten. Evelyn can, in Deck's words, 'be safe in her mammy's care and culinary tutelage'.[27] Her written appropriation of the recipes, however, represents a way to keep Sipsey as a secondary figure, an inspiration which shrinks into the background behind the establishment of a larger (white) 'Southern identity'. In *Fried Green Tomatoes*, aspects of an idealised regional identity are celebrated as a cultural construction which is, to borrow Hope J. Norman and Louise Simon's words, 'inseparable from food'.[28] This commemoration, however, seems to be based on the white woman's appropriation of antebellum and postbellum racial relationships.

As Flagg re-appropriates the figure of the black woman cook, the similarities between Sipsey and the representation of the iconographic mammy become even more significant if one considers the novel's historical setting. In cultural terms the Thirties witnessed the reappearance of African Americans as domestic characters in a large number of novels and films. In literary texts like Fannie Hurst's *Imitation of Life* (1933) and Margaret Mitchell's famous *Gone with the Wind* (1934), and in a variety of films starring child-star Shirley Temple—including *The Littlest Rebel* (1935) and *Rebecca of Sunnybrook Farm* (1938)—images of black domestic servants proliferated. The mammy figure, in particular, was a favourite in the Depression years. Her most famous incarnation was perhaps achieved by Hattie McDaniel in the film version of *Gone with the Wind* (1939) as the continuously present domestic offering food and support to 'her' white folk. Donald Bogle labels the Thirties as the 'age of the negro servant', claiming that 'no other period [. . .] could boast more black faces carrying mops or lifting pots and pans than the Depression years'.[29] With their jolly nature and constant smile, the kitchen servants of the Thirties uplifted the white readers and audiences of the Depression era. As a loyal kitchen servant, Sipsey in *Fried Green Tomatoes* similarly mixes her kitchen duties with a desire to keep everyone's spirits high and maintain a friendly atmosphere in the café:

> Ruth was hanging her picture of the Last Supper. Sipsey stopped sweeping and studied that picture for a while, and then she asked, 'Miz Ruth, who's that sitting up there with Mr. Jesus?' [. . .] 'Why, Sipsey, that's Mr. Jesus and the Brethren.' Sipsey looked back at her and said, 'Oh. Uh-huh. I thought Miz Mary just had the one boy,' and went on sweeping. We 'bout died laughing. Sipsey knew exactly who that was in the picture. She just liked to play with people. (50)

Sipsey's feigned naivety appears to cause amusement, while, simultaneously, it maintains her position as an inferior character who belongs in the kitchen, 'sweeping'. This validates Bogle's claim that the mammy characters of the Thirties, with their humorous accents, loyalty and 'incredible antics', 'demonstrated that nothing in life was ever completely hopeless'.[30]

The description and role of Sipsey in *Fried Green Tomatoes* seems thus inspired and informed not only by the mammy images of the antebellum South, but also by their re-elaboration and function during the Depression years. It must be noted, however, that Flagg's appropriation of the African American woman confirms some stereotypical aspects of this long-established mythology whilst subverting others. For instance, the physical description Flagg gives of Sipsey does depart in some significant respects from the traditional portrayal of the Thirties mammy: '[she] was a skinny little thing, and funny' (48). Flagg's decision to alter one of the principal characteristics of the iconographic thick-waisted mammy is, sadly, not developed in other areas. Ninny affirms that Sipsey 'was still cooking over at the café well up into her eighties' (50). Her determination in the kitchen is meant to mirror her zest for life and undying dedication towards her white family. This element appears to validate Lisa Anderson's claim that 'the figure of the mammy' is 'modified and dignified in white-constructed images [over the years], but semiotically remains the same. Her position is still defined by her race'.[31]

As Flagg's description of Sipsey bears the marks of racial typecasting, the presence of a mammy-like figure at the café constructs an air of emotional stability for the inhabitants of Whistle Stop. However, while the café signifies female friendships for white people in both the Depression era (Idgie and Ruth) and the novel's present (Ninny and Evelyn), there is an important historical element that should not be overlooked, as Sipsey's food also maintains the black community's connection to slavery. Here we need to look closely at the menu: 'grits, ham and red-eye gravy [. . .] fried green tomatoes; fried okra; collard or turnip greens; black-eyed peas; candied yams; butter beans and lima beans' (4). Most of the foods served constitute the main examples of what is commonly known by the African American community as 'soul food'. In the plantation economy, easy access to food supplies was limited, and for the slaves, it was often a matter of quantity rather than quality. The food grown by the slaves was the black woman's only usable material to cook a meal for her family. Marvalene Hughes points out that 'the survival-oriented black woman trusted her creative skills to make something out of nothing. She acquired the unique survival ability to cook all parts of nothing'.[32] For example, green tomatoes were dismissed by the white masters, but were used by black women and subsequently transformed into a staple food for the African American community. Although physically they were, as Carole Counihan points out, 'subordinating their freedom to a '"soulless" mass', the cooks and consumers of 'soul food' were seen as ultimately liberated in spirit.[33] The distribution of soul food to white consumers over one century of American history has been so conspicuous in certain geographical areas that African American dishes have become culinary symbols of Southern states. Geographically, that is where 'soul food' still remains part of the African American family's cookbook, keeping the memory of slavery alive and showing, in Counihan's words, how food became an indication of 'black ethnic identity'.[34] Cultural colonisation, however, has threatened to transform soul food into 'Southern food' and *Fried Green Tomatoes* seems, unwittingly, to contribute to this process. In the novel, soul food is interpreted as a symbol of the white-owned Whistle Stop, while Sipsey and her daughter-in-law Onzell are left largely marginalised in the narrative. They are often confined to the café, 'frying chicken and slicing green tomatoes' (20), only occasionally sticking their heads out 'of the kitchen door' (208). This marginalisation is doubly disappointing given that the soul food motivates and inspires most of the characters in the narrative. Whilst eating for the white women is a somatic trigger for nostalgic memories of Depression-era bonding, soul food at the café remains symbolically poisoned by the historical trauma of slavery and racial segregation.

In spite of Flagg's general marginalisation of Sipsey in the story, the black woman's historical link with slavery is crucially maintained and connected to the actual food she prepares at the café. We are told that her 'mother'd been a slave' (48) and as a result, Sipsey 'had all those old-timy superstitions' and was 'scared to death of spells' (48). It soon becomes clear that Sipsey's superstitions are particularly vivid when it comes to food:

> The thing she was the most deathly afraid of in the world was the heads of animals. If you brought her a chicken [. . .] of if big George

killed a hog, she wouldn't touch it or cook it until she'd buried the head out in the garden. She said that if you didn't bury the head, the spirit of the animal would enter your body and cause you to go completely insane. (48)

Flagg here constructs connections between food practices and religious-based beliefs. Food is presented as playing an important part in carrying out spiritual rituals and displaying particular beliefs. In *Fried Green Tomatoes*, Flagg specifically builds a link between Sipsey's food 'superstitions' and the religious practices that were common among slaves of African origin in America. Although Flagg does not name any particular religion or belief, Sipsey's desire to cut off a dead animal's head to banish its spirit hints at voodoo practices. Glenda Carpio argues that 'as a cultural practice transported by enslaved Africans', voodoo tradition maintains 'an unwritten record of slavery'.[35] Especially when it involves food and animal slaughter, voodoo recalls a 'history of cultural dislocation and enslavement'.[36] Voodoo is a concrete reminder of the trauma of slavery and the historical referent for the subjugation of a whole ethnic group. Sipsey's voodoo-like, animal cooking routine constructs a link between African religious practices, antebellum slavery and 1930s Alabama. Voodoo cuisine might be interpreted, therefore, as a symbol of the desire displayed by enslaved people to maintain their customs even in times of struggle.

Sipsey's culinary practices—strongly related as they are to voodoo rituals—appear particularly significant when they are associated with her behaviour as a 'protector' of white women and children. This becomes significant when she 'cannibalises' someone who threatens the family. When Ruth's estranged husband, Frank Bennett, arrives at Whistle Stop to claim his child, Sipsey punishes him accordingly:

She [Sipsey] jumped back up again and lunged at him. 'You leave dat baby alone! Dat's Miz Ruth's baby!' [. . .] he opened the door and put the baby—who had not made a sound—into the front seat, and was climbing in when all of a sudden he heard a sound behind him [. . .] the sound he had heard was that of a five-pound skillet hitting his own thick Irish hair, a fraction of a second before his skull split open. He was dead before he hit the ground, and Sipsey was headed back inside with the baby. (364)

Sipsey's murder of Bennett exemplifies her desire to protect the members of her white family. It is also significant that she kills him with a 'skillet', a utensil which symbolically couples her protective instincts with her cooking abilities. This element becomes somewhat ironic when, later in the novel, Sipsey's famous 'skillet cornbread' is described as 'so good, it will kill you' (397). When her son Big George arrives to dispose of the white man's body, however, Sipsey's actions are revelatory: 'His mother had chopped that man's head off and buried it somewhere [. . .] he was all white and pink, just like those hogs after they'd been boiled and all their hair had come off' (366). Sipsey treats Frank Bennett as an animal—he even gets explicitly compared by Flagg to a 'hog'—and cuts off his head in order to ensure his spirit will not come back to haunt her. Eventually, Bennett's body is cooked and served as part of the barbecue at the café whereupon it receives compliments from the customers as being the 'best hog' they had ever consumed. Here we see how Flagg recalls *American Pyscho* as the two share the metaphor of violence and cannibalism in order to expose poignant critiques of socio-cultural and political organisation.

The treatment of Frank Bennett's body, however, uncovers further elements of racial signification in *Fried Green Tomatoes*. Underneath the veneer of constructing the punishment of Bennett as justified on Sipsey and Big George's part, the cannibalistic act may prove problematic. One cannot help but identify two sides to Sipsey's act: although it is put forward as legitimate revenge for racial subjugation, it also confirms the idea of black people as dangerously 'Other' in their practices. Conceptually, cannibalism provides, in Maggie Kilgour's terms, 'clear boundaries between groups'.[37] Those boundaries designate the civilised from the savage, the normal from the abnormal, the 'right' from the 'wrong'. The threat of cannibalism is what legitimated the colonial subjugation of indigenous populations as inferior and barbaric. On the one hand, in depicting Sipsey and Big George as possible cannibals, Flagg appears to be confirming a long-standing cultural stereotype that associates 'black people' with savagery and barbarism. On the other hand, however, one could interpret the voodoo killing of the white man as a justifiable act of race revenge on the part of Sipsey and Big George. Bennett's body is 'fed' to the café's white customers and therefore confirms their status as 'cannibals'. Sipsey's application of voodoo practices on the white man's body could be interpreted as vindicated by her historical past as a victim of slavery. Her act of voodoo revenge appears to validate Franz Fanon's claim that 'face to face with the white man, the negro has [. . .] a vengeance to exact'.[38] Bennett's body is consumed in reprisal for the way in which a whole ethnic and racial group was exploited in the South. Applying voodoo culinary practices on Bennett's body, therefore, acknowledges Sipsey's history of suffering as an African American. The voodoo ritual provides the reader with a countermemory to the constructed figure of the Aunt Jemima mammy, which shifts her from a nostalgic kitchen worker to a historical slave. As a cooking practice inspired by voodoo beliefs, the beheading and cannibalisation of Bennett removes the mammy-like Sipsey from the embellished context of the antebellum South and establishes her as a product of the horror of slavery.

A TASTE OF THE LAND AND THE PEOPLE

Although the racial and economic politics in *Fried Green Tomatoes* cast a shadow over Flagg's interpretation of food as a symbol of community bonding, the text's desire to exalt regional cuisine is worthy of notice. In the novel, one does get a sense of how the food comes to represent the land, its people and its customs. Although Flagg keeps this contention inexplicit, the prospect that food is intended to 'carry the flavour' of the region is allowable. Whilst Flagg leaves this possibility in embryonic state, the politics of regional taste are fully unravelled by Rebecca Wells in *Divine Secrets of the Ya-Ya Sisterhood* (1996). The novel follows the life of Siddalee Walker—affectionately called Sidda—and her turbulent relationship with her charming and neurotic mother, Mrs. Vivi Walker. A famous playwright and engaged to marry her New York fiancé, Connor, Sidda must reconcile her memories of growing up in South Louisiana, which were darkened by her parents' unhappy marriage. Plagued by doubt about the possibility of marrying, Sidda receives the help of her mother's closest friends—Teensy, Caro and Necie, also known as 'the Ya-Yas'—in the form of her mother's scrapbook, entitled the 'Divine Secrets of the Ya-Ya Sisterhood'. Through the information supplied by the book, Sidda begins to gain an understanding of her mother's choices, her love for their native Louisiana and her wish for happiness and love.

Given its nature as a clear example of Southern literature—a quality shared with Flagg's novel—*Divine Secrets* entangles food and eating thickly into the narrative. The novel proudly displays an array of dishes typical of the Southern Louisiana region: from '*boudin* balls' to 'petite pecan tarts' and '*croissants*' as part of the daily 'petit *dejéuner*'.[39] The dishes described by Wells have a distinct Cajun flavour, giving a hint to the book's desire to engage with a particular sense of regional and ethnic identity. Indeed, the examples of Cajun cuisine presented in the novel are instrumental in delineating a specific sense of cultural affiliation; the novel does not simply engage with a general sense of Creole-inspired Louisiana cookery, but—specifically—wishes to delve into the socio-cultural background of the Cajun community in the fictional town of Pecan Grove. The Cajun community in Louisiana is said to display a different kind of cultural habits, which are instrumental in separating them other ethnic groups in Louisiana, especially those dwelling in the city of New Orleans. 'Cajun country'—as Paige Gutierrez describes it—is in fact said to lie 'to the southwest, west and northwest of the city'.[40] Geographical location, however, is but the beginning of the many differences that separate the Cajun community from the rest of Louisiana (not to say the United States).

The Cajun community in Louisiana is derived from the descendants of the Acadians, a group of farm workers of French heritage who had settled in the Southern region of Canada. When British rule took over parts of Canada, the Acadians were forced to move into the United States and, after a long and strenuous journey, settled in the Southern parts of what is Louisiana today. Particularly, the Acadians took over sections of the swamplands of the region, which have since been known as the *bayou*. With time, Acadians also expanded into surrounding towns, establishing the existence of a thick and thriving community. As the Acadians settled in Louisiana, however, they did more than simply bring a set of French customs to the area. The Acadian population merged with the region so much that the Acadian way of life became synonymous with the bayou, encompassing elements which ranged from speaking French to eating habits. The Cajuns—the word itself said to be a distortion of the term Acadian—are the descendants of those French peasant settlers. The impact of Cajun culture on the area is so unavoidable that this 'interplay between ethnicity and region' is implicitly 'recognised in the Louisiana state legislature's designation' of an area of Southern Louisiana as 'Acadiana'—a term in itself derived from the fusion of 'Acadian' and 'Louisiana'.[41]

Although there are many examples of Cajun cuisine through the *Divine Secrets*, the interplay between region and ethnicity does not become more visible than when Wells engages with descriptions of crayfish consumption. Crayfish dishes—from stews to grills and soups—accompany several events within the novel and culminate in the emblematic crayfish *étouffée*, a dish which is clearly given more than a simple gastronomic value within the story. The connection between crayfish and Southern Louisiana identity in the novel should not come as a surprise. Crayfish—or, to be ethnically specific, 'crawfish'—is indeed viewed in America as a living part of the Cajun community; crawfish is produced in great quantities in Southern Louisiana and statistics have estimated that 'almost ninety percent of the crawfish harvest is consumed in Acadiana' .[42] The impact of this particular ingredient, however, goes beyond its assured and constant presence in Cajun dishes. The crawfish—as geographically proper as it is to the state of Louisiana—encapsulates the whole system of Cajun culture, its approach to life and its desire to maintain itself separate from the other side of mainstream America. Gutierrez argues that the crawfish 'exists both as part of nature, in the form of a living animal, and as part of culture, when it is transformed by cooking into food'. The dual role of the crayfish—as both a creature native to Louisiana and a staple ingredient of local cooking—has allowed the crustacean to become the ideal 'ethnic emblem' of the Cajun community. The Cajun, therefore, proudly claims to be 'the primary heir' to the 'cultural and technological knowledge pertinent to crawfish foodways in the United States'.[43]

The crayfish is often visualised in *Divine Secrets* as a symbol of the Cajun community, particularly of the way of life which is prominent in the bayou. The perfect Cajun—still closely attached to French Creole customs, including both speaking French and cooking Cajun style dishes—is embodied in the character of Genevieve St.Clair Whitman, Teensy' mother. It is clear in the story that all the Ya-Yas absolutely adore Genevieve, whose charismatic personality rarely leaves anyone untouched. Genevieve is often portrayed as 'wearing a turban', while she is 'dancing and singing' around the house' (366). Throughout the novel, Genevieve is depicted as a true Cajun who grew up in the bayou near Marksville and is always speaking in her strange 'Cajun patois' (366). The tendency to speak French emerges as clear sign of Genevieve's Cajun identity, but it is not self-standing; its presence is constantly accompanied by the cooking of Cajun crayfish dishes—particularly *étouffée*. It is made clear that both the French patois and crawfish are used as symbolic indicators of Genevieve's ethnic affiliation with the bayou. This idea seems to confirm Linda Brown and Kay Mussell's idea that regional group identity can be defined as 'process' rather than a series of 'static markers, therefore placing a focus 'on the internal and external meaning of group interaction'.[44]

In cultural terms, the association between linguistic preference and food allows us critical scope into the construction of ethnic and regional affiliation. Howard Wight Marshall points out that 'like dialect', food traditions 'are main components in the intricate and impulsive system that joins culture and geography into regional' identity.[45] In the case of Genevieve, her 'regional' affiliation is not simply a matter of geography; her native provenance from the bayou is but the beginning of the malleable system which allows her to see herself—and to be seen by others—as 'Cajun'. The speaking of French patois merges with the cooking of crayfish in order to create a specific ethnic identity which has its origins (as we have seen previously) in the history of Acadian settlements in Louisiana. Once this is merged with the attachment to the bayou lands itself, what emerges is a sense of regional identity. This outlook on regional culinary identity allows us to see the 'metaphorical power' of ethnicity and its sense of specific 'mutability'.[46] Regionality—and, specifically in this case, Cajun regionality—is revealed as a dynamic process in which traditional dishes are instrumental for the maintenance of a specific ethnic character.

Nonetheless, it is a clear argument that crayfish, as much as it provides a regional symbol for the Cajuns of Louisiana, also functions as a clear cultural isolator. In historical terms, the crayfish maintained its culinary impact on the Cajun community in Louisiana even when, with the advent of the twentieth century, mainstream American legislation forced the use of English in education, official services and the media. By the time World War II had ended, the French speaking Cajuns found themselves isolated and in a social position not unlike that of the 'newly arrived' immigrant. The new legislature, of course, promised to bring prosperity, but its desire for homogenisation also 'threatened to destroy what was 'traditional and meaningful in the old' Cajun lifestyle.[47] Faced with cultural isolation from the rest of America, the attached to crayfish proved to be a helpful tool which allowed the Cajuns to cling on to their social tradition. It is said that local Cajuns often joke about how Louisiana hides 'behind the crayfish curtain' separated both gastronomically and culturally from Anglo-American Louisiana, where crayfish, as Gutierrez reminds us, is 'often ignored or even scorned as food'.[48]

The prejudice against the French-speaking Cajuns is clearly communicated in *Divine Secrets*. The dislike for all kinds of Cajun tradition comes from Mr. Whitman, Genevieve's husband; he is said to be constantly making 'fun of Genevieve's accent'—he even forbids 'bayou French' to 'be spoken in his house' (219). The culinary dishes prepared by Genevieve clearly receive the same treatment, although Mr. Whitman rarely refuses to eat them. The dislike for bayou customs by Anglo-speaking Louisiana residents can be explained in socio-historical terms. As mainstream America hit the Cajun parts of Louisiana, the newly established superior social class was that of the English-speaking Americans. As state law officially banned French from being spoken, the 'sophisticated' Anglo-American 'outsiders' began to openly ridicule local customs. As bayou language, dishes and customs originated in farming circumstances, the Anglo-Americans associated anything Cajun with poverty and ignorance.

It is clear, however, that Wells sets out to re-address this question and give rightful dignity to the Cajun tradition of South Louisiana whilst clinging on to a sense of regional identity. In the story, Mr Whitman is disliked by the Ya-Yas—especially Vivi—while Genevieve is kept in the highest regard by all four girls. Indeed, it is Genevieve that gives the girls their group names, referring to them as 'Gumbo Ya-Ya', meaning 'everybody talking at the same time' (72). Wells' almost political stance in favour of 'homely' Cajun culture seems to join the social motives and actions which are proper to the Council for the Development of French in Louisiana. The Council itself, founded in 1969, was inspired by the ethnic revival wave which took place in the Sixties and vowed to promote the existence of Cajun culture in Louisiana, which included speaking French and eating local crayfish dishes as 'key rallying symbols' of their regional conservation movement.[49]

Due to its culinary and economic importance to the area, crawfish is actually used by Cajuns as a commercialised symbol. The 'image' of the crawfish can actually be found in an array of souvenirs in Southern Louisiana, which properly associated with a Cajun-orientated way of life. The traveller leaving Cajun country from airports and train station will be presented with large quantities of 'crayfish iconography', from 'plastic crawfish key chains and combs' to real crawfish frozen into acrylic paperweights shaped like the state of Louisiana'.[50] Wells is clearly sensitive to this commercial exploitation of the Cajun symbol of Louisiana; she makes a nod to it in the novel as Chick, Teensy's husband, is portrayed 'wearing an apron emblazoned with a crayfish that reads: "Suck de heads!"' (379).

With crawfish's powerful cultural significance in mind, it is not a surprise that Wells chooses it as a communicative vector for Sidda to materialise memories of her mother in Louisiana. In an attempt to reconcile mother and daughter, the Ya-Yas visit Sidda at her holiday home on the lake. As a skilfully orchestrated reminder of life in Southern Louisiana, the Ya-Yas bring a pot of the famous *étouffée*, Genevieve's signature specialty, prepared by Vivi herself. As Sidda becomes reacquainted with Vivi's crawfish *étouffée*, each waft of scent and flavour particle from the dish produces a cascade of sensorial associations:

> With her first bite of crayfish *étouffée*, Sidda could see her mother in the kitchen at Pecan Grove. She saw Vivi first melting butter in a large cast-iron skillet, the slowly stirring flour into the butter, and coking the roux until it became a chestnut brown. She smelled the onion, celery, and green peppers as Vivi added them to the roux. She saw the dish change colour as Vivi added the crayfish tails, along with fresh parsley, cayenne pepper, and generous shakes of the ever-present Tabasco bottle. (423)

The re-familiarisation with the taste and smell of Vivi's dish releases a series of mnemonic traces for Sidda. It is this association of ideas that enables past experiences to be brought back into consciousness through memory. In his phenomenological account of the senses, Maurice Merleau-Ponty observes that the sensory knowledge of memories 'appears as a system of substitutions in which one impression announces others without ever justifying the announcement'.[51] As the sensorial memories of the crayfish *étouffée* announce themselves to her consciousness, Sidda's current spatio-temporal position—namely, the present—is substituted by remembrance of her time in the kitchen with her mother.

The sensation produced in Sidda by the interplay of the *étouffée*'s taste and smell is not simply the autonomous occurrence of a sensual response. Through its evocative associations the taste is articulated as a recognisable sensation which is connected to something else, a temporal and spatial location: 'she saw [. . .] she smelled' (423). Thanks to an elaborate series of sensorial associations, Sidda re-experiences the cooking of the *étouffée* as if it was happening at that precise moment. The taste of the dish is attributed a meaning which relies on sensorial data *and* the value of previous experience. The associated concept deriving from gustatory stimuli enables Sidda to re-establish a personal relationship with the eating of the *étouffée*. The taste of the dish is retrieved from 'memory' together with a series of episodic associations—'Vivi first melting the butter in a large cast-iron skillet, then slowly stirring flour into the butter' (423). The connection between a particular taste and a specific temporal moment here seems to validate David Sutton's claim that tastes and smells 'easily connect with episodic [. . .] memories'.[52]

The nuances of taste experienced by Sidda—which allow her to visualise her mother's kitchen, in a moment of synestetic connection—can be seen not only as a direct consequence of anatomically dictated sensory organisation, but as a product of her emotional attachment to the symbolic potency of the *étouffée*. Korsmeyer points out that 'the sensations of the mouth are so relative to the individual that there is no way to adjudicate among them'.[53] Having said this, however, Korsmeyer warns us against sensory relativism, arguing that 'tastes are also subject to the pressures of social change'.[54] In the case of Sidda, the pressure of social change is related to detachment from her mother and the arguments that have caused a break between them; this clearly affected Sidda's personality and her ability to make decisions about her own future (including the prospect of marrying Connor). And it is precisely her close attachment to her mother and Louisiana—and the conflicted pain of being separated from them—which creates a special liking for the *étouffée*. Sidda's taste buds are trained to recognise the taste of the dish and she is still able to appreciate it on several levels—in view of its symbolic value for regional identity and maternal love. Eating the *étouffée* is here understood as an embodied practice of memory, a performance that brings with it the bittersweet taste of the past and the melancholia of the present. Appreciation for the taste of the crayfish dish—stimulated by the mnemonic recollection of Vivi and Pecan Grove—becomes a memory practice in itself which, in Hallam and Hockey's words, is 'reworked in the context of the present'.[55]

There is indeed a sense of re-discovery accompanying the reawakening of Sidda's senses while eating the crawfish dish. When it comes to locally-produced foods—especially something as regionally inscribed as crawfish—there are certain taste and smell qualities that become culturally attributed to the product. The same qualities are treated as the expression of a group of practices belonging to the land in which it was produced. As a result, an association can exist in images and memories between the particular taste of a consumable product and the rural environment in which it was produced. Amy Trubek remarks that 'the moment when the Earth travels to the mouth is a time of reckoning with its local memory and identity'.[56] Although Trubek adds a layer of unnecessary mysticism to the practice of eating, her considerations on the relationship between food, soil and cultural remembrance remain valuable. In *Divine Secrets*, the taste of Vivi's crawfish *étouffée* becomes evocative for Sidda of not only a person and events but, also, of the rural attributes of the 'place' where the dish originated. Wells writes of how 'with each bite, Sidda tasted her homeland' (423). Wells also describes the sensorial qualities generated by the dish through its specific associations with rural ingredients from Cajun country, such as 'roux', 'onion, celery and peppers', along with 'fresh parsley, cayenne pepper' (423).

It seems here that the physiology of taste is joined with the idiosyncrasy of place; the land of origin—exemplified and embodied in specific elements defining Cajun cuisine, such as cayenne pepper and the typical roux—is imprinted on the taste of the *étouffée*. The dish, therefore, becomes iconographic, embodying, in Trubek's words, '*the lieux de memoire*'.[57] Wells establishes a vivid connection between the life in South Louisiana, culinary practices and the gustatory impulses experienced by Sidda when eating the *étouffée*. This phenomenon, creating a link between land and taste, is known in French as *goût du terroir*. According to Trubek, a sense of *terroir*—perhaps poorly translated as the English word 'place'—appears 'when something has a particular flavour that can be attributed to the soil, or the typical tastes and habits that come from a region or rural area'.[58] In this way, *goût du terroir* becomes understood, even more specifically, as the evocation of a precise geographical location—its grass, soil and water— through the consumption of a particular product that was produced there. In *Divine Secrets*, Sidda's associations between the sensorial qualities caused by the *étouffée* and its site of production—her 'homeland'—can be seen as evoking not only a taste, but a very specific *goût du terroir*, which brings with it the memory of a different way of life. That memory is inevitably linked to a general understanding of regional existence which, for Sidda, finds its embodiment in the local production of Cajun dishes.

And yet, it must not be thought that the *terroir* of Vivi's *étouffée* is simply an intrinsic quality of the dish. Trubek reminds us that 'the natural environment influences the flavours of food, but ultimately the cultural domain [. . .] creates the *goût du terroir*'.[59] The *goût du terroir* evoked in Sidda's memory by the dish is a product not only of physiological responses then, but also of a desire for remembrance, a need to re-experience the land and relive bygone times with her mother in Louisiana. It is not surprising, then, that Sidda claims to taste 'her mother's love' (423) as she consumes Vivi's signature dish. This mirrors Trubek's idea that '*terroir* is often associated with [. . .] roots, a person's history with a certain place'.[60] The gustatory moment, therefore, 'mediates [. . .] and incorporates people's belief that [they] [. . .] possess [. . .] a connection to the land'.[61]

One other essential element must also be pointed out about Wells' description of seemingly authentic Cajun cuisine. When visualising the preparation of the *étouffée*, a list of careful ingredients is provided, from the peppers, to onions and the ever-important roux—a mixture of flour, butter and flour which 'serves as the basis' of South Louisiana cooking.[62] Yet, there is nothing inherent to the basic ingredients themselves that identifies them as Cajun; onions, for instance, are a staple ingredients of cuisines from different regions and countries. The same can be said, of course, about parsley, butter and peppers. Their taste is recognisable in many dishes originating from the Southern states of America and do not openly spell Cajun or even 'Louisiana' in any way. Indeed, apart from the typically Cajun crawfish, the dish does not proudly show any particular sensorial qualities that classify its provenance. Even the characteristic roux is not proper only to South Louisiana cooking, but can be found—in different varieties—in several examples of broader Louisiana cuisine, especially in the New Orleans area. One needs to wonder, then, what does make the dish typically Cajun and how the identity of the South Louisiana region is imprinted on that taste and smell of the dish for Sidda.

To find an answer, one needs to think of not only the taste, but the cultural significance of the ingredients and how South Louisiana people actually perceive them. One could begin by saying that the ingredients in Vivi's dish are considered Cajun because they are produced locally and because they are consumed widely and in large quantities in South Louisiana. This initial explanation, however, would not be completely satisfying. The power of the ingredients lies in the way they are put together; Gutierrez reminds us that 'some frequently eaten and locally produced ingredients' are associated with South Louisiana 'only if they are cooked a certain way'.[63] Onion, peppers, parsley and butter are not necessarily examples of Southern Lousisiana cuisine, but the way they are mixed with roux and crawfish makes them so. The 'performance' of the dish, it would seem, is as important in assembling the dish as the taste of the ingredients themselves. The cultural interaction between ingredients and preparation provides an explanation to why Wells dedicates attention to Vivi's movements and precise assemblage of the dish. It is in that combination that we find the value of regional cuisine; therein lies the core of what is Cajun. This confirms Gutierrez's assertion that in examples of regional cuisine, 'cooking style is more important than the use of particular ingredients'.[64] The significance of the ingredients derives not simply from their taste, but from the ethnic value they hold within a specific community. Here we see how the senses can cease to be simple physiological process and become part of culture. Regional cuisine in *Divine Secrets*, therefore, is not composed of a strict list of ingredients and instructions, but is formed and performed by cultural, ethnic and familial attachment to a specifically recognisable dish.

As Wells dissects the culinary components of Cajun cuisine, she is also partial to showing how a sense of regional identity is able to reach the natives of a particular area even when they are away from home. In the novel, regional affiliation is communicated through the Ya-Yas' attachment to coffee, a beverage they cannot live with even when they go to visit Sidda. It should not come as a surprise that Wells chooses coffee as a particularly culturally-enriched beverage to signify the almost mystical presence of South Louisiana tradition within the story. Gutierrez reminds us that 'of all beverages used by Cajuns today, dark roast coffee is most closely associated with Cajuns and their region'. This particularly regional perception does not only belong to outsiders, but is proper to the inhabitants of Southern Louisiana, who see roast coffee as part of their culinary identity. Cajuns tend to be very strict about the quality of their coffee, which they claim must be dark and strong. It is also believed by Cajuns that 'their' coffee is superior to that of other regions—that includes, of course, other Louisiana regions, particularly New Orleans. Gutierrez attests to the fact that most Cajuns insist on taking 'their own coffee with them whenever they travel outside of Louisiana'. The fact that they Ya-Yas bring their own packet of coffee with them testifies to a desire to maintain a connection to their region and perhaps even 'feel at home' wherever they go. It is also indicative that the Ya-Yas specify the brand of coffee they brought, 'Community French' (286). The brand is in fact in fact the 'most popular' in South Louisiana as it is manufactured—although not grown—in the area of Baton Rouge.[65] The Cajun desire to drink one's own coffee seems to translate here into a need to maintain a cultural attachment to specific everyday habits, which is an integral part of regional identity. In addition, one must consider the possibility that Wells may be making a humorous suggestion about the Cajun attitude towards coffee, mocking—albeit in an affectionate manner—the conviction that South Louisiana strong coffee is actually superior.

However, it is not just the presence of the coffee that communicates its regional value to the Ya-Yas; preparation and serving methods seem to play a significant part as well. As the coffee packet emerges from Necie's bag, it is immediately offered to Sidda as a welcome party addition. Although Sidda is not formally 'the guest' at the cabin, the coffee drinking ceremony designates her as such in the eyes of the Ya-Yas. This attitude is also consistent with hosting habits observed in South Louisiana at coffee time. The serving of coffee to guest is 'perhaps the most strictly formalised' of all Cajun food events.[66] Attention is clearly given to the way the beverage is put together and presented. The Ya-Yas present Sidda with a 'demitasse' cup (286), obeying to a simple but effective serving ritual which has its origins in France and it is still part of coffee drinking in Louisiana. The adherence to particular presentation and drinking ceremony communicate the coffee's value as a regional symbol; its offering functions—in an almost mystical way—as the worshipping of a particular lifestyle that is associated with the Ya-Yas regional affiliation. As the coffee is offered to Sidda, so is the idea of Louisiana itself, a reminder of the woman's hometown and her ethnic, cultural and social origins.

Indeed, the concept of region becomes particularly relevant in *Divine Secrets* as it is connected to the idea of 'going home'. The idea of home in itself is not portrayed as an abstract concept of belonging or a static, material visualisation of a building in which close relatives live; the idea of home is visualised through familiar routines and practices which find their ideal embodiment is patterns of consumption. As particular dishes, drinks and ingredients serve to identify Louisiana as a region to Sidda, so do they aid her reconciliation with her estranged home within that region. When Sidda and Connor visit the family's home in Louisiana—in a planned attempt at reconciliation with Vivi—they arrive precisely during Vivi's birthday party. As the gathering welcomes Sidda, it is made clear that food takes on a peculiar function. The guests are offered 'some cold shrimp and fried frog legs', coming straight from a 'Cajun cooker' which is 'set up nearby' (508). Sidda describes the event as a 'birthday crayfish boil' (509), leaving no doubt about both the nature of the food served or how the evening is supposed to unfold.

While Sidda and Connor mingle with friends and members of the family, the particular nature of the dishes served highlights their role as a line of demarcation for regional identity. As the food is offered to Connor, he is affectionately referred to as the 'Yankee' (506); his momentary—and well-hidden—embarrassment about the food served highlights him as the outsider. The locality of the food here is used as an example of regional affiliation; the Louisiana guests show pride for their region as they offer their most definitive dishes, which are a testament to a whole way of life. In order to advance the symbolic function of food within the group, Connor is then asked by the other guests and family members to 'help' himself (508). Consuming crayfish and frogs legs becomes a medium through which the social impact and 'scale of the region' are 'articulated' into the group dynamics.[67] Wells seems to suggest that behind crayfish and other 'local' dishes one can identify the local community, the regional group which finds identification through culinary routine and food consumption. Bell and Valentine argue that the region is also partly made of 'imagination', an idea of affiliation with the land which is constantly perpetrated by those who live in it.[68] In *Divine Secrets*, that perpetration takes place through exemplary Cajun dishes, which are used as a beacon to simultaneously welcome outsiders into the home community and highlight feelings of regional pride.

Nonetheless, the true value of the region as 'home' in Wells' novel is revealed as Sidda makes peace with her mother, on the porch of their family home. Food, predictably, plays a star role in the episode. As a welcoming gesture, Vivi prepares a plate of food for her daughter: 'She handed Sidda a glass of champagne and a plate piled high with boiled crayfish, new potatoes, corn on the cob, and hunks of buttered French bread' (509). The selection of items offered to Sidda is revelatory on several levels. Firstly, the champagne brings with it memories of Genevieve, as we are told on several occasions throughout the novel that it was her favourite drink. Genevieve's memory lingers above Vivi and Sidda not only as a reminder of a dearly departed, but also as a signifier of Cajun identity. Secondly, the presence of specific items such as the unmissable crayfish and its many cultural associations define the ensemble as part of a precise South Louisiana culinary system. And yet, it is not just the food offered which claims a homecoming function for Sidda. Indeed, it is the act of eating it—together with her mother—which has a definitive effect on the daughter. As Vivi worries about how Sidda is going to eat the food, her daughter claims that she has 'not forgotten how to suck the heads of a Louisiana crayfish' and that she would not forget 'wherever' she goes (509). The fact that Sidda claims to 'have not forgotten' demands the presence of a system of culinary and cultural recognition which identifies the boiled crayfish as part of her home region. As she proceeds to 'shell the crayfish' (509), Sidda also engages with a particular practice which is closely associated with routines and habits of Southern Louisiana.

The crayfish alone does not communicate region; neither does Sidda's presence on her family porch. The 'sense of place'—unforgettable and part of Sidda's return home—emerges as a careful combination of location, food and practice. Her 'coming home' is not simply confined to a geographical place, the mingling with local people or the offering of Cajun dishes. As the crayfish is consumed, Sidda also finds a moment of communion with her mother, as their differences are momentarily erased and they put an end to their emotional conflict. In eating the food, Sidda symbolically recognises her affiliation to Louisiana, her home, her mother and her ways. Region—and its relationship to home—is communicated by Wells as the product of both a 'natural landscape' and a 'peopled landscape', which are exposed and fused through the medium of food.[69]

Attachment to food practices, as put forward by both Flagg and Wells, emerges as the key ingredient in literary depictions of life in the South. The feeling of locality obtained from it can be interpreted as 'the hallmark' of 'regional identity', as patterns of consumption are articulated within a precise social and geographical frame.[70] The fiction allows an insight into cultural conceptions of not only place, but also social identities, which revolves around relationships with people, flavours and the land. The 'sense of place' in the novels is developed through complicated notions of belonging and culinary preference, which, in turn, are able to expose intricate layers of social, ethnic, economic and racial politics. The region—here exposed in its varying Southern incarnations—takes on a symbolic role, while cultural, physical and historical dimensions expose, as Barbara Allen puts it, complex structures of 'both kinships networks and ownership patterns'.[71]

3 Race and History

> Black-eyed peas and rice or 'Hoppin' John', even collard greens and pig's feet, are not so much arbitrary predilections of the 'nigra' as they are symbolic defiance: we shall celebrate ourselves on a day of our choosing in honor of those events and souls who are an honor to us.
>
> —Ntozake Shange, *If I Can Cook/You Know God Can*[1]

It is important to remember that, because of very specific historical repercussions, the state of 'being African American' differs greatly from other experiences of exchange and immigration in the United States. Historically, African Americans have faced first the misery of slavery and then the agony of segregation, which put their experience as Americans in a different, yet interrelated category to that of other ethnic groups in the country. In the Sixties, the Civil Rights Movement brought attention to African American art forms that had been neglected, stereotyped or misinterpreted by mainstream American trends. Issues of cultural definition became paramount in an effort to provide a channel for African American expression which could be understood and given the dignity it deserved. The list of art forms redefined as African American in the late twentieth century includes, of course, literature. 'African American literature', argues Psyche Williams-Forson, 'has been the one place where black people have been able to define themselves with and against the order of the day'.[2] Fiction, in particular, has taken on a very particular cultural meaning for African Americans, in which 'the signs of cultural hegemony, food politics and delineations of power are omnipresent'.[3]

Although it is now not only a well-known term, but also an acknowledged embedment of African American foodways, the rubric definition of the ubiquitous 'soul food' are actually relatively new. The term, itself, and its emergence, are actually connected to waves of cultural nationalism which swept African American groups in the early Sixties. Renowned poet Amiri Baraka is credited with having coined the term in order to describe a specifically African American sense of legacy, which could—and arguably should—be separated from overarching definitions of Southern food. Encapsulating not only ingredients, but also the weight of history and experience which came with culinary heritage, soul food became, as William Frank Mitchell puts it, 'the perfect symbol for black cultural revolution'.[4]

Particular dishes, which had belonged to African American culinary traditions for centuries, were exemplified as being connected to African American across the wide spectrum of cultural and ethnic diversity. The idea of soul food was—and still is—perceived as a collection of culinary elements through which all black people could, and should, identify in the face of white-ethnic oppression. According to Mitchell, prime examples of 'soul food', symbolically recognised as such, include: 'Fried chicken, barbecued ribs, pork chops, fried fish, collard greens, candied sweet potatoes, potato salad [and] cornbread'. Emphasising a strong past lineage, the newly-labeled 'soul food' brought with it the ability to construct emblematic connections between African Americans. The 'sense of history' featured in certain black dishes promised to also provide 'an affirmation of community' to all its members.[5] In the tumultuous and belligerent era of the Sixties and Seventies Black Power philosophy, the foodways promoted by the culturally-created 'soul food' constructed a renewed feeling of loyalty, strengthening a sense of identity which greatly aided the achievements of the Civil Rights Movement.

In spite of the historical differences in the creation of African American sub-groups, it is my intention not to treat instances of food in African American fiction—and the writing itself—separate and in isolation from 'the broader range of multiethnic culinary writing in the United States'.[6] Following the example of eminent critics of African American writing, such as Rafia Zafar and Doris Witt, I aim to consider the fiction of African Americans, and its approach to food politics, in relation to the greater spectrum of American fiction. Nonetheless, it important to pay attention to aspiration and challenges which may characterise (without generalisation) the use of food and culinary metaphors in contemporary African American fiction. The sense of both ambition and confrontation could be inherent 'to the efforts' that African American writers engage with in order to 'articulate the meaning of blackness in the so-called global era'.[7]

In the Sixties and Seventies, the slogan of 'Black Power'—prominent among many African American groups—emphasised racial pride and the creation of black political and cultural institutions to cultivate and promote black collective interests and values. Possibly as a result of this expression of political goals—which included the fight against oppression and the achievement of separate and independent black institutions—a newborn interest in African American cuisine and culinary habits became a very noticeable feature in a number of texts by contemporary black writers. Joining a noticeable cultural trend which included the emergence of ethnic cookbooks, it is possible to argue that African American writers show a wide-ranging interest in 'the recuperation' of black foodways, from preparation methods to iconic foods which epitomise the African American experience in an over-arching manner.[8] In spite of emancipation, urbanization, and migration to the cities of the North, African Americans have preserved their foods and cooking methods. In the mid-twentieth century, African American foods began to be produced for the mass market, and many 'soul food restaurants' have opened in the United States.

In recent years, it has been the case in the United States that a large number of young, black professional have proved and confirmed that success—in both social and economic terms—is not only compatible but also continuous with African American restaurants monopolising on black culture and culinary traditions. This particular position is exposed by Bebe Moore Campbell in her novel *Brothers and Sisters* (1994). Campbell articulates the 'black restaurant' in the mainstream and shows it as an essential part of the African American experience. The novel highlights the importance of consuming rural, simple and 'direct' food, which carries concepts of comfort associated with it. The value of African American dishes is portrayed as an essential part of Esther Jackson, the novel's protagonist, who is a very independent and successful banker in Los Angeles. Although she lives happily in California, whenever Esther goes home to Washington, D.C., she is compelled to consume the 'local' black food, which is part of her childhood both culturally and socially: 'I must go to the Grille and have my fried chicken and greens and world famous biscuits. And following that, I must go over to Georgia Avenue and have a drink or two at Traces'.[9]

Nonetheless, however, one must bear in mind that the growing interest in black culinary ways—particularly noticeable in post-1980 fiction—also constitutes a clear-cut critique and social unveiling of a possible of 'homogenising conceptions of blackness'.[10] In drawing attention to sub-ethnic trends, recipes and culinary nuances, a number of African American writers manage to uncover expectation surrounding not only notions of blackness, but also pre-conceptions about black fiction. The texts themselves, as a result, respond 'to concerns about the loss of unique cultural traditions under the pervasive pressure' of mainstream cultural industry.[11]

A wide-spread interest in African American cuisine and its different incarnations—as exemplified, as we will see, in the work of Toni Morrison, Ntozake Shange and Gloria Naylor—has been stimulated (at least in part) by, on the one hand, the cultural explosion of 'ethnic restaurants', from Creole to Caribbean and Southern cuisine. On the other, the desire to focus on specific traditional foodways in African American writing responds to a wide-spread 'traffic in the iconography of ethnic multiplicity' that Witt identifies as 'a distinguishing and problematic feature' of the late-capitalist marketplace.[12] Charged with culturally-inscribed connotations and historical associations reaching back to the times of slavery, the foods which feature in African American fiction often function as signs which, 'hidden and embedded in the language', transforms literature into a 'fruitful site' for simultaneous self-definition and ethnic expression.[13]

RACIAL COMMODITIES

Toni Morrison's use of food metaphors in her novels is notorious. She often employs food and eating in order to dissect not only to unveil perspectives on race, gender and history, but also the state of African Americans within the wider American compass. In an interview, Morrison commented on her constructions of 'blackness' and 'white', stating that 'there is a lot of juice to be extracted from plumy reminiscences of "individual" and "freedom" if the tree upon which such fruit hangs is a black population forced to polar opposites'.[14] With this idea in mind, one can see how Morrison's elaborate use of food in her work speaks loudly of the greater connotations that eating—or, sometimes, not eating—takes on for members of the African American community. Whilst approaching the symbolic significance of food in Morrison's work, one can follow Lynn Marie Houston's suggestion, claiming that eating and cooking are 'frequently presented' in the novels as figurative representations of 'racial power struggle'.[15]

In particular, images of 'hunger' emerge as instrumental in Morrison's constructions of character, community and racial divisions. Some of Morrison's novels have received sizeable critical attention in terms of food. Works such as *Beloved* (1987) and *Song of Solomon* (1977) have been favourite examples among literary critics of how Morrison can build a particular relationship with food, unveiling the importance of consumption as a means to construct, dissect or annihilate conceptions of the African American self. Beyond the thought of physical hunger, one can identify different types of hunger that need to be considered; examples of 'emotional' or 'psychological' become metaphorical interpretations for 'memory, history, voice and sexual appetites'.[16] Hunger is conveyed by Morrison through mixed feelings of joy and despair, and she is able to render feelings of strength. Houston has affectively pointed out that in *Song of Solomon*, Milkman Dead discovers that feeling of hunger have an exercising effect on him; in *Beloved*, on the other hand, Denver Suggs finds hunger debilitating and it has a silencing effect on her. *Beloved* also deals with hunger as associated to maternal love, as Sethe needs to feed her hungry children and feel that she is nurturing them. Morrison has a skilful way to manipulate hunger in her novels, so that her characters, whether they are African American slaves on the run or members of a racially-right community, 'reveal ways of thinking about their relationships to the world around them through food'.[17]

Extremely important to discussions of African American 'hunger' in Morrison's novels is the critically overlooked presence of sugar. Indeed, one can find the conspicuous appearance of several sweet foods, from sugar, candy and chocolate to an array of delicious pies. In *Jazz* (1992), Joe spends a lot of money on peppermint sweets and candy; he even describes his sexual passion for his lover in terms of sweetness, calling Dorcas his special 'candy box'.[18] As the lovers' relationship falls apart, Joe expresses his heartache not for Dorcas as such, but for the 'sweetness' she provided for him. In Morrison's earlier text *Sula* (1974), the war veteran Plum refuses to consume nutritious food and instead has his room as full of sugary snacks: 'there in the corner was a half-eaten store-bought cherry pie. Balled-up candy wrappers and empty pop bottles peeped from under the dresser'.[19]

The lack of nourishment in Plum's diet prefigures his final physical degradation and demise. His inability to integrate into society is mirrored in his desire for sweet foods, which fail to nourish him on either a physical or psychological level. Sugary foods, one might venture to say, are taken by Morrison to be a powerful and malleable metaphor for a sense of insatiability and lack of fufillment.

Sugar is, for African Americans, a historically complicated foodstuff. Eminent sugar historian Richard Follett has described the oppressive social forms of nineteenth-century Louisiana's own sugar industry. Follett evokes a productive mode which constituted 'one of the most rapacious and exploitative regimes' of African Americans in 'the South'. The sugar worker—usually a slave—was subject to being disciplined by multiple means; these ranged from bells, clocks and whistles (which portioned out the day's labour) to a strict enforcement of spatial control within the plantation. Even though the sugarhouse transformed over the course of the nineteenth century, it still lingered as a dangerous and highly regimented environment, dominated by the 'constant clattering of conveyor belts shuttling canes and semidry sucrose across the mill floor'.[20]

Although Follett's account is passionate and compelling, it could also seem exaggerated by the impact of contemporary racial and class sympathies. To discount this suggestion, one should then consider that descriptions of the hellish sugarhouse also occur in historical documents. In 1884 George Cable, an eminent social journalist, offered a number of visually aggressive images as he evokes 'the battery of huge caldrons, with their yellow juice boiling like a sea, half-hidden in clouds of steam; the half-clad, shining negroes swinging the gigantic utensils with which the seething flood is dipped from kettle to kettle'.[21] It is worth recalling here, *en passant*, that the distinctly gothic, almost Dantean cauldron descriptions used by Cable in reference to plantation work is reminiscent of the imagery used by Karl Marx—a contemporary of Cable—in order to illustrate the workings of capitalism. Marx describes the capitalist master as a 'vampire' who 'sucks out [. . .] blood and brains and throws them into the *cauldron of capital*'.[22] Although the social and political circumstances approached by Cable and Marx carry distinct and profound differences, the shared imagery of 'cauldron' draws attention to issues of exploitation involved in a discussion of labour economies. As one approaches the historical outlook of the American plantation, it is important to consider the enslavement of African Americans not only as a despicable act of human degradation, but also as an important economic strategy on the white masters' part.

As we transfer our attention back to Morrison's fiction, we see that the cultural and historical relevance of sweet commodities was already signalled in her earliest work, published in the Seventies. Indeed, the racially conflicted use of the sugary is prominent in *The Bluest Eyes* (1970), Morrison's first novel. In the text, obtaining sugary foods for African Americans becomes symptomatic for the utopian possession of 'all-American' qualities, such as the movie star look of 'the bluest eyes'. Elizabeth House argues that Morrison uses sweet food imagery in order to render conflicts between 'two sets of values'.[23] In this respect, Pauline's 'sweet treat obsession' is particularly revelatory. While sitting at the movies, she spends her time examining idealized representations of white America. As she does so, Pauline eats candy almost incessantly; it becomes impossible here not to see how Morrison constructs an imagistic association between the 'sweetness' of the candy and the 'sweetness' of being white. As she watches white images of perfection, Pauline craves more and more sugary sweets, an indulgent appeal that offers very little (momentary) satisfaction and little sustenance. Pauline, one could argue, is not simply nurturing her hunger—which, clearly cannot be satiated by eating 'empty' candy. Indeed, she is also feeding her desire for whiteness; she challenges her own feeling of identity as the colour of her skin prevents from obtaining both the physical and social advantages of what she sees as associated with the white race. In a way, sugar acts as a surrogate for the desired racial equality. Subverting the historical stereotype which associated African American with the production, and not the consumption, of sugar, Pauline uses candy as a commodity which promises to fulfil her desired sense of self.

Nonetheless, Morrison seems keen to maintain that both erasing a history of sugary enslavement and transforming the black social psyche into white are not simple achievements. As Pauline consumes large quantities of sweet treats, she cracks her tooth on a piece of candy: 'I was sitting right back in my seat, and I taken a big bite of that candy and it pulled a tooth right out of my mouth. I could of cried'.[24] The breaking of the tooth is Morrison's initial, powerful warning of the danger represented by Pauline's racialised, sweet hunger. Emma Parker suggests that Pauline's 'broken tooth points to the destructive nature of the disease system of values which has conditioned her into a sense of worthlessness'.[25] The rotten tooth is symbolic of Pauline's social and psychological decay. On the one hand, the broken tooth signifies her inability to actually 'consume' the white fantasy and therefore become it. As a powerful embodiment of failed racial introjection, the broken tooth acts as a reminder of the history which connects African Americans to sugar and an indication of the dangers which come from being incorporated into an unbalanced fantasy of possession. On the other hand, the rotten tooth—which is revealed only after Pauline bites too violently into the candy—functions as Morrison's figurative representation of the 'rotten' nature of some members of the African American community, who not only dream of white perfection, but also accept their inferior social position. As the tooth disintegrates, so does Pauline's sense of achievement; as she is rendered unable to obtain a sense of 'sweet whiteness', her tears seal her demise as they wash away the hope to rise above her history.

As Morrison unveils the possibly disintegrating nature of black womanhood in *The Bluest Eyes*, she also continues to employ the medium of 'sweet foods' in order to dissect Pauline's issues with her African American selfhood later in the novel. Indeed, it is through her job that Pauline is able to materialise her subjected position within the white world. After the broken tooth episode, Pauline forgets her desires for whiteness and internalises 'her sweet hunger' as a wish to become the best pie maker. In her essay 'Age, Race, Class and Sex', Audre Lorde sharply employs a sweet food metaphor and claims that, for large number of African Americans, oppression is 'as American as apple pie'.[26] Aligning herself with the sense of sweet oppression described by Lorde, Pauline takes great pride in her work as a cook in a white household, realising white fantasies of iconic Aunt Jemina's love and perfection. Her delicious blueberry cobbler completes her warped picture of the domestic ideal. Her employer, Mr. Fisher, even comments that he 'would rather sell her blueberry cobbler than real estate' (125). One can see here how Morrison displays a representational affinity with Flagg in showing the racialised nature of kitchen politics and portraying the black woman as a stereotyped cook. However, while Flagg does not fully engage with the conceptual and historical implications of representing African American women as 'ideal cooks'—indeed, those implications are only exposed by reading *Fried Green Tomatoes* against its own narrative intentions—Morrison is openly keen to expose how particular food images can maintain the racial status quo in the wider American imagery. Pauline's culinary ability is viewed as a sellable product, therefore mirroring the function as 'commodity' that her African ancestors held within the plantation economy. Through the presence of sugary food, Morrison unveils how social creations of African American labourers and white employers still perpetuate—although in a mutated outlook—the financial constructs which maintained racial hierarchies at the time of slavery. Instead of challenging the racial conflicts raised by the production and consumption of sugary treats, Pauline wears her subordination proudly, giving voice to Morrison's concern about the state of working-class African Americans in the early Seventies.

Morrison's use of racialised sugar politics in her fiction draws attention to the historically charged relationship between African Americans and racial segregation. In gesturing towards the past of an entire group in the United States, however, Morrison is not alone in merging food with history and racial politics. In the post-2000 era, the trauma of slavery remains alive in African American fiction and it often emerges thematically as food customs are unveiled as potent racial signifier. This is the case in Edward P. Jones' *The Known World* (2004). The novel is a powerful and successful attempt at offering a self-conscious insight into not only African American slave life, but also the repercussions it had on establishing what is now understood as common African American foodways. The novel also wishes to draw attention to issues of cultural and culinary aberration that Jones identifies as part of prohibition systems, lying at the heart of African American oppression. *The Known World* narrates the story of Henry Townsend, a young and wealthy African American plantation owner in ante-bellum Virginia. Using the figure of Henry as a storytelling glue—and recounting the issues that unfold in his plantation after his death—Jones not only offers a critique of slave life, but also sends a powerful historical message regarding oppression of other races and cultural groups. Displaying an impressive ability to replicate African American vernacular in the written word, Jones dedicates close attention to slave eating habits and customs. In so doing, he reaches out to the figure of 'the slave' in a new manner, offering not the memory of a by-gone era, but a very contemporary glimpse into the slave experience.

In Jones' novel, Moses, the plantation overseer and the first slave Henry ever bought, is portrayed eating 'eating dirt' at the beginning of the novel:

> Moses closed his eyes and bent down and took a pinch of the soil and ate it with no more thought than if it were a spot of cornbread. He worked the dirt around his mouth and swallowed [. . .] He was the only man in the realm, slave or free, who ate dirt, but while the bondage women . . . ate it [. . .] for that something that ash cakes and apples and fatback did not give their bodies, he ate it not only to discover the strengths and weaknesses of the field, but because the eating tied him to the only thing in his small world that meant almost as much as his own life.[27]

It is possible to find a connection here between the fertility of the soil and the sexual potency of manhood. Wayne Flynt reminds us that many African slaves in the United States believed that eating soil 'increased sexual prowess'.[28] This belief seems to be reinforced by Jones. After Moses has consumed the soil, he lies on the ground, undressing 'down to his nakedness' (3). As he lies naked, he establishes an almost spiritual connection with the ground and the rain that falls gently on his face. Taken by the beauty of the moment (and in an unexpected turn of events), Moses begins to masturbate whilst still on the ground; he then closes his eyes and feels empowered by the experience. Here we see an example of Freudian introjection. In psychoanalytical terms, the mouth represents the initial source of sensual pleasure: the infant sucks the mother's breast and derives pleasure from it. Oral gratification is seen as the earliest manifestation of sexuality and is referred to by Freud as the 'oral' stage.[29] As the child grows, erotic gratification is transferred from the mouth to genitalia. This process of transference seems to be still happening in Moses. He consumes the soil—associated with an idea of prosperity, fecundity and worth—in order to enhance his sexual potency. It is also interesting that Moses is said to be stepping 'into the 'woods' before lying on the ground; In *Introductory Lectures to Psychoanalysis*, Freud proposes that the idea of woods and forest is always associated, in imagistic terms, with female genitalia.[30] Moses' masturbatory act seals a conceptual connection between his life and that of the soil, establishing a sense of longevity which is contained in the feminised ground.

As one explores Jones' use of soil-eating as a metaphor for sexuality in bondage, the novel also unveils a socio-historical critique of slaves' eating habits and their perceived usefulness. The practice of geophagy—or soil-eating—has a long-standing history in West Africa. The oldest evidence of soil-eating being practised by humans has been found in the pre-history site of Kalambo Falls, on the border between Zambia and Tanzania.[31] Although many instances of soil-eating can still be found throughout the world, the practice was taken to the Unites States (unsurprisingly) through the slave trade. Indeed, geophagy—also known in the Southern states as 'clay eating'–is strongly associated with minority groups and continues to have the stigma of being an eating habit of the old African slaves. The practice was so common among the slaves that, in many areas, they were given the depreciative nick-name of 'clay-eaters'. Needless to say, soil-eating was extremely frowned upon by the white community, which associated it with ideas of social inferiority. In 1851, Dr Samuel Cartwright—an eminent physician of the time—went as far as saying that 'pica' (or clay-eating) belonged to a particular list of 'negro diseases'; Dr Cartwright even gave dirt-eating an official scientific name, 'Cochexia Africana'.[32] As a result of the misconceptions and stereotypes that surrounded soil-eating (or chewing) in the nineteenth century, white Southerners perceived the West African practice with contempt, forgetting that pica has a long tradition in Western history 'dating back to the Greeks'.[33]

Jones, however, does more than just commenting on the cultural and issues surrounding a practice which was common among West African groups during the times of slavery in the South. Through dissecting the practice of 'soil eating', Jones offers a critique of the slaves' lives, how they were kept and what sustenance they received. Jones' attention to geophagy may actually be related to an evaluation of the physical and emotional state of the slaves on Henry's plantation. Historians have noted a close relationship between the slaves' poor diet and disease. Schneider and Schneider point out that the slaves had to live on rationed portions of 'rice, fatback, cornmeal, and soft pork'.[34] Jones tells us on a number of occasions that the slaves must survive on 'poor food' (25)—also referred openly to as 'slave food' (17)—which is given from their masters, consisting mainly of 'plenty of fatback and ash cakes and the occasional mouthful of rape or kale' (17). As he describes their poor diet, Jones also draws attention to many of the slaves' ailments, which range from common 'skin burns' to 'toothache' (122). Instances of blindness and stomach-ache—and even physical disability–are also portrayed as common throughout the novel. It must be noted, however, that Jones does not imply that the slaves in *The Known World* are malnourished and under-fed. The consequences of their poor diet are not related necessarily to how much food they receive, but to the quality. Schneider and Schneider argue that the slaves' diet, as poor in nutrition as it was, rendered them 'vulnerable to blindness, sore eyes, skin irritations and toothaches'.[35] With this idea in mind, Jones may be commenting, through issues of physical nutrition, on the emotional state of the African Americans in bondage. Their ailments are a metaphorical transposition of their emotionally imprisoned state. In this framework, then, once could argue that the sustenance coming from eating dirt is of an emotional nature. Clay-eating—emerging as giving a type of nourishment that is described by Jones as 'incomprehensible' (1)—is a practice that keeps a symbolic connection to not only the slaves' land of origin, but to the tradition, ways of life and, most importantly, freedom that went with it.

RECIPES AND MAGIC

The sensitivity to slave food customs is a widespread characteristic in contemporary African American fiction. However, while Jones is interested in exploring slave life through a lucid twenty-first century perspective, other writers prefer to use cooking as a narrative tool which makes the historical heritage of black food prominent in contemporary life. This is the case of Ntozake Shange. Her fiction shows a propensity to exalt connections between past and present; denying claims of racial minority, she draws attention to the historical struggle of African Americans as a point of departure, a connection from which contemporary black people—especially women—can draw strength and inspiration in order to live fulfilling lives.

In the Seventies, Shange achieved notoriety for her theatrical representations of the experiences of African American women; she is best known for her first dramatic production, *for colored girls who have considered suicide / when the rainbow is enuf* (1975). In this work—which did receive mixed reactions from critics at the time—she incorporates poetic monologue into a dramatic performance, a form that Shange herself termed the 'choreopoem' and which has also been referred to as 'staged poetry'. Her writing style is unusual and striking, merging elements of poetry, dance, and music into dramatic monologues. Throughout her career, Shange has been simultaneously praised and criticized for the ways in which she unravels the intersection of race and gender oppression. Her portrayals of relationships between African American women and men, in particular, have been widely challenged. Shange's depictions of African American men have often been disparaged as unsympathetic and one-sided; particularly in *for colored girls*, the men often serve as obstacles in the journey to self-affirmation that African American women find themselves on. Indeed, Shange often seems to suggest that men should not 'exist', in order for black women to achieve individuality and self-awareness. While Shange focuses on the difficulties experienced by her African American characters, she also manages to maintain an aura of triumph over their circumstances, often unveiling forms of inner strength and, eventually, rejoicing over the friendships which can be established between women.

Shange's fiction shares the genre-mixing forms which compose her dramatic pieces. Recalling the stylistic qualities of her poems and plays, her novels incorporate a variety of forms, such as recipes, dreams, songs, magical spells and letters in a pastiche format, rather than in a conventional linear narrative. This is particularly true of *Sassafrass, Cypress and Indigo* (1982). Set mainly in the coastal district of South Carolina, the novel concentrates on the lives of three African American sisters, who all have particular and yet interconnected talents. Sassafrass, the eldest, is a poet and a weaver. Cypress is a dancer who leaves home to 'discover herself' and discover new ways of living in the world. Indigo, the youngest sister, is described as a child of Charleston—with 'too much of the South in her'.[36] She makes beautiful dolls, plays the violin and has the gift of 'magic'. It is made clear by Shange that every single experience in sisters' lives is looked at as amazing and worth of note. Indigo, in particular, projects her sense of self and her wish to celebrate experience. For instance, she is portrayed staging the time-honoured transition into womanhood for her dolls. Although the event provides Indigo with an opportunity for expression, her particular approach to life is not always understood or shared by those around her, especially her mother: '"Indigo, I don't want to hear another word about it . . ." her Mamma says, "I'm not setting the table with my Sunday china for fifteen dolls who got their period today"' (20). Overall, *Sassafrass, Cypress and Indigo* is very experimental; Shange combines elements of tradition with innovation, spirituality with obsession, joy with grief, in order to express African American women's experiences in idiosyncratic and unequivocal terms.

Shange's novel has been described by Doris Grumbach as a 'narrative potpourri', into which the author 'tosses all the graphic elements of Southern black life: wonderful recipes . . . spells and potions (how to rid oneself of the scent of evil), prescriptions (how to care for open wounds when they hurt), letters from Mama to her beloved but straying and erring daughters, full of calm reason and uncritical love, always advising accommodation to the hostility and blindness of the white world)'.[37] In an interview, Shange herself admitted that the recipes she included in the novel were intended to be an integral part of the plot: 'You have to read the entire recipes— ingredients and procedures—because if you don't, you don't really know what's going on with those girls'.[38] Her characters in *Sassafrass, Cypress and Indigo* cook for a variety of reasons: sometimes to celebrate and comfort, often to mourn and, on occasions, even to seduce. Shange claims that the recipes are meant to offer a sense of involvement for the reader, as if they were coordinates towards finding a place in the characters' lives: 'I didn't want readers to skip over the recipes, or they would lose that sense," she said. "I wanted those recipes to create a place to be'.[39]

The recipes, however, serve as much more than a storytelling device. The foods presented in the novel are clear examples of what is usually known as 'soul food', the food of the African American cuisine which evolved into a form of ethnic gastronomy charged with the weight of history. This is mirrored in the sisters' cooking of a 'Kwanza recipe' (120), testifying to connections between modern life, soul food and the celebration on an African festivity. Patricia Clark charts the connection between the maintenance of African culinary traditions and the cultural and geographical shift for the slaves: 'Africans uprooted from ancestral soil, stripped of material culture, and victimized by brutal contact with various European nations were compelled not only to maintain their cultural heritage at a meta (as opposed to a material) level but also to apprehend the operative metaphysics of various alien cultures'.[40]

In *Sassafrass, Cypress and Indigo*, Shange makes explicitly the idea that black women cooks of the United States—and the dishes they continue to prepare—have a celebrated and highly historical quality. That state of historical importance is transmitted by African American women through their recipes, which can potentially be interpreted as what Judith Carney terms as a form of gender-specific 'indigenous knowledge system'.[41] The African American recipes are portrayed as the embodied representation of traditional preparation methods; as they are enacted and remembered, they identify foodways throughout several regions of Africa from which they originated. By stressing the historical importance that 'soul food' holds for the African American women, Shange highlights how food and recipes testify to the suffering that past black slaves endured when they crossed the Atlantic during the three-hundred-year period of the trade. In *Sassafrass, Cypress and Indigo*, the strength and sense of self which the sisters derive from their cooking is a contemporary representation of the slave experience and their resilience; this position on African American food traditions reminds the reader what was 'primary' to the slaves' survival was the 'work of consciousness', a desire to desire which, as it became embodied in the food, provided a material form of 'counter intelligence'.[42]

The presence of the slave ancestors is felt throughout the novel, and becomes particularly evident in the merging of recipes, magic and spells: 'And now they were all ancient and African [. . .] it's so magic folks feel their ancestors coming up out of the earth to be in the realms of their descendants' (114). As the sisters play music, dance and cook, their actions reverberate through the walls of history: 'The slaves who were ourselves aided Indigo's mission, connecting soul and song, experience and unremembered rhythms' (45). Shange's lyrical ways create a poetic environment in which the importance of tribal communal ways—which encapsulates modes of cooking, singing and dancing—reawakens the importance of African tradition, from which the three sisters draw the strength to face the everyday and the courage to develop as individual black women. The memory of bygone slaves is recalled—sometimes forcefully imposed and demanded—on several occasions, as examples of slave food, chanting and music provides what Arlene Elder identifies as black and female ' signifying commentaries' on Western conventions and dialogue.[43] The unpredictable stylistic form of the novel—as it conjures recipes, poetry and spells—only aids the formation of African American identity and infuses 'a clear woman' voice' into the expression of black 'culture and experience'.⁴⁴

As the voices of the historically marginalised are given an embodied culinary permanence by Sassafrass, Cypress and Indigo, rice emerges as a prominent and primary foodstuff in the novel and dominates many of the annotated recipes. Upon her return to her mother's home, Cypress declares that she craves 'some red sauce & rice with shrimp' (48); Sassafrass, we are told, is often fixed 'on the idea of a rice casserole', as she finally records her own famous 'Rice Casserole #36' (74). Many recipes contain rice as a staple, and the sisters take it so for granted that many of their instructions simply read: 'cook rice as usual' (74). Towards the end of the novel, Sassafrass' sense of African heritage is also communicated through rice, as her epiphany of identity comes to be with the sounds of drums and the smells of 'incense, smoke, whiskey and rice' (196). As she consumes soul food and listens to the people at the African Centre chant, she finds herself thinking that 'the slaves would have been singing like that' (196).

Rice is a distinctively West African primary food. In their struggles of passage and survival, the African slaves brought their knowledge and usages of the grain to the new continent with them. Indeed, it was through the ongoing cultivation of rice that slaves 'reinforced an African identity by adapting a favourite dietary staple'.⁴⁵ One could notice the emergence of a characteristic rice culture. As the knowledge of how to grow and cook rice was transferred across the Atlantic, so was 'an entire cultural system, from production to consumption'.⁴⁶ The effect of slave rice cultures were—and arguably still are—particularly visible in South Carolina, where rice growing was made an essential part of the slaves' daily life. In historical and geographical terms, one could see the reasons for this; Judith Carney has identified it as the result of a particular group of West Africans (who regularly grew and consumed rice) being forced and grouped into particular areas of the South. This 'diffusion of skills' was able to characterise particular ethnic groups which later had a great impact of what is now seen as the regional cuisine of South Carolina.⁴⁷

It is possible to identify this potent cultural function in Shange's novel. In creating a historical and spiritual connection between the sisters' dishes and the original staple cooking of West Africa, Shange establishes a direct link between pre-slavery West African cuisine, slave food and the modern African American woman. However, in spite of Shange's detailed description of culinary trans-historical affinity, one cannot help but see her particular approach to African American cuisine as possibly reductive. Having analysed the development of culinary habits among slaves in America, Mintz and Price have drawn attention to the possibility that contemporary African American foodways are in fact the result of ongoing cultural change. This position suggests that 'cultural fragmentation and the formation of plantation societies of slaves from disparate ethnic origins resulted in syncretic cultures'.[48] Over the years, slaves managed to survive by developing forms of hybrid cultures. Amalgamation, adaptation and modification proved to be important elements in constructing a new culinary system which, whilst still relying on old West African traditions, necessarily called for new additions in order to survive. It is possible to argue, then, that current African American culinary ways are the result of not a direct link with the old continent, but a hybrid formation of African and 'American'. Carney suggests that 'the social experience of being African and slave proved far more significant in structuring black cultures [. . .] than any traits or retentions with specific African ethnic groups'.[49] The idea of 'African American' dishes was therefore generated as a product of not only tradition, but of new cultural ways within the plantation economy.

In this light, and going against the grain of the novel itself, Shange's efforts to identify African American foodways as a spiritual manifestation of strictly West African culinary traditions fails to satisfy. The impact of life in America—and the cultural impact of slavery—is ignored in favour of a radical stance of black mysticism and geographical separation. There may be some conceptual and historical issues with trying to identify pure African traits in the varied and distinctive black cuisine of the United States. Indeed, Shange's novel fails to recognise the impact of not only diversification, but also culinary blending and assimilation which, over the centuries, have moulded the current (and yet evolving nature) of African American cuisine throughout the Unites states. Shange's desire to explain contemporary African American food ways as a pure and untarnished descendant of West African culinary traditions poses a number of ideological questions which, sadly, her novel fails to resolve.

Nonetheless, Shange's novel is worth of praise for its eloquent aspiration to show how individuals managed to survive, even in the most dreadful hardship, and pass on their memories and experience through the medium of food. In bestowing ancestral power on food and recipes, *Sassafrass, Cypress and Indigo* draws attention to the need for current generations to remember the past and acknowledge, as they continue to cook and consume African American food, that over years of dread individuals 'evolved ways of thinking, ways of manipulating nature' with their hands, in order to ensure 'the availability of food for survival'.[50]

Working as meaningful expression of generational aspirations, the recipes are completely interweaved into the plot of Shange's novel. They accompany the events in the sisters' lives. They highlight the importance of the occasion and place emphasis on the beauty of the everyday. As a testament to practice and existence, the recipes contain knowledge of the past and, at the same time, come to represent a trans-temporal coordinate from which to begin understanding the sisters' lives and the social situations they experience while cooking. The annotated recipes in Shange's novel provide an insight into Sassafrass, Cypress and Indigo's inner sense of self. This claim becomes evident when the annotated recipes are mixed with the sisters' own moods, desires and reactions to everyday occurrences: Sassafrass and her mother become emotionally involves as they recall a recipe for 'Catfish/ The Way Albert Liked It' (54). When living in New York, Cypress's narrative is mixed with her 'Meal for Manhattan Nights, barbecued lamb Manhattan 3–4 pounds leg of lamb, 3 cup blackstrap molasses 2 cans tomato sauce 2 stalks celery' (174). In integrating everyday events with recipes, Shange encapsulates not only the sisters' lives, but also their personalities. Recording and performing everyday acts of cookery here could be interpreted, in Janet Theophano's words, as an act of 'autobiographical writing and self-representation'.[51]

Indeed, the most striking element of Shange's writing is perhaps its unstable blending—from one sentence to the next—of recipe instruction and personal meditation. In this sense, the novel almost reads as an autobiography for the characters, an almost metaphysical chance to explore the sisters as living entities. This discursive heterogeneity—and, indeed, the style in which the text itself is written—clearly evokes the blurring of boundaries identified by Tracie Marie Kelly in examples of the 'autobiographical cookbook'. Kelly describes this genre as 'a complex pastiche of recipes, personal anecdotes, family history, public history, photographs, even family trees'.[52] In this type of biographical text, 'recipes play an integral part in the revelation of the personal history'.[53] This is the style in which American writer Alice B. Toklas wrote her famous *Cook Book* (1954). Here, Toklas offers a very detailed chronicle of the years she spent travelling with Gertrude Stein; the food recipes are fully intertwined with the memories, so that the two things, as Kelly argues, 'could not be separated'.[54]

This act of culinary and autobiographical creativity is one of the concepts on which Shange builds the narrative in *Sassafrass, Cypress and Indigo*. The sisters' reactions to the dishes, the way they give instructions and the moods which accompany them are as important as the events themselves. It is this interaction between event and recipe that characterises the text as an autobiographical cookbook existing within a novel. Kelly concludes that 'the divisions between functions of cooking, history and storytelling blur' and 'the reader may wonder [. . .] whether the recipes are the primary texts and the other devices incidental, or the reverse'.[55] In the case of Shange's novel, the answer to this conundrum can be difficult to pin down.

The portrayal of their everyday life is conveyed by every recipe, every event, every piece of information included in the text. This element confirms how recipes function as autobiography and, as Janet Floyd and Laurel Forster put it, interacts with personal 'spheres of daily experience'.[56] Food is always present even, when not being cooked or eaten. The fact that Indigo stuffs her dolls with rice is very noteworthy. Her mystical personality—which creates spells and makes her speak with dolls—is grounded in history as rice (the staple slave food) is joined with hints of imagination in order to give an outlet to her creativity. The recipes mark the passing of the sisters' lives, presenting themselves as a chronological presence, a social and emotional coordinate. Margaret Randall argues that recipes can be interpreted as 'diaries, in which fabric are woven the obstinate threads of quest for social justice, humour and love'.[57] The recipes create a historical account of the everyday, a domestic rendition of women's lives. The recipes' function as 'personal manuscript' allows Shange to offer an additional—perhaps alternative—account of everyday events within the story. In this regard, Shange appears to validate Theophano's contention that, through remembering culinary ways, women have given history and memory a permanent lodging'.[58]

It is not being implied here, however, that the recipes in *Sassafrass, Cypress and Indigo* offer a form of black female history; this would be a dangerous assertion to make. Not only would it create a political gap between, as Janet Todd puts it, 'male public and civil history and female herstory', but it would also validate the claim that the political, religious and economic factors creating history are 'men's domain alone'.[59] Rather, one can see the recipes as the archive of everyday occurrences, offering a different perspective on events and writing the domestic sphere—which has traditionally belonged to women and has been sadly ignored—into the pages of history.

While Shange unveils how Sassafrass, Cypress and Indigo's recipes act as a declaration of personal history, she also unravels how the recipe book is part of a collective history as well. Writing about the practice of recipe collection, Jessahym Neuhaus points out that recipes and cookbooks 'reveal much about the societies that produce them'.[60] If this assertion is to be believed as true, then the African-inspired recipes in Shange's novel become emblematic for the women's sense of self, female heritage and, especially, a sense of sisterhood. Indeed, cooking food—and recording its recipe—is also interpreted in the novel as a gift. That gift is intended to be an endowment of confidence and sense of purpose for the black woman and the African American community as a whole. The recipes are the gift of history, of emotion, of posterity. Marcel Mauss suggests that 'to give something is to give a part of oneself [. . .] in this system of ideas one gives away what is in reality a part of one's nature and substance, while to receive something is to receive a part of someone's spiritual essence'.[61] It could be argued that the food cooked by the sisters transmits a message to whoever eats it. Each culinary gift contains the essence of the giver—one might say even a part of 'self'—and a sense of accomplishment derives from this exchange of what Martyn Lee defines as 'psychic energy'.[62] The investment of this energy is what ultimately bonds the giver to the receiver, in a cycle of sisterhood.

Ultimately, the three sisters leave the recipes to symbolise the cyclical nature of female existence, and possible lead other women to full personal identification. Ursula King points out that 'the experience of sisterhood is understood as a new way of being which may include implicit religious elements: elements of faith and hope, of a vision, as well as liberating features'.[63] Portraying a struggle between repressive social taboos and the benevolent liberation of female legacy, Shange unveils food as an essential instrument in the construction of a separate social identity and the rejection of authoritarian regimes. Interpreted as an autobiographical writing practice steeped in the gender struggles of South Carolina in the early Eighties, the recipes in *Sassafrass, Cypress and Indigo* keep the conceptual nature of the text anchored to the material world, as its reading assists the preparation of food. Shange's treatment of the recipes confirms Floyd and Foster's assertion that cookbooks provide records of 'historical and cultural moments'.[64]

As the value of the recipes begins to shape visions of sisterhood and historical legacy in the novel, the text also makes connections between cooking and spiritual development. Indeed, the concept of 'recipe' is put next to the annotated list of Indigo's 'magical' spells, as mystical rituals blend with everyday culinary practices. While sitting in the kitchen, or consuming her mother's food, Indigo often records her incantations, intended to either cure an ailment, or celebrate a particularly seminal moment in a woman's life. Her spells unequivocally include eating and drinking as principal components:

> IF YOUR BELOVED HAS EYES FOR ANOTHER: Fill your pillow with 2 handfuls of damiana leaves. Do this 3 days in a row. On the fourth day, use one handful of the damiana leaves to make tea. Drink 2 cups' (12); MARVELOUS MENSTRUATING MOMENTS ... Don't be angry with your body if she's not letting go of the flow. Eat strawberries, make strawberry tea with the leaves to facilitate the flow. To increase the flow, drink squaw weed tea. For soothing before your blood flows, drink some black snakeroot or valerian tea. For cramps, chew wild ginger (16); TO RID ONESELF OF THE SCENT OF EVIL: Drink a strong mix of lemon tea and honey. This, if you've not cheated, should bring sweat to your brow. This is the poison the offender has left lurking' (26).

In spite of the unavoidable predictability of Indigo's magical endeavours and mystical connection with the past, Shange's ambitious amalgamation of recipes and magic is worthy of notice and praise. Conceptually, one can find a recognizable affinity here between recipes and spells. They both rely on the assemblage of ingredients and they both demand specific instructions to be followed. As the recipe is written down, one could almost see how the instructions are 'chanted' as they are recorded, strengthening the conceptual connection between food preparation and magic. Ron Scapp and Brian Seitz argue that cooking and eating 'embody some of the most dramatic philosophical conundrums, including the puzzling divisions and linkages between culture and nature as well as those between appearance and reality'.[65] Although Scapp and Seitz's assertion seems too mystical and overly dramatic in its interpretation, one needs to consider how, in their conceptual existence, cooking and spell chanting bear traditional similarities, both in their usages and their creations.

The style adopted and the literary devices employed in *Sassafrass, Cypress and Indigo*—including the mixture of recipes and cooking with magical and spiritual occurrences—place the novel in the realm of magic realism, a genre that, as Barbara Cooper argues, 'strives to capture the paradox of the unity of opposites, [as] it contests polarities such as history versus magic, the pre-colonial versus the post-industrial present, and life versus death'.[66] As a genre, magical realism relies on the careful (and sometimes extraordinary) mixture of the supernatural with what is seen as 'real'; in this creative context, food (it would seem) proves to be the ideal choice. Food functions not only as a successful storytelling medium, but also as a sensual connector which allows Shange to smoothly meld together the mystical and 'real' aspects of each chapter. The presence of a contemporary narrative voice also allows Shange to merge real events with the fantastic element, without questioning their credibility.

Just as she stresses the formative importance of food and cooking in women's lives, Shange also leaves no doubt about her ideas concerning femininity: at the beginning of the novel she declares that 'where there is a woman there is magic' (3). Later, she announces that a woman is a mystical 'river' and her 'banks are red honey where the moon wanders' (16). It is through food preparation, mixed with a great deal of mysticism that the novel awakens female spirituality, which seems to have been passed on to her from ancestral spirits.

Although Shange's perception of the magical nature of the feminine experience could generate scepticism on a number of levels, her desire to mix food, female spirituality and magical enterprise is not a solitary standpoint. As Meinrad Craighead argues, 'a woman's spiritual quest awakens her to forces of energy within herself, deeply connecting her with the cyclic movements of creation and with other foremothers. (. . .) Feminine existence transforms matter, giving from elemental energy, cooking and boiling, bearing and healing'.[67] The connection between magical practices and food, in particular, has been explored by anthropologists and food historians as part of a series of evolutionary processes in primitive societies. Food was perceived as the most adaptable ritual offering. Freud remarks that when food is used in magic it 'has to serve the most varied purposes [and] it must protect the individual from his enemies and from dangers'.[68] Joanne Harris goes as far as offering a clear representation of food preparation as a magical enterprise:

> There is a kind of sorcery in all cooking: in the choosing of ingredients, the process of mixing, grating, melting, infusing, and flavouring, the recipes taken from ancient books, the traditional utensils—the pestle and mortar with which my mother made her incense turned to a more homely purpose, her spices and aromatics giving up their subtleties to a baser, more sensual magic.[69]

'Magic' seems to have survived through the ages as a social and spiritual practice which allows its practitioners to adapt to situations and spiritualise elements of the natural world. Shange may be suggesting that Indigo's culinary sorcery mixes the creation of food with realising human desires. Freud reminds us how 'it is easy to perceive the motives which lead men to practice magic: they are human wishes'.[70] Indigo's desire and ability to manipulate the natural ingredients transforms the practice of cooking from the mere provision of foodstuffs to an organised ritual which belongs to the realm of magical practice. Cooking is offered as a highly embodied activity whose outcome is seen as 'magical' because it provides the women with a sort of 'historical comfort'. It gives them a sense of identity. Shange proposes that the transformation of the natural elements in food becomes part of a mystical process that spiritualises the act of eating. Indigo's 'magical food is transformed into the final product of an original mystical 'wish'. Shange's interpretation of culinary spirituality shows affinity with Ronald Hutton's claim that magic 'consists of a control worked by humans over nature by the use of spiritual forces, so that the end result is expected to lie within the will of the person or persons working the ritual'.[71]

The value of recipes as not only a symbol of cultural and ethnic affiliation, but as an expression of female subjectivity and daily development, is signalled in several other examples of contemporary African American fiction. In *Linden Hills* (1985), for instance, Gloria Naylor dedicates close attention to how recipes can open a gate into understanding people's lives—especially women's—and how that understanding is connected to a historicised discovery of individual progression and group and belonging. The novel—often defined as 'modern vision of Dante's Inferno'[72]—narrates the life of Mrs. Willa Needed, an unhappy inhabitant of Linden Hills, a predominantly African American middle-class suburb. Through Willa's daily tribulations and encounters with racial and gender oppression, Naylor unveils the sins of a whole community which, in Dantean fashion, are eventually punished by their own sense of righteousness and moral obligation. Willa, in particular, in put through an emotional journey which aids her personal development and allows us to see herself as an independent and worthy entity. Upon the birth of their first child, Mr. Needed is displeased with the baby's light skin colour. Suspecting Willa of cheating—an accusation which has no foundation in reality—Mr. Needed traps Willa and her baby into a tunnel and agrees to feed Willa only after the infant has died. Whilst experiencing the horror of entrapment and confined solitude, Willa discovers a box containing a selection of diaries, journals, bibles and notes which belonged to previous Needed wives. In particular, Willa becomes fascinated with the history of the second Needed wife, Evelyn Creton, who lived almost a century before.

Evelyn's life is patched together in the novel through a collection of personal cookbooks, which contains not only cooking instructions, but also the woman's thoughts and observations. Naylor uses food and eating metaphors here in order to encapsulate the ambivalence of Evelyn's condition. It soon emerges that Evelyn attempted to control events in her world through food, 'as she roasted her meats and canned her apple butter, year after year'.[73] Treating cooking as a manipulative art, she prepared enormous meals in order to win her husband's attention. Unable to obtain his love, Evelyn resorted to grinding up various aphrodisiacs in the dishes she served him. When neither of her initial culinary device worked, she eventually starved herself to death by eating small quantities of food and consuming large doses of laxatives—concoctions for which she leaves several recipes in her cookbooks. Through hard-written recipes within the pages and other pieces of personal paper paraphernalia, Willa comes to understand Evelyn as a marginalised wife who tries to achieve a sense of purpose through preparing food—especially inventing her own recipes—and showing a definite 'desperation for recording' (149). Echoing the sense of every day culinary history put forward by Shange, Naylor seems to be implying that the history of women—especially African American women—is not always found in history books and official archives but in oral wisdom, in kitchen narrative and in the seemingly mundane records of women's daily lives.

Nonetheless, the sense of feminine creativity and desire to maintain a historical connection with people and places, which comprises much of Shange's approach to food and cooking, is dramatically subverted by Naylor in *Linden Hills*. The female practices of cooking and compiling recipe books is merged with feelings of inadequacy and happiness. We are told of how an unconscious rebellion against her subsidiary situation began to ferment inside Evelyn and manifested itself in the development of food loathing. According to Hilde Bruch, food rejection is characterised by 'an all-pervasive sense of ineffectiveness, a feeling that one's actions, thoughts and feelings do not originate within the self but rather are passive reflections of external expectations and demands'.[74] Evelyn's sense of culinary and emotional impotence extended to a physical extent, so that her condition gradually presented itself as an eating disorder, which eventually killed her. One could argue that her sense of ambivalence about her gendered social position was internalised through food loathing and an uncontrollable desire to be 'purged'. Clearly, the idea of purging here should not be interpreted as a simple physical endeavour, but as a desire to expel what she dislikes, her marginalised status as unloved woman and wife.

The equivocal attitude that links women and food, on both individual and public levels, is particularly evident in women with eating disorders. Feminist sociologists in particular have pointed out that the social pressure imposed on women and their relationship with cooking and feeding can endanger their subjectivity and sense of function. In Western societies, thinness is promoted as beautiful. Starvation—or its converse, overeating—in women mirrors feelings of inadequacy within an environment that promotes expectations about proper ways of being, living, looking and thinking. In *Fat is a Feminist Issue*, Susie Orbach points out that any 'obsession with food carries with it an enormous amount of self-disgust, loathing and shame'.[75]

The particular psychological connection between food loathing and self-loathing has been found to be the acting agent in the creation of repressive neurosis. This condition is evident in Evelyn in *Linden Hills*. According to Freud, 'one of the vicissitudes an instinctual impulse may undergo is to meet with resistances [. . .] under certain conditions, the impulse then passes into the state of repression'.[76] The initial desire to love and be loved by her husband—constituting an emotional need—is slowly substituted in Evelyn for her need to please him through her culinary abilities. In Freudian terms we might say that 'rejection based on judgement will be found to be a good method to adopt against an instinctual impulse'.[77] It could be argued that the 'external stimuli' of her husband's emotional rejection initiates a process of repression that will result in neurosis; the reaction to the external situation becomes a repressed instinct and, therefore, seemingly disappears from Evelyn's consciousness. That disappearance, however, proves to be only temporary. In Freud's terms again, 'it may happen that an external stimulus becomes internalised—for example, by eating into and destroying some bodily organ—so that a new source of constant excitation and increase of tension arises'.[78] As even her culinary attempts of seduction fail, Evelyn represses her desire for love and sublimates it into an obsession with writing recipes and, paradoxically, purging her body from food.

As Naylor unveils connections between gendered divisions and alimentary disturbance, one could argue that Evelyn experienced a chain of substitutions and displacements. Her eating disorder—comprising of food loathing and a need to purify her body—was the displaced substitute for her denied affection. In this way, Evelyn's anxieties about disintegrating marriage are displaced onto foodstuffs. Her desire to be a perfect cook and her eventual repulsion of all food can therefore be seen as an alimentary phobia generated by repressed anxieties associated with the frustrating nature of her gender position. In constructing Evelyn's story of self-loathing and emotional disintegration, *Linden Hills* achieves a level of self-conscious interrogation of the fusion between kitchen economy and African American gender politics which takes us beyond Shange's vaguely utopian sense of culinary and mystical womanhood. Naylor's account is powerful in that it draws attention to the resilience of the African American woman in an everyday situation. After her imprisonment extends for days, no mystical power is offered to rescue Willa—she does not possess the arguable culinary and spiritual abilities presented by Indigo in Shange's novel. Naylor's approach to a sense of African American femininity does not indulge in fantasies of mystical connections; the trans-generational bond felt by Willa with the previous Needed wives, and the sense of simultaneous joy and despair which emerges from it does not call for ritualised sorcery. Instead, it highlights Naylor's desire to inscribe women in the pages of history through what defines them as human individuals. There is magic in Naylor's text, but it is not sorcery; it is the magic of the everyday, which reveals itself to be a connector to a sense of self and stability. Food here acts not only as the anchor to the past, but also as the perpetrator of female strength.

SOUL FOOD, ON THE BARBECUE

Naylor is particularly interested in showing how food bears a special historical relevance for African Americans, and how examples of 'soul food' carry cultural associations which can form a divide between different social classes of African Americans in contemporary society. Daily habits and iconic cooking practices are interpreted as representation of black heritage; that heritage, however, is not viewed by Naylor as a straightforward, homogenous concept, but as a multi-faceted notion with different nuances and incarnations. This particular concept is explored by Naylor in *Bailey's Café* (1992). Rejecting the all-encompassing vision of black womanhood put forward by Shange and gesturing towards the culinary stratification suggested by Morrison, Naylor uses food as an active ingredient in her dissection of African American identity as a culturally inscribed conception.

Since its publication, *Bailey's Café* has received much attention not only as a clear development in Naylor's work, but as an unmissable part of contemporary African American fiction. In the novel, Naylor constructs a powerful narrative, evocative of many cultural and ethnic aspects which have often been viewed as ichnographically definitive of African American communities, such as jazz music and soul food. Coherence in the story is often maintained by recalling elements of music, which give the titles to the chapter, such as 'Maestro, if you please . . . ', 'Eve's Song and 'The Vamp'. Bailey, the narrator of the story and proprietor of the eponymous café, speaks directly to the reader—or his musical 'audience'—and tells tragic stories of the women and men who he now recognises as his regular customers.

Foodways take on a particular social, cultural and racial relevance in the segment on the story of Jesse Bell, one of the café's habitual presences. Jesse is described by Bailey as a 'nice' person, with a 'good-natured' laughter that comes from 'deep down'.[79] As it does happen for many of the café's patrons, one night Jesse opens up to Bailey—and the reader—and tells her tale. A young black woman who comes from a working-class family in 'the docks' (120), Jesse manages to marry into the Kings, a wealthy, upper class family of Sugar Hill, Harlem. Although the two families share the same race—they are both African American—it becomes immediately apparent that there are deeply-rooted social differences between the two. Jesse's inadequate social position is highlighted frequently by Uncle Eli, the powerful head of the King clan, who sees Jesse as belonging to an inferior rank of African Americans. The deep divergence between the Jesse's way of living and the Kings become particularly evident in their approach to food. Throughout the story, Jesse comments on how the Kings, including her husband, are used to eating differently. In the beginning, Jesse is keen to cook for her own family the way she was taught to:

> 'My biggest problem was at the dinner table. A new bride, mind you, so I'm putting on the hog, don't you know. Frying catfish. Washing and chopping collard greens. Baking biscuits. Smothering pork chops till they cried for mercy. Macaroni salad with homemade mayonnaise' (126).

The presence of Southern black food in Harlem testifies to the urban exodus undertaken by thousands of African Americans in the post-bellum period. The long-standing West African tradition of cooking all edible parts of plants and animals aided the slaves' survival once in the United States. In a manner that exceeded the Europeans' occasional use of leafy green vegetables, African slaves regularly prepared the leaves of plants—especially the now iconic collards—by simmering them in oil and spices. In addition, they also creatively prepared and cooked corn and its meal; Herbert Cavey and Wayne Einsach remind us that cornmeal was, together with pork, 'one of the most prevalent foods available to slaves' and regularly appears 'in most plantation rationing logs'.[80] From corn, slaves made corn bread, grits (bleached and hulled corn kernels), ash cakes (cornmeal flatbread baked in hot ashes), and hush puppies (deep-fried cornmeal with onions and spices). In similar fashion, the slaves were known to use parts of the animal which were discarded by the masters, including pig's snout, feet and ears and parts of the cow such as the tail—therefore creating one of the most well-known African American dishes, oxtail soup.

However, Jesse's eating habits and ways of cooking are deprecated by Uncle Eli, who continues to 'pick and pick at his food' every time he is at Jesse's table (126). Confused about her cooking skills, Jesse presents he husband with her specialty, 'a platter of cornbread and a steaming bowl of oxtail soup' (126). When her husband fails to recognise even what kind of meat the soup is made with, the issues with her cooking becomes clear to Jesse: 'Uncle Eli never let the Kings eat like that. He called it slave food—that old Uncle Tom' (126). Uncle Eli completely controls not only the Kings, but also their regular diet. His refusal of what he calls 'slave food' is instrumental in separating the King family from Jesse. The refusal is obviously not of the food as sustenance, and it does not have anything to do with matters of gustatory taste. Uncle Eli, a wealthy African American man, rejects traditional examples of African American cuisine because of their association with slavery. Far from being worried about painful historical memories, Uncle Eli does not want to be associated with a social rank of blacks which he rates as inferior. Quintessential examples of black cuisine such as 'collard greens' and 'cornbread' become the vector to describe a particularly ethnic tradition, showing roots in West Africa, which Uncle Eli refuses to acknowledge and accept as part of his racial group's historical background. In so doing, Uncle Eli creates a social and cultural stratification between groups of African Americans, which transcend race and rely on ethnic affiliation—mirrored in food choices—in order to emerge.

In terms of intra-race social stratification, the pit barbecue episode becomes particularly interesting in the novel. Set on showing Jesse's inferiority to the entire social scene, Uncle Eli organises a barbecue to which he also invites the Bell family. Jesse feels uneasy and concerned about the Bells' presence at the party: 'they git suckered into that cookout Uncle Eli threw. I warned them not to come. I had a bad, bad feeling about the whole thing. Why would Uncle Eli invite the Bells to celebrate with the Kings?' (131). His motives, however, are quickly discovered by Jesse herself, as Uncle Eli tells 'her people' to 'come two hours later than he told everybody else—and telling'em to bring all the food and liquor they wanted' (131). Despite his seemingly genuine desire to consume the Bells' food, Uncle Eli cunningly plans a separate, well-catered party: 'He'd already rented this big striped tent to set up in [the] back yard and hired waiters and a cook. They brought in one of those prophane grills' (131). It is made clear by Jesse that Uncle Eli 'could have easily put the tent' over her 'special made barbecue pit in the corner of the garden' (131), but that would have clashed with his plans for ' grilled mushrooms, smoked cheese and that kind of shit on silver trays' (131). Doubting even that that kind of party could be called a 'cookout' (131), Jesse cannot but watch as her family appears, bringing 'the things they were supposed to bring: a crate of spareribs and about thirty chickens that Mother had cut up and soaked overnight in her special sauce; bowls of potato salad, coleslaw; cases and cases of beer' (131). The difference- in the approach to the concept of cookout cements the split in social affiliation between the Kings and the Bells; although the Bells' idea of a pit barbecue—with coleslaw, beer and marinated chicken—seems to fit perfectly with what most people would associate with a barbecue, especially in the South, it is made clear that it does not fir the occasion and the social situation which was carefully set up by Uncle Eli. As the Bell family prepare to cook, they are refused access to the hired cook's propane grill; their only option is to use the barbecue pit outside the tent, facing the rain which has mercilessly begun falling on the party. The barbecue pit is treated here as an example of a lower social standard; this feeling of deprecation is clearly perceived by Jesse as her family tries to 'light up the fire' in the open pit (132), while the other guests to the party watch them 'like they were a bunch of trained monkeys at the zoo' (132).

The sense of disapproval felt by the upper-class guests at Uncle Eli's party goes hand in hand with the history and social development of the barbecue pit as a way of cooking. Here we need to turn to the origins of the barbecue itself, as known in the modern United States. In the eastern colonies the mingling of Native American, Anglo and African cultures produced a hybrid cuisine that included, among other things, barbecued food. A large number of the African slaves who came to the colonial South—particularly in the Carolinas—arrived from the West Indies, where, as linguistic evidence suggests, the 'barbecue' originated. The term developed, together with other native American influences, from the Native Caribbean *barbacoa*, a word used to identify 'the framework of sticks' that raised and cooked fish and meat 'above the fire'.[81] The technique of cooking 'over the fire' was imported in North America through the slave trade and adapted to pre-existing cooking techniques. Thus, enslaved Africans may have learned some culinary techniques, including the pit barbecue, from the West Indies. When cooking over a fire, American slaves began to baste their meats with sauce instead of serving the sauce on the side, as had been the practice in Africa. Regional differences in livestock and food availability caused 'barbecue' to mean pork in the eastern United States and beef in the western United States.

Although there are many instances in American history of the pit barbecue being enjoyed 'by president after president', the impression remains, as Andrew Warnes suggests, that it is a 'strange black element'.[82] Steeped in the history of African Americans, and their culinary ways in the pre- and post-Civil War periods, the pit barbecue manages to conjure up ideas of America which is much less Eurocentric. Owing to both West African and Native American culinary traditions, the pit barbecue holds a connection with the smells and tastes of black cuisine. Recalling colonial culinary memories and keeping African traditions alive, the pit barbecue holds an imagistic connection with mischievous 'savage implications', constantly luxuriating—as Warnes playfully suggests—'in its own barbaric status'.[83]

In maintaining its connection to a particular strand of Southern/African American cookways, the pit barbecue, as Sydney Mintz puts it, is one of those food categories 'around which people communicate daily to each other who they are . . . validating group membership'.[84] Just as it can make people feel part of the same group, as they light a fire in the pit and roast ribs and chicken in the open air, so can the pit barbecue alienate those who are unfamiliar with the practice, as a result of social, cultural or racial divisions.

It is carefully suggested by Naylor that in *Bailey's Café* the aptly named 'King family' and their guests have somehow 'forgotten'—or decided to forget—how to appreciate the pit barbecue, a practice which connects them to their wider and encompassing past as African Americans. Adopting culinary practices that are not only a testament to a higher social status, but also a counter-colonisation of European food-ways, the Kings prefer to have 'cookouts' which allows them to 'wear fancy clothes' and drink from their champagne glasses' (131). Naylor uses the image of a socially marginalised food practice in order to convey the separation of the Bell family; the pit barbecue functions as a conceptual connection between what is disliked in culinary terms and what is despised in the interlinked social, racial and cultural sphere.

As Naylor unveils socio-culturally inscribed prejudices within the King clan, she also seems to be engaging with the pit barbecue in terms of 'invented tradition'. Although she does not explicitly expose the pit barbecue as connected to the colonial and ante-bellum periods, one can see a desire to establish not only the barbecue itself, but also what goes with it as a definable African American practice. Jesse associates the idea of the pit barbecue to what she calls 'my people' (131). That concept of 'people' and belonging appears to be trans-chronological; there is a sense here that through the pit barbecue Jesse is able to feel a connection not only to 'her people' intended as her immediate family, but a larger past and present ethnic tradition that encapsulates African Americans from slavery times. In these terms, the idea of a 'pit barbecue' is 'invented' because it carries with it a meaning that transcends its function as a culinary practice and stretches into the feeling of boding and kinship that connects people with a shared ethnicity, race and past. Elizabeth Pleck argues that, like all forms of invented traditions, the pit barbecue functions for African Americans as 'a ritual implying continuity with the past', meeting 'the needs of people in the present' for 'structure' and 'unchanging' variants.[85]

It must be noted here that Uncle Eli does not shun the idea of a 'cookout' itself, but does reject the specific concept of a 'pit barbecue'. There is a slight hint here that, in Uncle Eli's eyes, the pit barbecue is too unrefined, 'too savage' and, paradoxically, 'too black'. Far from evoking the all-American conception of the 'civilised barbecue'—a perfect match for the Fourth of July celebrations—the pit barbecue is interpreted as a despicable example of slave savagery. The cultural and ethnic character of the pit barbecue could be seen at the basis of the Kings' dislike for the practice. In the wider American spectrum, the pit barbecue continues to be associated with 'inferior' culinary practices, its transitory nature a materialised example of its unreliability and inconsequence. Associated with paper cups and cardboard plates rather than fine china, the pit barbecue is 'disposable' in concept; the plastic cutlery and cartons which accompany a pit barbecue cookout appear to almost 'conspire' with the 'auspicious memorials' of the culinary elite, 'enforcing the verdict' that the pit barbecue 'deserves' very little respect.[86] The transient nature of the barbecue comes to signify the equally disposable nature of the Bells family in the eyes of Uncle Eli and the Kings.

Nonetheless, the Bells maintain an almost emotional connection with the pit barbecue as a culinary practice; refusing to leave 'with their tails between their legs' (132) and displaying the 'ties of authority' that Eric Hobsbawn recognises as part of an 'invented tradition', the Bells persevere in wanting to have the whole pit barbecue experience.[87] Although their time and effort is not ultimately rewarded, and the fire in the pit is never actually lit, they do not join the elegant cookout under the tent and decide to consume their food in the rain. Naylor seems to be suggesting that the desire to have a pit barbecue, in the face of struggle and social disdain, goes hand in hand with a sense of 'being African American' and appreciating the past. This explanation owns a lot to the nature of the pit barbecue and how it is treated, both socially and culturally, in the wider American culinary scope. Warnes suggests that, in spite of the fact that many 'custodians' of American culinary heritage 'continue to ignore' it, the pit barbecue proudly wants 'such arbiters of good taste and judgment to hold their distance'.[88] Echoing the African American refusal to perish and later to be put down—symbolically rendered through a definitely black culinary practice—the Bells do not concede to social pressure and revel in the tradition which represents their ethnic belonging. By rejecting the convention of the industrialised Western world—identified by the Kings' propane grill—the Bell family are uncompromisingly proud of their outcast status, which encapsulates the efforts and resistance of a whole racial and cultural group.

The segment on Jesse Bell and the pit barbecue unveils Naylor's preoccupations with African American culinary traditions and the possible disappearance of black foodways as a result of modernisation and globalisation. Naylor's concerns about the state of African American identities run throughout the text and are intersected with food on numerous occasions until the very end. Nonetheless, the final pages of the novel do not offer a satisfying finale to the events narrated throughout, nor do they allow Naylor to conclude with a lucid evaluation of racial, social and cultural politics. In an ordinary fashion, the final part of the novel does shed some light on the overall culinary politics of the text, but it does so by leaving the narrative almost incomplete and, to some extent, the reader dissatisfied. Indeed, the novel parts from its 'audience' with an unresolved closure. Maxine Lavon Montgomery argues that this is not simply part of the story's generally indecisive nature, in terms of plot and chronology. Montgomery draws attention to how the novel's indefinite ending 'serves to encourage a participatory involvement from the reader/audience and is a strategy present in much of African American writing'.[89] In the end, even Bailey, the seemingly all-knowing narrator and proprietor of the café, is unable to provide an adequate conclusion to the people's narratives that comprise the written text. Contrastingly, he simply asks the reader/audience to identify with the characters' unfortunate tales: 'If this was like that sappy violin music on Make-Believe Ballroom, we could wrap it all up with a lot of happy endings to leave you feeling real good that you took the time to listen,' Bailey claims in his final section. 'But I don't believe that life is supposed to make you feel good, or to make you feel miserable either. Life is just supposed to make you feel' (219).

Although it might appear as an unorthodox suggestion, I propose that in order to fully understand the final treatment of food and African American identity in *Bailey's Café*, one needs to return to its opening pages. It is indeed not accidental that Naylor picks a 'café' as a place in which stories unfold and on occasions merge. The café, in itself, can be interpreted as a symbol of community (an interpretation which, as we have seen in Chapter 2, is clear and persistent in Flagg's *Fried Green Tomatoes*). The pervasive nature of the café, however, is much more complicated in Naylor. In challenging the enduringly cohesive quality of African American food, the novel also poses questions regarding the homogenous and ethnically binding power exercised by the culinary. It is made clear from the beginning that people do not necessarily visit Bailey's Café for the quality food—which is said to be 'not very good.' Bailey himself is not described as a fine cook, unlike Shange's sisters in *Sassafrass, Cypress and Indigo*. Bailey does not posess almost magical and historically-charged abilities to cook the most quintessential African American food. Instead of using recipes which have been passed down from generation to generation of black cooks, Bailey admits to having 'picked up' his 'cooking skills from the Navy mess where you're taught a little more grease and salt should answer any complaints' (3). Even his café helper Nadine—although actually known to make a peach cobbler which is 'close to spectacular' (4)—does not care for pleasing friends and customers and is said to be making her signature dish 'when the mood hits her' (4). The customers 'don't come for the food', nor do they come 'for the atmosphere'; Bailey, for his part, admits that 'he didn't start' in the catering business 'to make a living', as 'personal charm'–he is very adamant to stress—is not his 'strong point' (4).

Bailey's (and Nadine's) outlook and attitude is not that of the spiritual, family orientated African American cook, which has strongly survived as a popularised stereotype with, perhaps, both white and black readers alike. In similar fashion, there is no exaltation of African American food as holding the secret to self-affirmation or offering a pseudo-mystical link to bygone eras. At Bailey's Café, food signals the everyday, but also does not promise to offer resolution, in the manner in which it does in Shange's work. We are told clearly by Naylor that Bailey remains 'at this grill' for a very clearly reason, but that reason is unfortunately not expressed. As he begins his narration, Bailey himself claims that there cannot be a 'one sentence answer' (4); nonetheless, in spite of a number of whole narratives unfolding over many passages—which promise to deliver a clear-conclusion—a clear insight into the characters is not provided, even in the final part of the novel. All that the reader is left with in the end are (paradoxically) Bailey's instructions at the very beginning of the text. Having taken the time 'to listen' (as Bailey puts it), to the explanation as to why people continue to go to a café where the food is of poor quality is still found in what is said by the narrator in the opening pages of the novel: 'The answer is who I am and who the customers are' (4). It is this idea of 'unclear conclusion' which will remain alive in the final pages of the novel, as Bailey makes his farewells and, in a circular fashion, takes the reader back to the very beginning.

Eventually, *Bailey's Café*—both the novel overall and the physical establishment within it—proposes an outlook on the culinary as it does in life; it does not offer the reader any hope for long-term conciliation and refuses to believe that any cultural or ethnic pretext can provide a generalised, acceptable conclusion for a whole group. In its stance on food and existence, *Bailey's Café* is conceptually lucid and does not indulge in utopian fantasies of affirmation. The past and the present coexist in the culinary as they do in life. Reflection is what is required and resolution—as much as it is desired by both the characters and the reader—cannot be found in an overarching sense of what it means to be African American. Montgomery points out that 'Naylor's particular triumph as a contemporary African American woman writer' has a lot to do with her ability to move 'beyond the one-dimensional' portraits of African American men, women and traditions.[90] Individuality, existing without losing sight of the past and its influences, is called for and demanded. Naylor does not explicitly sing the beauty of African American culture and foodways in the manner which defines Shange's work, nor does she condemn aspects of it which have often been made famous for all the wrong reasons. In the early Nineties, Naylor is able to achieve a gastro-political clarity regarding African Americans which Shange, in the early Eighties, was incapable or unwilling to grasp.

And yet, in their desire to express the multi-faceted state of being African American, Shange and Naylor's novels show similarities. This, of course, goes beyond the shared use of the colour 'indigo', appearing on several occasions in both texts as either a character name or a mood description. It is a well-known fact that Shange's work was a huge inspiration for Naylor's writing and that inspiration left its mark. Shange shows an unsurpassed ability to retreat 'into her past'.[91] In *Sassafrass, Cypress and Indigo*, she is able to use food in order to 'verbalise' black 'women's memories' and experiences, stressing the importance of the past and a desire to live the present to its full potential. Expanding the interdependence of geographical attachment, personal knowledge and culinary experience, the relationship between African Americans, food and memory is given permanent historical lodging. The importance of culinary memories is revealed in its being a medium for the integration of the domestic into a greater historical register. In a similar attempt, Naylor moves beyond ethnic stereotypes in *Bailey's Café* and offers an insight into the lives of 'alienated characters'.[92] Food figures as a defining element of the characters' lives, which, whilst maintaining a quiet presence and a subdued connection to both past and present, is able to make the 'disparate voices' of black people audible to a wider audience.

4 Immigrant Identities

> They'll be hungry because everyone who "comesover" is hungry; for home, for family, for the old smells and touches and tastes . . . I sense the distances between places, the country house and suburbs, even between America and Jordan, start to disintegrate. Geography turns liquid. There is something is us connecting every person to every other person.
>
> —Diana Abu-Jaber, *The Language of Baklava*[1]

The various interpretations of food, cuisine and identity in contemporary American fiction transform the idea of a 'culinary community' into a malleable concept. As a social, cultural and geographical phenomenon, immigration emerges as a particularly important variant in the presentation of food and culinary customs in what has often been (broadly) referred to as 'immigrant fiction' in the popular imagination. In 1980, Tina de Rosa's successful novel *Paper Fish* offered an insight into the importance of culinary customs for Italian-American communities and drew attention to how, through shared practices, identifiable dishes and cultural representations of 'preparing the dinner', food continues to be inextricably linked to immigrant and ethnic sensibilities in contemporary American culture.[2] Overall, there is a sense that, in immigrant fictions, the display of a particular cuisine becomes 'a daily and visceral experience through which people imagine themselves as belonging to a unified and homogenous community, be it nation, village, ethnicity, class or religion'.[3] As we noted in the previous chapters, culinary differences throw socio-cultural boundaries into sharp relief. What is acceptable and what is not—what is edible and what is disgusting—can be interpreted as evidence of a group's distinction and organisation; these elements are ultimately what construct the cultural boundaries of taste. In *Food, the Body and the Self*, Lupton argues that 'food and culinary practices hold an extraordinary power in defining the boundaries between "us" and "them"'.[4] The relationships and boundaries between cultures, races and food are at the heart of *The Book of Salt* (2003). Asian American novelist Monique Truong explores the issues of culinary cultural boundaries and expands the idea of familiar—or, more precisely, acceptable—food. The focus on food conceptually confirms Wenying Xu's contention that 'culinary and alimentary motifs [. . .] abound in Asian American Literature'.[5]

However, the relationship between culinary tropes and Asian American literature could be problematic; the need to re-affirm eating habits might come from the fact that Asian Americans have been, to borrow Xu's words, 'racialised, gendered, and classed through their involvement with food'.[6] *The Book of Salt* follows the life of a chef, Binh, who works first as a *garde-manger* in his native Vietnam and then as a live-in cook in Paris. Binh's employers in France are fictionalised versions of Gertrude Stein and Alice B. Toklas, a couple renowned for their romantic partnership, literary collaborations and great interest in culinary experimentation. A large section of *The Book of Salt* is set in Vietnam during the French colonial occupation and food plays a central role in defining the physical and symbolic boundaries around national and racial identity. Xu reminds us that in a colonial context, 'food and eating become necessary not only for the sake of realism but also for the symbolism of the ontological character'.[7] Xu appears to be suggesting that the display of food habits and eating preferences in colonial situations becomes a significant part in the establishment of a person's psychological, cultural and ethnic identity. Food preferences and cuisine in *The Book of Salt* become a means of self-definition, a source of social value and an embodiment of 'taste'. The symbolism of salt unveils libidinal and racial anxieties in Binh's life as a colonial subject. The preparation and consumption of food confers a sense of national belonging upon the French colonists and is put in opposition with the 'Oriental'. Echoing Flagg's interpretation of food as a racial classifier, the food community in Truong's self-conscious novel uncovers how culinary preferences can act as an element of social and racial distinction. The text plays on culinary tensions between cultural factions; Truong turns the banning of certain foodstuffs into an issue of national and class identity. In the social community of *The Book of Salt*, the French ruling group maintains a distance from the oppressed native through displaying different food preferences. Those preferences are not based on actual gustatory taste, but are used as an element of socio-cultural distinction. Culinary preferences are categorised according to national acculturation and highlight the effects of ethnocentric prejudice on social experience.

One of the key foodstuffs in Truong's novel, as the title itself suggests, is salt. Salt appears repeatedly in Binh's life-story and connects the experience of cooking, tasting, travelling and even belonging. This prominence is noteworthy though hardly unique since, as Mark Kurlansky observes, in all ages 'salt has been invested with a significance far exceeding that inherent in its natural properties, interesting and important as they are'.[8] Truong sprinkles references to salt throughout the narrative: 'intrigue, like salt, is best if it is there from the beginning'[9]; 'salt enhances the sweetness' (185); and 'she had added a spoonful of salt to the water to help cleanse the wound' (201). Despite salt's constant presence in the narrative, its most significant appearance occurs when Binh—living in Paris—receives a letter from Vietnam, sent by his brother Anh Minh:

> I sniffed the envelope before opening it. It smelled of a faraway city, pungent with an anticipation for rain [. . .] I was certain to find the familiar sting of salt, but what I needed to know was what kind: kitchen, sweat, tears or sea. (5)

Salt forms a crystalline bond between the various components in Binh's life from his job as a cook in France ('sweat' in the 'kitchen') to his departure from his homeland ('tears' and 'sea'). Perhaps the most crucial feature of the symbolic salt in the letter is its provenance from Vietnam, Binh's home country. The letter itself is testimony to that, accompanied as it is by Anh Minh's suggestion: 'It's time for you to come home to Viet-Nam' (8). The idea of a painful 'return' to the homeland of Vietnam is juxtaposed with salt and connotations of suffering and struggle as well as that which is left behind and abandoned. This group of associations is intricately interwoven with the Biblical parable of Sodom and Gomorrah. A Western and Christian exegesis is sanctioned here by the fact that Binh is raised in a family of 'Vietnamese Catholics' (165). In the Book of Genesis, God sends two angels to warn Lot of the imminent destruction of Sodom and Gomorrah. Lot is instructed to take his wife and sons and leave the cities at once without looking back. However, as the family is leaving, Lot's wife looks back and as punishment for her transgression she is transformed into a pillar of salt:

> The sun was risen upon the earth when Lot entered into Zoar. (24) Then the LORD rained upon Sodom and upon Gomorrah brimstone and fire from the LORD out of heaven; (25) And he overthrew those cities, and all the plain, and all the inhabitants of the cities, and that which grew upon the ground. (26) But his wife looked back from behind him, and she became a pillar of salt.[10]

Sodom and Gomorrah are of course mythically associated with sexual deviance and the former dead city has given its name to the act of anal intercourse ('sodomy'). In *The Book of Salt*, Binh is forced to flee Vietnam once his homosexuality is made public and the 'sting of salt' suggests a punishment that will be inflicted for 'looking back' or returning to the homeland. The salt in the letter from Anh Minh signifies bodily excretions (sweat and tears), taboo desires and the threat of judgement, ostracism and castigation.[11] Through salt imagery, Binh's queerness is joined, in Xu's terms, with 'factors of race, class and coloniality'.[12]

In Truong's novel, not only is salt linked to a history of sexual repression, it is also imbricated with the history of French colonial oppression in Southeast Asia. The phrase 'sweat, tears and sea' symbolises the travails of occupied Vietnam. Kurlansky reminds us of how, on first arriving in Vietnam, the French disapproved of the food-preserving techniques used by the Vietnamese which were mainly based on the practice of salting. The

French demonised Vietnamese preserved food, especially fish, as 'rotten'.[13] This hostility towards salt involved a certain historical amnesia on the part of the French colonists. Since the fourteenth century, France itself found in salt a valuable product for export. By the eighteenth century, as Kurlansky notes, it was believed that France 'made the world's best salt'.[14] At home and abroad the French Crown relied heavily on revenue raised by salt taxes. The *gabelle* was a complex system of unpopular taxes and its most despised element was the *sel au devoir*, or salt duty. As Kurlansky elucidates: '[e]very person over the age of eight was required to purchase seven kilograms of salt each year at a fixed government price'.[15] Towards the end of the eighteenth century, as revolutionary ideas were fermenting, crimes against the *gabelle* became punishable by death. Kurlansky goes so far as to suggest that the salt law in France 'was not the singular cause of revolution, but it became a symbol of all the injustices of government'.[16] Although the *gabelle* was abolished after the Revolution, it was reinstated by Napoleon Bonaparte and remained in force until after the end of the Second World War. Throughout French history, therefore, there has often been 'a direct correlation between salt taxes and despots'.[17] The reaction of the French colonists to salt in Vietnam is related to a history of political and financial control. Just as the pre-revolutionary *gabelle* played a crucial role in the corruption that proved fatal to the French monarchy, salt imagery in Truong's novel is pivotal to its critique of French colonialism.

Binh's memories of his life in Vietnam are haunted by experiences of political and cultural oppression that are mixed with salt and other foodstuffs. At the Governor-General's house in Saigon, Binh receives a stern lecture from his brother Anh Minh on the importance of keeping local Vietnamese food separate from French cuisine:

> these French chefs were purists, classically, trained, from families of chefs going back at least a century. Minh the Sous Chef agreed that it was probably better this way. After all, the *chef de cuisine* at the Continental Palace Hotel in Saigon [. . .] had to be dismissed because he was serving dishes obscured by lemongrass and straw mushrooms. He also slipped pieces of rambutan and jackfruit into the sorbets. (42)

The desire of the French colonists to maintain the cuisine at the Continental Palace as purely French as possible is part of a strategy for preserving cultural identity. Paul Fieldhouse points out that national cuisine is 'used to denote a style of cooking with distinctive foods, preparation and techniques [. . .] because it is "normal" it is [. . .] thought of as [. . .] an aspect of group identity'.[18] The rules imposed by the French colonial community are clearly motivated by a desire to preserve the 'purity' of French food. The contaminations of 'lemongrass' and 'straw mushrooms' are less a matter of flavour than of national culture. As Lupton reminds us: 'food itself is a term which makes cultural distinctions between acceptable and non-acceptable organic matter for human consumption, and as such, is used to denote different material in different cultures'.[19] The decision of the chef to 'obscure' French dishes with 'abnormal' Vietnamese ingredients threatens group identity by traversing cultural boundaries. This subversive mélange takes place, Truong tells us, at 'one of the most fashionable hotels in all of Indochina' (43). According to Joanne Finkelstein, dining out involves 'the mediation of social relations through images of what is currently valued, acceptable and fashionable'[20]. While functioning as a token of group identity, then, food can also act as a badge of individuality. In this way, the public dining space might act as an inventory of an individual's 'private world'.[21] Dining out—especially in what is regarded as a 'fashionable' space—becomes a significant statement of self-representation. Individuals believe that restaurants, as Roy Wood argues, will help them 'realise certain desires [and] these are not simply objective desires—for good food and service—but expectations that the restaurant will satisfy deeper emotional desires for status and belongingness'.[22]

What emerges as extremely significant from the incident at the Palace Hotel is the severity of the French reaction to the 'obscured' dishes: 'the clientele was outraged, demanded that the natives in the kitchen be immediately dismissed if not jailed [. . .] yes, the Continental sent the man packing!' (42). The attitudes towards the renegade chef—and his outlawed Vietnamese ingredients—clearly transcends mere matters of culinary taste and recalls Pasi Falk's observation that 'within one culture, there may be a number of sets of rules which define the boundaries between forbidden and permitted foodstuffs, related to stage in the life-cycle, place, gender and social class'.[23] As typical ingredients in Vietnamese cuisine, lemongrass and straw mushrooms come to embody the native way of life, its culture and its beliefs. By adding the two local ingredients, the chef at the Continental Palace 'infects' French food with a Vietnamese presence. The reaction of the Palace restaurant's clientele thus underlines the role that food can play as a key marker of cultural difference. The customers at the Continental Palace are 'shocked' and 'outraged' by the way their meals have been 'obscured' (42). The mixing of ingredients in dishes is haunted by colonial paranoia concerning cultural contamination and hybridity. The insistence that everything be cooked the 'French way' and 'as if in France' is not merely a matter of culinary preference, but is informed by ethnocentrism and fear of cultural miscegenation (46). Truong's exploration of national cuisine seems to validate Fieldhouse's claim that 'the flavour of the food is [often] irrelevant [. . .] culture tells us what is fit to eat and ethnocentricity ensures that we obey'.[24]

While issues of national identity dominate the kitchen realm in *The Book of Salt*, one could also move towards interpreting the diners' distaste for Vietnamese cuisine and ingredients as an issue of social and economic class. Taste and the desire for any individual commodity—in particular food here—are important elements in the process of class formation and reproduction. In the words of Alan Warde: 'classes can be identified by their consumption patterns [. . .] and consumer behaviour can be explained in terms of the role of display and social judgement in the formation of class identities'.[25] As the 'ruling' class in Vietnam, the French colonialists in Truong's novel seek to maintain distance from the lower classes by expressing an amplified distaste for Vietnamese foodstuffs (the rambutan, the lemongrass and the straw mushrooms). The desire to maintain the purity of French dishes dovetails colonialist propaganda and class distinctions. In *Distinction* and elsewhere in his critical oeuvre, Pierre Bourdieu explores the relationship between patterns of consumption, the expression of social status, class positions and the concept of 'habitus'.[26] The 'habitus', as discussed briefly in my introduction, is that which connects a person's social position with an equivalent position in 'the universe of lifestyles' and, consequently, 'makes it possible to account both for classifiable practices and products and for the judgements [. . .] which make the practices into a system of distinctive signs'.[27] In Bourdieu's terms then, the French colonists' salt-phobia and exaggerated aversion to traditional Vietnamese ingredients belong to a signifying system which generates social distinctions and consolidates class structure: 'taste is the source of the system of distinctive features which cannot fail to be perceived as a systematic expression of a particular class of conditions of existence'.[28] The outrage caused by the presence of Vietnamese foodstuffs in 'French' dishes is then a key symbol of the social divisions that Truong exposes as pervasive in colonial Vietnam. The lemongrass, the straw mushrooms and the rambutan do not of course pose physical threat, but they menace to pollute as agents in a process of cultural and class-based loathing. In *Distinction*, Bourdieu discusses how distaste for another cultural group's foods expresses and enforces social division: 'tastes are perhaps first and foremost distastes, disgust provoked by the taste of others [. . .] [a form of] aesthetic intolerance'. The intolerance shown by the French community towards native food is paradigmatic of the dualistic colonial psyche: 'us' and 'them', 'pure' and 'polluted', 'inside' and 'outside'. Crossing the boundary between categories, as the Vietnamese chef does, thus threatens the very process of boundary-making. As Bourdieu points out, food 'distinguishes in an essential way, since taste is the basis of all that one has—people and things—and all that one is for others, whereby one classifies oneself and is classified by others'.[29]

Whilst the forbidding of Vietnamese food acts to maintain national and class boundaries, *The Book of Salt* also displays the French desire to designate the native Vietnamese as devious, dangerous and 'incensed' (42). Truong underscores the subversive nature of the renegade chef's conduct at the Continental Palace Hotel by describing him as 'slipping' rambutan and jackfruit into the sorbets. The choice of the word 'slip' carries obvious connotations of secrecy, potions and poisons; it implies secrecy and the breaking of rules. As Kristeva points out, 'it is not lack of cleanliness or health that causes abjection but what disturbs identity, system, order [. . .] what does not respect borders, positions, rules'.[30] Kristeva also observes that social disgust is often associated with 'the traitor, the liar, the criminal with a good conscience [. . .] any crime, because it draws attention to the fragility of the law, is abject, but premeditated crime [. . .] [is] even more so'.³¹ The chef's act of secretly slipping a prohibited ingredient inside a French dish is no mere culinary indiscretion and might be linked symbolically and politically to the secret and 'polluting' acts of 'culture mixing'. The 'treacherous' chef causes outrage, shock and abjection not only because he breaks social rules, but because his crime is concealed, thoughtfully prepared: 'abjection is immoral, sinister, scheming, and shady [. . .] a terror that dissembles, a hatred that smiles'.³²

In this context, then, the rejection of Vietnamese food takes us back to abjection, or, to be more specific, 'Asian abjection'. This concept, which finds its theoretical foundation in discourses on Orientalism, highlights cultural differences as a way to establish domination and oppression. According to Edward Said, Orientalism consists of a collection of false assumptions underlying Western attitudes towards the East: 'Orientalism is all aggression, activity, judgement, will-to-truth'.³³ In a colonial environment, the authority of the Western colonisers is foregrounded by their difference from the 'Oriental', the native inhabitant of a country who is perceived stereotypically as devious, unlawful and unreliable. It is precisely this difference that functions as a social marker and constructs a sense of superiority for the colonisers, whilst, at the same time, justifying subjugation and social subordination of the natives. Iris Young describes racial abjection as a form of oppression that is executed as a structural 'immobilisation' of a particular group.³⁴ The emergence of a colonial 'self', therefore, is dependent on the construction of the 'non-self'—in this case, a native, 'Oriental' counterpart. The treatment of Vietnamese food in *The Book of Salt* represents an example of how Asian abjection designates an area for the unviable. Understood as part of the 'deviant nature' of the Oriental, the local food is rejected precisely for its being 'Vietnamese', and therefore the opposite of all that is 'French'. This idea is reinforced in the novel by various examples of how the colonists do not accept a Vietnamese chef at all and always demand a French one: 'Anh Minh [. . .] insisted that after Monsieur and Madame had tasted his *omelette á la bourbonnaise*, his *coupe ambassadrice*, his *crème marquise*, they would have no need to send for a French *chef de cuisine* [. . .] [but] a young Jean Blériot arrived from France to don the coveted title' (14). The presence of Vietnamese food at the Continental Palace designates the boundary between the lawful and the outlaw, the colonial and the native, the Occidental and the Oriental. Through food rejection, the French colonists construct, in Judith Butler's words, the 'unliveable' and the imaginary limit of the 'subject's domain'.³⁵

As Truong unveils the racial abject dimension of food consumption in *The Book of Salt*, she also hints at how the cultural horror of ingesting 'infected' Vietnamese food is irrevocably related to broader concepts of selfhood—in this particular instance, a strong sense of 'Frenchness'. The food preparations for Madame's birthday at the Governor-General's house represent a carefully orchestrated example in this regard:

> For her birthday dinner, Madame wanted her eggs in the snow, but she would not have any of Indochina's milk in the snow. "Simply too much of a risk" she said. "I've heard that the Nationalists have been feeding the cows here a weed so noxious that the milk, if consumed in sufficient amounts, would turn a perfectly healthy woman barren". (47)

Madame's concerns here underline the efficacy of Lupton's work on *Food, the Body and the Self*. Eating involves a 'process of incorporation [that] is inextricably linked to subjectivity'—food, in simple terms, becomes part of the self—and is thus a potential source of 'great anxiety and risk [. . .] a sense of danger [. . .] in relation to bodily boundaries'.[36] Indeed, food carries an important symbolic function, inasmuch as the fragile limits of the body are concerned. As a substance that enters the body, and becomes part of it, food is a highly liminal substance. Whilst analysing the effect that food and ingestion can have on the production of subjectivity, Lupton argues that 'as the process of incorporation is inextricably linked to subjectivity it is the source of great anxiety and risk [. . .] by incorporating food into one's body, that food is made to become self'[37]. Madame fears that the ingestion of local milk might sterilise a 'perfectly healthy woman' and needless to say 'the woman' that Madame and old Chaboux had in their minds was, of course, French. Madame added this piece of unsolicited horror and bodily affront to Mother France just in case old Chaboux dared to balk at this task' (47). The milk's poison attacks on two fronts to threaten both bodily and national boundaries: infertility for the mother and a potential reverse colonisation of the motherland. The endangered victim would imbibe the hatred which inspired the Nationalists to poison the milk. By taking in the 'infected milk', Madame would also ingest the surrounding colonial world and its political threats to her position which would make her 'barren'.[38] Although Truong does not establish definitively whether Madame's fears about alimentary violations have any basis in fact, the fantasy itself is potent enough. Claude Fischler has pointed out that the alimentary incorporation of a dubious substance may lead to contamination, transformation from within and therefore, an overall dispossession of the self.[39] The sterilisation of colonial French women threatens to destroy Mother France literally from within. Like the lemongrass, straw mushrooms and rambutan at the Continental Palace, the milk threatens borders, it pollutes the 'clean and proper' subject and undermines social structures. According to Kristeva,

> abjection is coextensive with social and symbolic order, on the individual as well as on the collective level [. . .] the logic of prohibition [. . .] founds the abject [. . .] defilement is what is jettisoned from the

symbolic system [. . .] [it] then becomes differentiated from a temporary agglomeration of individuals and, in short, constitutes a classification system or a structure [. . .] the potency of pollution is therefore [. . .] proportional to the potency of the prohibition that founds it.[40]

In this light, once could view Madame's fervent prohibition against the polluting Indochinese milk as an attempt to reinforce the potency of the Symbolic by expelling a substance that traditionally signifies the Semiotic or Imaginary.

While *The Book of Salt* unravels how the cultural integrity of the colonial body is threatened by 'noxious' foreign foods and exotic deviance, Truong also implicitly uncovers the techno-political function of alimentary regulation and creates a parallel between the paradigmatic colonial body and the French State. Within colonial and patriarchal discourse, the body of course performs a crucial role in establishing and maintaining relations of power around cultural and social boundaries. Janet Price and Margrit Shildrick point out that 'the colonial body politic [. . .] is concerned with the set of material elements and techniques through which power/knowledge relations are mapped on the individual body'.[41] In the light of those power relations, what is 'mapped' onto the body is not only the construction of rules, but also the presence of pragmatic associations between the body and its function as a political gateway. In *The Book of Salt*, Madame's fear of personal bodily harm—precisely, becoming barren through the consumption of polluting food supplied by the Nationalists—is interpreted as a 'bodily affront to Mother France' (47). Price and Shildrick have contended that 'the morphology of the body and the morphology of the state meet in an exercise of symbiotic mapping'.[42] Madame's intimate body politics might be read in the light of this contention as an exemplification of the French body politic (and vice versa). Madame's body is born of and gives birth to a Mother State which aims to reproduce its dominion over dependent colonies.[43] This symbiosis is, as Deleuze and Guattari suggest, part of an 'ancient platitude' which defines the State as an organism.[44] In the opening pages of Thomas Hobbes' *Leviathan* (1651), for example, the State is famously dissected into body parts and organs each corresponding to a different site of political power.[45] *The Book of Salt* offers both a continuation and critique of this 'ancient platitude'. Binh's experience as a colonial subject allows insights into the colonial imaginary in which the body/state functions as a closed and impenetrable system. Food plays an important role here as part of a system of regulatory injunctions and a potent signifier of invasive threats.

As a parallel to the French fear of being 'infected' by the Oriental, the 'colonisation' of the native body is portrayed as part of a politics of domination which are central to *The Book of Salt*. The abolition of local ingredients and cuisine in Vietnam represents an instance of Western control in the colonies and provides the novel's reader with an unforgettable lesson in what

Xu calls the 'fixity of colonial stratification'.⁴⁶ Truong is keen to use food metaphors elsewhere in order to show the extent to which Vietnamese elements are extirpated from Vietnam and replaced with French preferences:

> There are some French words that I have picked up quickly, in fact, words that I cannot remember not knowing. As if I had been born with them in my mouth, as if they were the seeds of a sour fruit that someone else ate and then ungraciously stuffed its remains into my mouth. (12)

Truong's equation of food with language exemplifies the brutality involved in colonising the Oriental 'Other'. The sour nature of colonial subjugation suffocates the knowledge of the native population—including Binh—just like unwanted, regurgitated food, which is then force fed to the oppressed. The seed of Westernisation is planted in the colonial body—or, more specifically, in the colonial mouth—and, like the sour fruits of a tree it branches, in Xu's words, to annihilate 'indigenous cultural consciousness'.⁴⁷

Nonetheless, stopping at the uses of food as a class, colonial and racial separator in *The Book of Salt* does not fully resolve how the novel unveils the hidden impact of American foreign politics. In spite of Truong's open engagement with French colonial politics and their impact on Vietnamese consciousness, it is necessary to go beyond the plot restrictions of the novel and enquire about the relationship that the novel holds to the Vietnamese invasion, American history and the eponymous salt. The discussions of how the French impose limitations on Vietnamese foodways in the novel could give way to a more specific critique of Truong's own conflicted separation from her native country and her identity as an American writer. The fictional presence of Stein and Toklas, two highly vocal American political activists and writers, questions the motives that may lie at the core of the text itself. Far from implying that *The Book of Salt* is a historical commentary on American-Vietnamese political relations—and the Vietnam War in particular—I suggest that the presence of salt within Truong's novel also creates a connection that speaks to a very specific part of American history. Indeed, tales of salt are intertwined with the development of the United States as a separate country. Salt is arguably considered a major factor in the outcome of many wars fought on American soil. During the War of Independence, salt took on 'acid' and 'sour quality'. The British used Americans who were loyal to the Crown to intercept the rebels' salt supply.⁴⁸ As any American vessel carrying salt was automatically subject to seizure, this action destroyed the rebels' ability to preserve food for prolonged periods of time. It has also been documented that, during the War of 1812, American soldiers in the field received salt and brine as payment because the new government could not afford to pay them with money. After the war ended, the Americans began to develop domestic salt sources in an effort to reduce dependence on imported goods. Salt mines in America became not only widespread, but also a hugely invaluable source of financial gain. John Paul

Zronik points out that the salt industry in America continued to grow until it became the biggest in the world'.[49] Salt, it would seem, has been greatly connected with America's bid for independence and its desire to expand into a powerful nation.

In the twentieth century, and during the years of the Cold War, salt's involvement with American politics took on a metaphorical meaning and extended into the creation of new legislations. In 1974, while the Vietnam War was taking its toll on the country, U.S. president Richard Nixon signed a treaty with the Soviet Union, limiting the number of strategic ballistic missile launchers at existing levels. The 'Strategic Arms Limitation Talks Agreement'—known more commonly as 'SALT'—gave way to a number of communications aimed at regulating political power and providing a form of armament control.[50] After the SALT treaty was signed, the United States began to drastically reduce their troop support in South Vietnam, putting an end to it in 1975. The term of 'salt', therefore, holds an important conceptual connection with American history and politics in the wider American imagination. Truong, one could argue, is feeding into that connection. In the novel, just as quickly as they had appeared in his life, Toklas and Stein 'abandon' Binh and return to America, seemingly promising to return to visit him, but equally and openly denying the possibility. Finding himself alone, Binh is left with nothing but 'the salt' of Vietnam and wondering what to do with his life:

> Salt, I thought. GertrudeStein, what kind? Kitchen, sweat, tears, or the sea. Madame, they are not all the same. Their stings, their smarts, their strengths, the distinctions among them are fine. Do you know, GertrudeStein, which one I have tastes on my tongue? A story is a gift, Madame, and you are welcome. (261)

With salt's historical metaphor in mind, it is not hard to see how Truong could be establishing a link here between the American writers abandoning the Vietnamese chef and American military forces fleeing Vietnam at the end of the war in 1975. The provocative suggestion here is that the United States left Vietnam in poor condition, 'Americanising' the country as they did so. Binh's final ruminations over the importance of salt also create a connection to Truong as an immigrant. One must not forget that, at the age of six, Truong left Vietnam with her mother and moved to the United States as a refugee of the Vietnam War. The 'salt' being tasted in the final pages of the novel is connected to the idea of migration, travelling and experiencing different countries, as the prospect of separation is introduced through the idea of 'tears' and 'sea'. Truong's sense of becoming American, therefore, is conceptually problematised in *The Book of Salt* through recalling a foodstuff that connects the United States to a history of war. Ultimately, Truong employs salt and its historical correlations in order to provide us with a poignant evaluation of Vietnam's own historical and political exploitation, from French colonisation to American politicised conquest. The author's own private history of Diaspora is embedded in the pages of the novel, as food takes on a confessional role and unveils questions of traumatic history and national identity.

CUISINE, TRADITION AND CULINARY GROUPS

If a close analysis of food in *The Book of Salt* opens discussions on how culinary attitudes—and the consumption of specific dishes become emblematic for national identity, cultural affiliation and community prejudice—it is now important to focus on how, in literary immigrant communities, the representation and experience of food are frequently framed by the concept of 'tradition'. 'Tradition' can be associated with types of ingredient, methods of food preparation and consumption as well as connotations of 'authenticity' and 'wholesomeness'. This cultural configuration is central to Amy Tan's highly acclaimed novel *The Joy Luck Club* (1989). Tan plays with the idea of tradition to render the importance of food in the formation of cultural identity. Recalling the idea of a 'national cuisine' suggested by Truong, *The Joy Luck Club* shows how immigrants use culinary tradition as a way to maintain a cultural connection with their country of origin. As was noted previously, there is an abundance of food imagery in Asian American literature. Xu reminds us that the representational regime associating Asian Americans and food traditions is not only a cultural matter, but also serves as 'a medium for casual and safe exchanges between Asian Americans and white strangers'.[51] In Tan's novel, issues of 'authenticity', cuisine and the construction of culinary groups, bearing a literary testimony to Alan Warde's sociological contention that 'a reaction to rapid cultural change is to reaffirm the value of tradition.'[52]

David Leiwei Li describes *The Joy Luck Club* concisely as a story of food, gender, generation and geography.[53] The narrative follows the lives and deaths of four Chinese women who emigrate to San Francisco—Suyuan, An-mei, Lindo and Ying-Ying—and their respective daughters—Jing-mei, Rose, Waverly and Lena—who, as second generation Chinese Americans, struggle to come to terms with their mixed cultural backgrounds. It should not come as a surprise that Tan chooses San Francisco as a setting for a story centred on food, immigration and trans-generational exchanges. Historically, San Francisco has played an important part in the settling and integration of Chinese immigrants in America—a part influenced by the city's geographical location, which places it in a favourable position connecting China to America. Economically, food production represented an important way in which the Chinese could find employment in California. Xu states that in the mid-1880s the Chinese in America were mainly involved in 'farming, fishing and cooking'.[54] By the late 1880s, 'Chinese immigrants made up between half and three-quarters of the cultivators of specialised vegetable crops', going as far as introducing new species of fruit such as the frost-resistant oranges which later boosted the citrus industry in both Florida and California.⁵⁵ Significantly, the historical relationship that Chinese Americans have with food has, to borrow Xu's words, 'little to do with the thrill of creation' and was mainly based on 'survival and adaptation'.⁵⁶ Food plays a pivotal role in the everyday lives of the women in Tan's novel, and on special occasions the dinner table emerges as a key social and symbolic site. Against a backdrop of rapidly changing social and cultural circumstances, resulting from emigration and marriage, Tan explores how the customs associated with meal times—food purchase and preparation, consumption and clearing-up—provide continuity and a base for individual and collective identity. 'The Joy Luck Club' itself provides ample opportunities for the women to meet, play Mah-jong and talk whilst feasting on various foods. This gathering, in Per Otnes's words, 'not only says "we share"', but it operates the actual sharing, being mediated by its various foodstuffs'.⁵⁷ Indeed, food is presented throughout the novel as a vital additive for selfhood, communication and community.

In terms of group identity, the dinner table, with its repertoire of culturally inscribed conventions, affords a performative arena in which social relations can be created, cemented or destroyed. Mealtimes represent significant occasions when groups are normally together and therefore provide opportunities, in Wood's words, 'to observe what is acceptable in terms of food-related behaviour'.⁵⁸ As a result, food tradition and customs are involved in a highly practical level of performance, so that the way in which the food is consumed can become just as important as the way in which it is prepared. In *The Joy Luck Club*, this is exemplified by the family meals at the Jong household. Waverly is invited to her parents' house for a celebratory birthday dinner and she decides to bring Rich— her Irish-American fiancé—in order to introduce him. Waverly's mother, Lindo, takes great pride in her culinary skills and decides to prepare her 'famous' eggplant and shredded pork using only the finest traditional ingredients: 'cooking was how my mother expressed her love, her pride, her power, her proof that she knew more [. . .] "Just be sure to tell her later that her cooking was the best you ever tasted [. . .]" I told Rich'.⁵⁹ The meal at the Jong house is meant to function as a performance which displays and confirms family roles. However, Rich's presence proves to be disruptive and the expected script cannot be followed. To begin with there is some suspicion and even resentment from family members due to the fact that Rich is 'not Chinese' (177). Rich's behaviour at the dinner table also highlights cultural boundaries between guest and host thus increasing the family's discomfort:

> When I offered Rich a fork, he insisted on using the slippery ivory chopsticks. He held them splayed like the knock-kneed legs of an ostrich while picking up a large chunk of sauce-coated eggplant. Halfway

between his plate and his open mouth, the chunk fell on his crisp white shirt and then slid into his crotch. (178)

Rich's attitude towards the eating of the food—when he finally does manage to eat it—accentuates his position as an outsider within the Jong family circle and a stranger to their food traditions: 'He then helped himself to big portions of the shrimp and snow peas, not realising he should have taken only a polite spoonful, until everybody had had a morsel' (178). Rich's final and most serious *faux pas* involves criticising Lindo's culinary skill:

> As it is Chinese custom, my mother always made disparaging remarks about her own cooking [. . .] This was our family's cue to eat some and proclaim it is the best she had ever made [. . .] But before we could do so, Rich said 'You know, all it needs is a little soy sauce' and he proceeded to pour a riverful of the salty black stuff on the platter, right before my mother's horrified eyes. (178)

The slight here is keenly felt as it extends beyond the food on the table to the mother, her family and their culture. Rich's behaviour highlights a clear breakdown in the customary process described by Wood: 'the giving and receiving of food is never a neutral act but affords opportunities for host and guest to demonstrate appropriate behaviour as benefits their roles'.[60]

The disastrous birthday meal at the Jong household is an instructive example of how the 'authentic' customs and traditions associated with specific food cultures play a crucial role in *The Joy Luck Club*. Traditional food evokes a raft of memories associated with specific ingredients, methods of preparation, people and places. The idea of an authentic, 'traditional' meal has as much to do with the associative mechanisms of cognition as it does with the ingredients themselves. As Lisa Heldke has proposed, 'authenticity is a property of the particular work of cuisine that is "happening" [. . .] and will involve [. . .] interpretation'.[61] The social gatherings held at Kweilin in *The Joy Luck Club* involve precisely this mixture of traditional cuisine, memory and interpretation. The story of the Ladies of Kweilin is significantly told in retrospect: after Suyuan's death, her daughter Jing-mei—also known as June—is asked to take her mother's place at the Joy Luck Club, a monthly gathering centred on feasting, sharing stories and playing Mah-jong. Jing-mei's memories of her mother's stories establish that the Club has a long history: 'My mother started the San Francisco version of the Joy Luck Club in 1949, two years before I was born' (20). In fact, the San Francisco Club serves as both a recreational outlet and a commemoration of an original Joy Luck Club in Kweilin. The club was founded by Suyuan and three female friends during the Japanese occupation. Tan's decision to expose the effects of colonialism on the construction of culinary communities recalls Truong's reflections on colonial food, cultural prejudice and taste in *The Book of Salt*. As it emerges from Suyuan's stories, the Japanese occupation of course re-shaped the lives of the Chinese. The Kweilin Ladies formed a close-knit group who celebrated their friendship with 'feasts':

> Each week one of us would host a party to raise money and to raise our spirits. The hostess had to serve special *dyansuin* foods to bring good fortune of all kinds—dumplings shaped like silver money ingots, long rice noodles for long life, boiled peanuts for conceiving sons, and, of course, many good-luck oranges for a plentiful, sweet life [. . .] What fine food we treated ourselves to with our meagre allowances! (23)

The traditional *dyanisuin* foods consumed by the Kweilin Ladies appears to serve as a reminder of cultural belief in a quickly changing historical situation, caused by the Japanese invasion. The associations made with the consumption of certain foods—their 'traditional' value in terms of luck, fertility and longevity—create an appeal because they represent a set of customs and beliefs which embody the stamina of a challenged social group. Serving and consuming traditional foods, embedded with powerful cultural connotations, could be interpreted as a displaced desire for consistency, security and, ultimately, the 'sweet life'. As Warde has argued: 'in the face of the [. . .] new, some people seek out authentic or shared sets of customs that can be protected, defended or reproduced'.[62] The foods consumed by the Ladies of Kweilin valorise and reinforce long-standing beliefs and practices challenged by the emergence of a new political and cultural authority imposed by the Japanese. The meals at Kweilin are portrayed as 'traditional' by Tan because they legitimate a way of life and collective beliefs which belong to happier times.

Suyuan's descriptions of the gatherings transform a meal into a 'party' (23), 'feast' (24) and 'banquet' (24) and emphasise the traditional meanings attached to certain foods such as 'good life' and 'good luck' (23). She thus confirms Roy Wood's observation that 'various forms of feasting serve to link individuals to the wider social fabric through shared understandings of cultural conventions'.[63] At the same time, it ought to be noted that Suyuan expresses reservations about aspects of the feast: 'the dumplings were stuffed mainly with stringy squash' (23). The participants consume inferior substitutes for traditional foods but apparently do not 'notice' the difference (23). The Japanese invasion has a profound impact on the everyday lives of the Kweilin Ladies and enforces culinary improvisation to contend with missing and downmarket ingredients. The fact that the participants in the feast do not comment on the inauthenticity of their meals may testify to a tactical reticence, or might suggest the extent to which the actual content of a traditional meal is secondary to its culturally inscribed meanings. In this instance, the concept of 'authenticity' in relation to food can be difficult to pin down.[64]

The consumption of certain 'traditional' foods at the Kweilin gatherings testifies to a need for stability and expresses a collective yearning to return to the better times before the Japanese occupation. In this context, the experience of 'traditional' dishes by the Ladies of Kweilin can be viewed as a collective exchange of information that begins with the encounter between food and the eater. According to John Dewey, in examples of traditional cuisine, 'the contributions made by the dish itself [. . .] are contributions to an experience, that are met by the contributions of the experiencer (the eater)'.[65] The 'hope to be lucky' is inscribed upon the act of eating though a constructed idea of traditional food. The same inscription, for the Ladies of Kweilin, becomes a conversation within a wider cultural frame. Their desire for 'luck' and 'good life' interacts with the attributes of the food and transforms 'authenticity' into a reciprocal relationship between the eaters and the dish. Dewey argues that in the collective experience of a particular dish, 'every individual brings [. . .] a way of seeing and feeling that in its interaction with old material creates something new, something previously not existing in experience'.[66] The Ladies' 'lost past' (24) becomes an integral part in the consumption of the dishes they prepare so that 'tradition' ceases to be a static list of qualities and becomes instead a dynamic element in the cultural experience of eating.

The ideas of 'tradition' and 'authenticity' are further problematised when 'The Joy Luck Club' crosses the Pacific and, on arrival in America, is greeted by a series of misconceptions and mythologies regarding Chinese culture. Tan is keen to emphasise that these misconceptions do not belong exclusively to 'the Americans'—many people of Chinese descent in the US appear themselves to have forgotten what it 'means' to be Chinese and unwittingly participate in an elaborate fantasy about their national identity. In this context, Tan explores the legitimacy of Chinese culinary traditions in San Francisco in relation to the experiences of different generations of mothers and daughters. A good example of this can be found in Lindo Jong's mental conversation with her daughter Waverly, who, according to her mother, has a completely distorted conception of Chinese culture, especially when it comes to culinary traditions. What seems to particularly haunt Lindo is the knowledge that Waverly is tempted to construct romanticised visions of 'being Chinese', which are inevitably related to food: 'Why do you always tell people that I met your father in the Cathay House [. . .] This is not sincere. This is not true! Your father was not a waiter, I never ate in that restaurant' (259). The manufactured nature of Chinese culinary traditions in America is further underlined by Tan: 'The Cathay House had a sign that said "Chinese Food", so only Americans went there before it was torn down [. . .] All nonsense. Why are you attracted to Chinese nonsense?'(259). In her mother's eyes, Waverly embellishes the idea of her family's Chinese traditions so that they can become palatable to 'the Americans' as idealised images. These conceptions include, of course, Chinese foods, restaurants and culinary customs. The idea that Chinese people should eat and work in a Chinese restaurant appears to be part of the traditional stereotype. Waverly seems to be employing cultural–particularly culinary—stereotypes in order to feel ethnically legitimised, thus reinforcing Warde's claim that 'behind invented traditions lurks the imagined community, a site [. . .] that promises collective security and group identity'.[67]

Conceptions about traditional Chinese food in *The Joy Luck Club* show, in Xu's words, 'the success of Western colonisation of the minds' of Eastern immigrants.[68] A further example of this takes place when Waverly, still a child growing up on the streets of San Francisco's Chinatown, exchanges culinary knowledge with a Caucasian tourist:

> Tourists never went to Hong Sing's, since the menu was printed only in Chinese. A Caucasian man with a big camera once posed me and my playmates in front of the restaurant. He had us move to the side of the picture window so the photo would capture the roasted duck with its head dangling from a juice-covered rope. After he took the picture, I told him he should go into Hong Sing's and eat dinner. When he smiled and asked me what he served, I shouted, "Guts and duck's feet and octopus gizzards!" Then I ran off with my friends. (91)

A number of significant elements emerge from this short episode. Firstly, the fact that the menu is written only in Chinese immediately exemplifies a desire to maintain Chinese culture—embodied in the food—separate from the 'American' way of life. Secondly, the Caucasian tourist's wish to photograph the duck in the window highlights his conceptions of what Chinese food is: his need to document the roast animal is symptomatic of his view of 'traditional' Chinese cuisine. The tourist's view of Chinese culture—which literally hangs off a 'juice-covered rope'—serves to maintain a cultural distance and perhaps even a sense of superiority. Leiwei Li argues that a sense of 'apparent tolerance' consolidates the idea of Chinese food and culture as a 'manipulable auxiliary to white interests'.[69] The idea of taking a photograph of 'foreign' people and food serves as a social marker which delineates the Chinese as different and alien.

Most significant of all, however, is Waverly's reaction to the tourist. His distrusting presuppositions of the restaurant's food already introduces an Orientalist view of Chinese food, which is probably expected to contain dubious ingredients. Xu argues that 'dietary accusations' against Chinese food 'litter [. . .] everyday conversations' in America, so that Chinese Americans are almost invariably 'portrayed through foodways'.[70] Waverly's reference to '[g]uts and duck's feet and octopus gizzards!' reveals a number of cultural conceptions which are part not only of the tourist's view, but also her own. The foods are highly stereotyped in terms of what a Caucasian might expect Chinese food to be.[71] The ingredients are used by Waverly as examples of 'disgusting' foodstuffs, which are meant to repel the tourist despite her previous invitation to enter the restaurant. Waverly constructs an idea of Chinese food for the 'outsider' which fully conforms to Orientalist stereotypes and shapes the vision of the Chinese as an ethnic minority. Frank Chin and Jeffrey Chan characterise racist stereotypes as a 'low maintenance engine of white supremacy' that shapes not only 'the mass society's perceptions' but also 'the subject minority' itself into 'becoming the stereotype'; they eventually 'live it, talk it, embrace it, measure groups and individual worth in its terms and believe it'.[72] Although a sense of mockery—which ridicules stereotypes—accompanies Waverly's description of typical Chinese foods, her idea of what is 'disgusting' is influenced, if not constructed, by the stereotype itself, as if she had been 'fed' it so much that she started believing it. Maintaining the difference between Chinese culinary preferences and the world of the Caucasian tourist represents a way through which she can defend her cultural belonging and, simultaneously, accept the social implications—namely stereotypes—that might come with her race. In soliciting Orientalist consent from the tourist, Waverly constructs an idea of Chinese food in which, as Leiwei Li argues, 'the stereotype and the subject become one'.[73]

Tan is keen to show how the West can romanticise Eastern culinary traditions and even construct an idea of Chinese food that is actually non-existent. This is particularly illustrated an episode involving fortune cookies. As a young immigrant from China, Lindo first finds a job in a cookie factory:

> This job in the cookie factory was one of the worst. Big black machines worked all day and night pouring little pancakes onto moving round griddles. The other women and I sat on high stools, and as the little pancakes went by, we had to grab them off the hot griddle just as they turned golden. We would put a strip of paper in the center, then fold the cookie in half and bend its arms back just as it turned hard. (262)

It is rather obvious that the 'cookie factory' is meant to be a 'fortune cookie factory' and, just as obviously, that Lindo does not know what they are. Fortune cookies—a 'Chinese' food known world-wide—are in fact an American-born invention. Although historians have found the inspiration for fortune cookies in fourteenth-century Chinese warfare—when soldiers slipped messages into mooncakes to help coordinate their actions—their first commercial appearance dates to the twentieth century. Culinary folklore has it that Canton native David Jung, a California baker, began making cookies with encouraging notes in them and handed them out to the poor. Tan humorously illustrates the non-Chinese origin of the cookies by adding confusion to Lindo's encounter with the food. When she learns the cookies' function from a fellow worker, Lindo remembers that she 'did not know what she meant' and was shocked by the thought that 'American people think Chinese people write these sayings' (262). Eventually, Lindo and her fellow worker agree that what is contained in so-called 'fortune cookies' are not 'fortunes', but simply 'bad instructions' (262). Tan implies here that with manufactured examples of Chinese cuisine in the West—like fortune cookies—the idea of Chinese food and Chinese community is filtered through American imagination and re-invented. The idea of Chinese culinary tradition is constructed through poor cultural representations and merged with a series of false expectations—like, for instance, the certainty that the Chinese speak of fortunes on a daily basis. Trinh Minh-ha has argued that in the re-elaboration of ethnic cuisine in a foreign country there is always a degree of 'planned authenticity', in which cuisine becomes a 'product of hegemony' and part of a universal standardisation.[74] In the case of Tan's fortune cookies, the suggestion of culinary authenticity is used as a pretext through which an idea of ethnicity can be sold for profit. A faux Chinese product is sold on the basis that is authentic and traditional and this idea is strengthened by the presence of mock-Chinese sayings. The thought of authentic Chinese food becomes a manufactured and marketable fiction and functions, in Yuan Yuan's words, as a 'signifier' which paradoxically 'divides' the immigrants from the new country and 'splits their identities'.[75]

Confused images of what traditional Chinese food 'should' be like are challenged more vigorously when Jing-mei—Suyuan's daughter—travels to China. After her mother's death, Jing-mei and her father plan this trip in order to get re-acquainted with long-lost members of their family. Jing-mei understands this journey in terms of 'becoming Chinese' (267): 'Today I realise I've never really known what it means to be Chinese. I am thirty-six years old. My mother is dead and I am on a train, carrying with me her dreams of coming home. I am going to China' (268). However, on arrival Jing-mei does not encounter the authentic and traditional China she had expected. The China she discovers clashes with her own expectations. The buildings, for example, appear too luxurious and lack the 'traditional'—or, in other words, impoverished—Chinese qualities Jing-mei had anticipated: 'The taxi stops and I assume we've arrived, but then I peer out at what looks like a grander version of the Hyatt Regency [. . .] and then I shake my head' (276). Edward Said argues that Orientalist visions are mainly based on a 'misinterpretation of some Oriental essence' that operate as reductively 'as representations usually do'.[76] That misinterpretation imposes a difference between the East and the West. In the case of Jing-mei, her imagination conjures representational mythologies of humility about China in order to differentiate it from the reality of her America.

Above all, however, Jing-mei's expectations about 'traditional' China seem to be connected with her Westernised expectations regarding food culture:

> 'What about dinner?' I ask. I have been envisioning my first real Chinese feast for many days already, a big banquet with one of those soups steaming out of a carved winter melon, chicken wrapped in clay. Peking duck, 'the works'. (278)

The description Tan offers of Jing-mei's culinary expectations is indeed revealing. Firstly, Jing-mei admits to envisioning not just Chinese food, but, specifically, 'real' Chinese food. The authenticity of the dishes is emphasised by the concomitant use of the words 'feast' and 'banquet'; these terms immediately communicate not only opulence and higher quality consumables, but, especially, a sense of celebration and therefore a gathering of people consuming food together. It is also significant that Jing-mei's descriptions of 'real' Chinese food echo the terminology used by her mother to describe the Kweilin culinary gatherings. Joanne Mäkelä points out that a real meal involves not only 'different ingredients and cooking methods combined in the right way', but also 'entails social sharing of food'.[77] Jing-mei's idealised vision of a proper Chinese meal encapsulates a very special list of foodstuffs, what she refers to as 'the works' (278). Jing-mei expects not merely authentic ingredients, but a 'real Chinese feast'—a social gathering which displays all the trappings of a previously lost Oriental etiquette. Her desire to consume idealised traditional food could mirror her need to define herself through her personal choices, which obviously include what she actively chooses to eat. Consuming traditional—perhaps forgotten—food dishes would encode a message which signifies cultural acceptance, and concomitantly, a stable personal identity.

However, instead of the food and ceremony which Jing-mei sees as a vital rite of passage in her journey towards 'becoming Chinese', her father decides on something more familiar:

> My father walks over and picks up a room service book [. . .] He flips through the pages quickly and then points to the menu. 'This is what they want' says my father. So it's decided. We are going to dine tonight in our rooms, with our family, sharing hamburgers, French fries and apple pie á la mode. (278)

The 'real Chinese feast' is replaced by an authentically Americanised eating experience: local cuisine is exchanged with 'anonymous' fast food. The resignation signalled by Jing-mei's flat statement—'it's decided'—is clearly symptomatic of a cultural disenchantment that goes beyond mere of culinary gratification. According to Warde, 'to claim that a practice is traditional is to deem it continuous over time and to accord it to some legitimacy because of its moral value'.[78] In place of a tradition which promises continuity, legitimacy and moral value, Jing-mei is offered a burger and fries. Through the image of the Americanised meal *par excellence*, Tan explores the idea that 'tradition' can be a manufactured invention. Jing-mei's orientalised vision of Chinese culinary tradition appears generated, on the one hand, by her mother's homesick memories about 'being Chinese' and, on the other, by her own desire to find something long-lasting and legitimate with which to associate now that her mother has passed away. As a result, the idea of tradition becomes embedded with the desire to maintain a culinary culture threatened by immigration, assimilation and evolution. Remembering traditional food—even if it is at risk of being culturally fabricated—is a way through which, in Bell and Valentine's words, ethnic groups have 'reproduced their identities over time'.[79]

CULINARY NOSTALGIA

H.D. Renner has commented on how 'immigrants cling to their own cooking, believing it to be the real thing of the country'. However, Renner goes on to inquire: 'How far is memory exact? [And] if memory is inaccurate, how much is this inaccuracy influenced by time?'[80] The possibility that, in immigrant communities, a remembered food habit could be the product of a constructed, nostalgic interpretation as opposed to an authentic tradition has to be admitted. Immigrant or ethnically inspired texts underline the extent to which memories, including body memories of food habits, are the product of an ongoing process of representation, rather than the authoritative repository of an authentic past. This highlights the validity of Renner's observation that in both cultural and psychological terms, 'an emigrant tends to forget the language of his fatherland before giving up his native food habits'.[81]

In immigrant communities, food memories figure as a central element for the recreation of everyday life. Writer Diana Abu-Jaber shows a particular propensity to connecting eating and cooking to the immigrant experience. Biographically, Abu-Jaber holds a complicated relationship with food, foodways and her own mixed-ethnic identity, being of Jordanian descent on her father's side and Irish-American on her mother's. In her memoir, *The Language of Baklava* (2005), she offers a poignant commentary of her relationship with her father, Bud, and his status as an immigrant. The presence or absence of particular consumables in the text shapes the emotional experience of everyday life. As the daughter of an American mother and a Jordanian father, Diana—the memorialised transposition of Abu-Jaber herself—lives her childhood in the United States and is caught between the commodities of her material, American life and her father's stories about an almost mythical, far away Jordan. Diana's meals are often examples of Jordanian cuisine, lovingly prepared by her father—affectionately referred to as 'Bud'—with a great sense of nostalgia and melancholia. The sadness of her father's immigrant condition is passed on through the memory of homemade food and commensal events: 'My father is a sweet, clueless immigrant . . . [he] misses the old country so much, it's like an ache in his blood. On his days off, he cooks and croons in Arabic to the frying liver and onion songs about missing the one you love'.[82] It is not difficult to see how *The Language of Baklava* represents Abu-Jaber's careful negotiation of her own identity, split between being 'an Arab' (as her father puts it) and being 'American'. The attachment to food is vitally significant, as eating functions as catalyst towards unravelling the relationship Diana holds to the memories of her father's Jordanian homeland.

A similar interpretation of food—and its value as a mnemonic and cultural medium in immigrant communities—can be identified in Abu-Jaber's fiction. The meaningful connection between recent immigration, food habits and memory is particularly dissected in *Crescent* (2003). In the novel, Sirine—a thirty-nine-year-old half-Iraqi, half-American chef—works at Nadia's Café, a culinary establishment which, while serving traditional Middle Eastern foods, also provides a site of social exchange for the Arabic community in Los Angeles (especially the vocally home-sick university students). The Iranian and Iraqi expatriates find solace in Sirine's authentic food, a reminder of their lives in the 'old country'. Throughout the novel, food memories and practices are used by Abu-Jaber not only to illustrate the culturally-specific immigrant attachment to recognisable 'home foods', but also to negotiate Sirine's conflicted relationship with her own identity and her relationship to the ways of the Iraqi community. Issues of cultural adaptation and assimilation are very prominent in *Crescent*; Abu-Jaber is keen to remind us, for instance, that many of the Middle Eastern immigrants have adapted their Arabic names into version which sound more 'American': 'His name is actually Sharq, which means *East*, but he has asked all his American friends to call him "Shark" instead. Sirine can't hear the difference in pronunciation, but he assured her there's a huge difference'.[83] In the process of building an 'American' identity, the Arabic community develops new names but is still keen to maintain its distinctive food culture and traditions.

Cooking foods from the 'old country' is portrayed, of course, a way to maintain ties with familiar ways of life. The attachment to familiar food memories and habits is especially evident in the immigrant who has only recently 'come over'. Solitude becomes an evident trait, as does the wish to eat Arab foods. Abu-Jaber writes:

> The loneliness of the Arab is a terrible thing; it is all-consuming. It is already present like a little shadow under the heart he lays his heart in his mother's lap; it threatens to swallow him whole when he leaves his own country. (21)

When immigrants 'leave home', Abu-Jaber adds, they 'fall in love' with their sadness' (143). A clear antidote to this sadness is represented by meeting with fellow Arabs and consuming favourite home foods, such as 'sfeehas—savoury pies stuffed with meat and spinach' (217), 'smoked frekkeh' and 'baba ghannuj' (220). The Arab students stress to Sirine that eating 'home foods' helps them with difficulty of being an immigrant, as they 'crave' the 'sort of friendship' which consists of 'days' of eating, 'coffee-drinking and talking' (22). One of the Arab students also explains to Sirine how 'painful it is to be an immigrant—even if it was what he'd wanted all his life—sometimes especially if it was what he'd wanted all his life' (22). Writing about 'home' and 'displacement', David Sutton explores the concept of *xenitia*: 'a condition of estrangement, absence, death or of loss of social relatedness [. . .] seen to characterise relations at home'.[84] This condition—experienced with particular intensity by migrants—incites a longing for 'home' in such a powerful way that it can manifest itself in physical and spiritual discomfort, accompanied by a general 'sense of disjunction'.[85] In *Crescent*, the Arab students' *xenitia* presents itself through their incessant desire to spend time with fellow immigrants and eat Middle Eastern foods.

This idea of solitude, paired with a desire for recognisable home foods, is also reiterated by Abu-Jaber in *The Language of Baklava*: 'They'll be hungry because everyone who "comesover" is hungry; for home, for family, for the old smells and touches and tastes'.[86] Immigrant 'hunger' is related to a general sense of anxiety associated with dislocation and the unfamiliar surroundings of a new country. In this context, the recreated smells and tastes of familiar cooking act both as a bond (with the old country) and a buffer (against the new). Arjun Appadurai has written about the role played by food in 'punctuating or periodising all our lives through repetitive "techniques of the body"'.[87] For the immigrant, the memory, recreation and consumption of familiar foods from the homeland offer precisely such a repetitive corporeal practice. In *Crescent*, familiar Arab foods offer precisely such a repetitive corporeal practice. Food preparation and consumption structures the rhythms of everyday life in a strange new environment by recreating those associated with the country of origin.[88]

The stability produced by culinary repetition (and the feeling of emotional relief that derives from it) is reinforced by memories and symbolic representations associated with food. The memory of home and homeland, of course, is intrinsically connected to the formation of a social self. Andreea Deciu Ritivoi argues that attachment to the concept of home 'require[s] a stock of memories that can be resuscitated over and over again'.[89] Abu-Jaber foregrounds the significance of food memories in this respect and also the way in which they are typically sugar-coated with nostalgia. This is evident in Han, the Iraqi professor exiled from his home country. Throughout his interactions with Sirine, Han cherishes memories of his childhood in Iraq:

> We had a well on our property. It was lined with big, crackling palm trees all around. All the Bedouin used to use it. I would stand in line with them holding two big metal pails and they would bring up the water using old-fashioned crank and spill the fresh water from the bucket into my pails. And I would drink a cup of the water as soon as it spilled out of the earth—it was so cold it could make my ears ring. And it tasted like—I don't know it was so good—it tasted like rocks and wind and pure . . . pure coldness. (69)

These romantic memories of family life keep Han connected to his past in Iraq and affect his current life in America but, Abu-Jaber insists, his memories are *highly* idealised: life in the 'old country' was not always 'pure' and jewelled with beautiful 'palm trees'. On several occasions, Han himself has to admit that living in Iraq was less than peaceful, as he talks about 'the Iraqi guard—the soldiers with automatic weapons, the crisp uniforms and slanted berets that he'd seen in the city streets, how he'd been afraid of them when he was a child' (82).

The nostalgic attachment to food memories and methods of preparation, however, finds its most distinctive incarnation in Sirine's relationship with her parents' old Iraqi recipes: 'Sirine learned about food from her parents. Even though her mother was American, her father always said that his wife thought about food like an Arab' (56). One must mention here, *en passant*, that it is perhaps necessary to surpass Abu-Jaber's subtle contention that Arabic foodways are more valuable than American ones and therefore should be adapted. In keeping with the power bestowed by novel upon immigrant culinary ways, the function played by food in Sirine's life (after her parents are in a fatal accident) is made explicit by Abu-Jaber: 'On the day she learned of their deaths, Sirine went into the kitchen and made an entire tray of stuffed grape leaves all by herself' (56). Detachment from her family—forced by death—causes Sirine to desire culinary experiences that are symbolic of her relationship with her parents. Natalie Davis and Randolph Starn remind us that memories can be a 'surrogate, or consolation for something that is missing'.[90] An object (or even a concept) to which memory is attached, therefore, becomes a symbolic replacement which occupies the space once occupied by a living person. In similar vein, Elizabeth Hallam and Jenny Hockey also propose that 'in the absence suggested by death' one can find objects that 'constitute systems of recall for persons [. . .] that have been threatened or traumatised by loss'.[91] In the case of Sirine's attachment to her childhood foods, the actual absence of her parents is filled by a culinary substitute. The same substitute is meant, in a circular fashion, to erase the lack created by death. The foods desired are not only a reminder, then, but an embodiment of life with Sirine's family.

When Sirine begins to work at Nadia's Café, her choice of dishes is hardly unexpected: she 'went through her parents' old recipes and began cooking the favourite—almost forgotten—dishes of her childhood. She felt as if she were returning to her parents' tiny kitchen and her earliest memories' (22). The fact that Sirine's favourite foods had been potentially 'forgotten' is of extreme importance. As a chef working in California, and having studied the art of French, Italian and 'American' cuisines, Sirine had been used to preparing what Abu-Jaber describes (somewhat cynically) as 'half-constructed salads with smoked mozzarella, capers, and sun-dried tomatoes' (92). It is implied here that Sirine had momentarily abandoned her Arabic culinary heritage in favour of Americanised cooking methods and, in turn, ways of living. Forgetting Arabic food might thus signify forgetting a whole system of rules of commensality, based on different ways of living and modes of consumption. In this context we may recall Nadia Seremetakis' suggestion that 'in the process of historical transformation, and cross cultural encounter, divergent sensory structures and commensalities can come into conflict with each other, and some are socially repressed, erased or exiled into [. . .] marginal experience'.[92] The foods of childhood begin to work for Sirine as an expression of an Iraqi material culture which she had exchanged for a different, American milieu.

Discussing immigrant food habits, Elisabeth Bronfen points out that in the nostalgic preparation of food all powers are focused on 'an idea, namely, the idealised concept of home and an obsessive notion of returning to this place'.[93] The relationship between Sirine and the foods she remembers from childhood is a particularly effective example of this dynamic. As she cooks Arabic foods which she remembers from childhood, her mind is also fixated on memories of cooking with her mother:

> Sirine's mother strained the salted yoghurt through cheesecloth to make creamy lebneh, stirred the onion and lentils together in a heavy iron pan to make mjeddrah [. . .] Sirine's earliest memory was sitting on a phone book on a kitchen chair, the sour-tart smell of pickled grape leaves in the air. (56)

The food remembered by Sirine functions as a medium which consolidates memories of the mother-daughter relationship. In Volume Two of *The Practice of Everyday Life*, Luce Giard reminds us that food and its preparation require 'a multiple memory: a memory of apprenticeship, of witnessed gestures and of consistencies'.[94] It is through this concept of 'apprenticeship' that the recipes encourage a system of experience and exchange. As Sirine begins to cook Arabic food, she displays a desire to feel close to her parents, symbolically embodied in food they used to cook and the recipes they have left behind. Beneath the desire to replicate this act, one can find a sense of nostalgia for Sirine's past. Ritivoi has observed that 'nostalgia occurs when the present seems deficient in contrast to the past but only if the past is somehow available in symbolic representations—images, objects, associations'.[95] The dishes cooked by Sirine function as a symbol of the past and as a catalyst to nostalgic recreation. Collective culinary memories are inevitably entangled with personal identity, so that the idea of separating the individual from the group is almost impossible. In *Crescent*, nostalgic culinary memories are part of an imagined group psychology and encourage the individual's sense of self. Sirine's food recollections here are fuelled by an underlying desire to return to the world of childhood and its associations with parental comfort.

The complex of emotions involved in the eating of Arabic foods, however, raises issues of reliability in relation to Sirine's interpretation of the food's qualities. As an adult, she declares the foods of her childhood to be 'perfect' (92), as she proceeds to replicate the effect in the dishes she prepares for the café. Seremetakis suggests consuming foods from one's childhood can evoke 'the sensory dimension of memory in exile and estrangement'.[96] Sirine's desire to consume 'home foods' presents itself as an evocative journey towards a historicised sensation. In this manner, painful feelings of culinary nostalgia are 'linked to the personal consequences of historicising sensory experience which is conceived as a [. . .] bodily and emotional journey'.[97] The appreciation of Arabic childhood food in *Crescent* is influenced by affective mechanisms and historical memory. As a result, food itself becomes a medium through which the sedimentations of the past remain alive in conjunction with the codified sensations of the present. James Fernandez points out that 'a domain of experience that is experienced as fragmented or deprived is re-valued by simply marking it for ritual participation'.[98] The cooking of childhood foods in *Crescent* is a secular ceremony, which symbolises the infusion of new (or, rather, old but forgotten) knowledge into Sirine's life. This concept appears to confirm Sutton's assertion that the desire accompanying culinary events can be satiated only 'through a sensory experience evoking local knowledge [and] at the same time [. . .] a domain of experience that has fallen into disuse'.[99]

Nonetheless, the distance between the actual historical past and its idealised evocation is underscored by Sirine's doubts regarding her Arab-American identity: the woman's nostalgic desire is quickly followed by a form of 'culinary pain', an inability to capture the past which manifests itself through her confused feelings about her own ethnicity. This element of doubt highlights the presence of two specific stages of food nostalgia. Svetlana Boym proposes an etymological interpretation of the word 'nostalgia' by dividing the term into two components, *nostos* (to return) and *algbia* (pain).[100] Following Boym's suggestion, nostalgia can be seen as producing two different stages, one 'restorative' and the other 'reflective'.[101] In *Crescent*, Sirine's decision to cook her parents' recipes is tacitly motivated by a need to remember happy times and thus constitutes a 'restorative' act. According to Boym, restorative nostalgia places emphasis on *nostos* and, in so doing, conveys a wish to 'rebuild the lost home and patch up the memory gaps'.[102] Sirine's memories of comforting childhood meals become the trigger for the restorative process—so that, in a rather circular manner, embellished memories generate more embellished memories.

However, this process of nostalgic restoration is interrupted by Sirine's Uncle who reminds her that it would be impossible to return to her childhood. The Uncle explains why he does not like talking about the past, which encompasses both the times spent in Iraq and the times in America when Sirine's parents were still alive: 'It means talking about the differences between then and now, and that's often a sad thing. And immigrants are always a bit sad right from the start anyway [. . .] but the big thing is that you can't go back'(143). Sirine's realisation that she cannot bring back her parents—or successfully return to Iraq as the daughter of an immigrant—generates uncertainty in her life and she begins to feel sad and confused, a condition she comes to share with her Uncle and the other Arab immigrants. At this juncture we shift from restorative to a reflective and essentially melancholic mode of nostalgia, producing *algbia*. Ritivoi remarks that 'reflective nostalgia zooms in on the difference between reality and simulacra, the original and the copy'.[103] Sirine's nostalgia for her parents, and an Iraqi homeland she has never known, highlights a demoralising acceptance which is proper to the immigrant in a foreign land. Nostalgia transforms itself from a need to restore to a painful, reflective meditation on what has been lost. Reflective nostalgia, as Ritivoi remarks, 'does not seek to return as much as it prefers to brood over the impossibility to return'.[104]

As issues of culinary recollection become prominent in *Crescent*, so do matters of cultural adaptation. In an attempt to show his interest in Sirine's American heritage, Han decides to cook her a romantic meal consisting of 'meatloaf dressed in sweet pools of ketchup', 'broccoli branches, mashed potatoes, spools of gravy' [and] 'sliced pillowy white bread' (77). Han shows a distinct excitement about his introduction to a different cuisine; the event, it is made obvious, is more than mere experimentation in the kitchen. Cooking 'American food' is interpreted here as a step towards assimilation into a new culture, an embodied way to find a common ground for interaction. The cooking of what is for Han 'foreign food' is described as 'a shift of ingredients like a move from a native tongue into a foreign language; butter instead of olive oil; potatoes instead of rice; beef instead of lamb' (77). Echoing Truong's representation of linguistic and culinary colonisation, Abu-Jaber interprets cooking American food as a transfer of expressive technique, an introduction to a different historicised commensal event which carries with it the ability to convey a whole cultural system. The encounter also has a significant tactile dimension:

> He [Han] slices off a sliver from the meat loaf in the pan and picks it up with his fingertips. He holds it to her lip. "Come on" he says. "*Min eedi*". *From my hand*. The thing intimate friends say to express the greatest of care. She [Serine] opens her mouth and remembers her father feeding her a bite of bread, *min eedi*, he said. And Han places the food in her mouth. (79)

When Han dispenses with cutlery, he displays how food can function as a historicised and culturally active substance, even in methods of consumption. In this framework, consuming the hand fed directly from one's hands places Han—and Sirine in turn—in a specific cultural system. That system exists within the history of a particular group.[105] Eating with one's hands is a return to the most primordial stages of historicised corporeality, when the act of eating was unmediated by cultural artefacts (such as cutlery). The meal cooked by Han is a mixture of new, Americanised cooking habits (embodied in the meatloaf) and his culinary memories as an Iraqi immigrant.

Roger Haden remarks that

> the culinary legacy of knowledge gained through the sense of taste has been one related to all practices, technologies and experiences that have affected taste [. . .] this represents our present-day archive of taste.[106]

In any archive of taste, favourite foods, along with their modes of preparation and consumption, are part of a network of socio-cultural influences that intersect on the body and help to shape subjectivity. In this context, Abu-Jaber's hand-fed meal—with its particular mixed-cultural nature and emotional attachment—is a testimony to how the sensorial aspect of commensality—particularly in the form of taste and touch—becomes a portal into cultural experience. The food becomes a historicised sensorial tool in itself which connects past and present through the embodied performance of eating. Nevertheless, it is important to point out that Abu-Jaber runs the risk here of over-romanticising the descriptions of the Arabic, hand-fed meal. The relationship between touch, historical memory and commensality is interpreted as characteristic to a culture that is detached from Americanised eating.[107] In this context, Susan Bordo argues that culture has a 'direct grip' on our bodily activities and it is through 'routine' and 'habitual activities' that social knowledge is generated.[108] For the migrant, food habits are not only a product of remembered knowledge, but also the consequence of acclimatisation.

KITCHEN NARRATIVES AND CULINARY CRYPTS

In examples from immigrant fiction, the importance of food memories is revealed in its being a medium for the integration of the domestic into a greater historical register. Blended with their cultural significance, food and drink have the ability to evoke a particular legacy of mnemonic experience. With its material connotations, food represents, as David Morgan puts it, 'an anchorage in the past, its strength deriving in part from the familial relationship in which the serving and preparing of the foods are located [. . .] Food serves as one of the links between historical time, individual time and household time'.[109] A similar claim seems to animate representations of food, memory, family and cooking methods in Leslie Pietrzyk's *Pears on a Willow Tree* (1998). The meaning of food in the novel is often connected to the presentation of the home—and the kitchen in particular.

The story focuses on four generations of Polish-American women—Rose, Helen, Ginger and Amy—and their personal journeys towards individuality and self-realisation. Pietrzyk employs food and cooking to connect the female members of the family in a manner that goes beyond mere biological relation. The process of culinary education is given particular attention; teaching how to make traditional Polish foods (and how recipes are passed on from one woman to the other) not only strengthens the bond between kinsfolk, but also valorises the domestic space in difficult times. Echoing an understanding of food which we previously encountered in Shange's work, the practice of cooking is amalgamated into a system which creates bonds transcending generations. Cooking methods are shown as a definitive way to unite granddaughters and grandmothers, past and present, the old and the new. This seems to validate Theophano's claim that the 'worldly relationship between kin [is] given permanence' in the recipe.[110] Pietrzyk is very sensitive to the fact that the kitchen is not simply a place where food is casually prepared, put together and consumed. That, to be sure, is the superficial role of the kitchen, a logistical presentation which Pietrzyk understands only as the surface of its anthropological function. It soon emerges from the text that the kitchen is a locus of exchange—psychological and material—which is particularly essential to the immigrant politics within the novel.

Within the circle of Marchewka women, Ginger is the exemplification of the rebellious, 'modern' daughter who has no time for her family's old-fashioned ways. She despises her close-knit family circle in Detroit and decides—to the shock of her mother, Helen—to move to Arizona, abandoning her family and the habitual ways with them. There is a suggestion in the novel that a sense of tradition is being lost within the Polish family. The attachment to particular foods is not as strong in rebellious Ginger as it is in the women from her family's previous generation. Living in Arizona, Ginger openly admits that she does not cook traditional Polish dishes and prefers to feed her children—Amy and Cal—simple and quick 'TV dinners'.[111]

It is suggested by Pietrzyk that culinary knowledge is being lost in the family and Ginger's disdain for traditional Polish cuisine and cooking methods is clearly an example of this. For Ginger's grandmother, Rose, the concept of cooking and the understanding of everyday life are inextricably linked. That link is not only representative of daily routines which facilitate endurance—one must eat to survive—but also signify the historical connection between her past in Poland and her life in America. Culinary knowledge, it would seem, is the thread which connects generations across oceans and times, marking a sense of purpose and belonging in the immigrant community. It is this desire to prioritise cooking as both a familiar and historical practice that moves Rose to teach Ginger how to make *pierogi*, a traditional dish of Polish dumplings. Rose learns with shock that Ginger 'had never learnt how to make *pierogi*' (20) and sees this as a clear lack of essential knowledge in her grand-daughter's life. The Grandmother is keen to teach Ginger the old ways of cooking, a way of showing patronage of culinary practices which has nothing to do with modernised systems which are seemingly associated with living in America. The competence that Rose displays with preparing food begins not only with the conceptualisation of the dish, but also develops into a real ability when it comes to dealing with raw materials. Grandmother Rose, one could argue, teaches cooking 'through the body'. Her teaching methods do not consist of long lists of ingredients or helpful suggestions; her movements and gestures compose the stock of knowledge that she wishes to communicate to the younger female members of the family. Culinary knowledge is presented as a repository of embodied memories. Rose perceives that ability to cook as an unmissable skill, a historical practice which is composed by a number of 'ancient' gestures.[112]

Ginger, on the other hand, is keen to modernise the process by infiltrating the use of modern technology into the practice of cooking. When discussing the amount of flour to be used in the making of *pierogi*, Ginger, enquires how many 'cups' (4) of the raw material she should put into the mixture. Rose quickly dismisses the use of modernised measuring systems such as 'cups' and claims that you should 'use your hands, to introduce yourself to the dough. Four handfuls, five, six' (4). A lot can be said of the way Rose responds to Ginger's technical suggestion. Firstly, one can recognise the value of the body in cooking practices; culinary knowledge is not mediated by external measuring systems, but is transmitted to both the food and the onlooker as part of an embodied involvement on the cook's part. This appears to confirm Luce Giard's assertion that homemade cooking allowed the cook to 'perfect her dexterity, and display her ingenuity'.[113] In *Pears on a Willow Tree*, cooking is offered as a personalised practice, leaving a lot of room of improvisation and highlighting the cook herself as an essential part of the culinary equation. Culinary knowledge is presented as intrinsically connected to past existence which, in this case, goes hand in hand with processes of migration and settlement in America. This side of culinary practices is revealed by Rose, as she shuns Americanised measurements and reminisces about cooking in Poland: 'We did not need measuring cups. We used our hands; we felt what we were doing instead of always thinking it' (4). The cooking lesson, it would seem, is nostalgically depicted as a performance and associated with the memory of all other cooking sessions that preceded it within the family, aligning with Steven Connor's idea that 'all everyday touch consumes when it touches; when we learn to grasp, we do it first of all in order to convey the objects to our mouths'[114].

It is also important to notice the recurrent use of the word 'we' when discussing cooking. Rose appears to be hinting at the fact that in the old, 'non-American' times, cooking was part of a communal systems which brought groups of people together—whether families, town or entire national groups—and allowed to find a common ground for affiliation and belonging. In this framework, measuring the flour with one's hands places Rose—and the whole of her family as a result—in a specific cultural system. That system exists within the history of a particular group. Individual and communal memory becomes interwoven with foodstuffs and culinary practices. When looking at Rose's dislike for measured technologies in favour of the immediacy of touch, we might recall Connor's assertion that the tactile 'informs [. . .] values, ideals and attitudes'.[115] When it comes to food, touch epitomises attitudes to social conduct, including rules about how the dishes should be prepared and consumed. In the cultural frame of the grandma's cooking lesson, the idea of touch—particularly with food—becomes associated with the idea of community. The tactile quality of Rose's cooking habits confirms Falk's idea that culinary memories involve 'at the same time the social history [and] the cultural history [. . .] of the body'.[116]

The most relevant element of Rose's response is that she claims to have 'felt' the flour in the old days, rather than measuring it. The old days, clearly, is just another expression for 'the old ways' and bears no chronological significance, since the grandmother is still applying the same methods in the present. The idea of 'feeling' the ingredients introduces a heightened embodied dimension to the practice of cooking. Sutton points out that traditional cooking requires the mobilisation of 'the resources of the body as well as of the mind'.[117] This process somehow entails that, as a cook, she is able to somehow construct a particular relationship with the foods, almost feeling the 'essence' of ingredients as much as the actual weight and consistence. This idea is stressed by the fact that Rose believes the cook's hands and the flour should be given' a good greeting' (5); it is impossible here to miss the possibility that the foods can actually 'speak' to the food. It is also implied here, of course, that Rose perceives the food almost as something that is alive and breathing, communicating information—in his case, the quantities to be used—and helpful culinary tips to the person doing the cooking. It is clear from Rose's remark that she understands cooking as a highly emotional and personal practice, which begins with the body and seeps thought to the mind, allowing the cook to establish an almost metaphysical connection with the culinary.

Rose continues her lesson by declaring that in the old days' cooks did not 'need' measurements and that they understood culinary practices in a different ways (5). It is suggested here—by the careful use of the past tense 'used to'—that the new generation, including Ginger, have somehow forgotten how to feel the food and require external technologies to allow them to cook. This appears to validate Sutton's claim that, in immigrant communities, practical knowledge finds ' necessary transmission' not 'thought a set of rules that could be abstracted and learned separate from practice', but through 'an embodied apprenticeship'.[118] Rose dismisses the use of precise measurements because she considers them a side effect of disembodied Americanisation; the 'cups' mediate between the body and the food and, therefore, remove the metaphysical connection that she believes must exist between the cook and the food. That connection, of course, goes beyond the simply practice of assembling dishes, but extends to a whole sense of purpose in the cook's life. The cups are not only representative of standardisation, but they are also symbolic of the loss of cultural connections to the practice of cooking.

There is a suggestion that 'the old ways'—implied here to preceded everything that is American and modernised—were to be preferred, because they allowed the human interaction within cooking to be the centre of attention and highlighted the importance of personal experience in the making of dishes. Seremetakis points out that, food 'is a temporal conduit' for culinary 'histories'.[119] Within the system of the Polish cooking lesson, cooking with one's hands testifies to a sense of community, witnesses the passing of time and authenticates the presence of individuals within a particular group. Sutton reminds us that the 'willingness to get one's hands dirty to mix one's substance with that of the food one is preparing, is a reflection of a dynamic social life'.[120] It is subtly implied that the sterile American ways—with their seemingly blank measuring systems and technological advances—fail to provide the embodied elements in food preparation. Grandma expresses a clear disdain for any kind of time-saving technique. As the *pierogi* cooking lesson begins, she warns Ginger not to 'all the time be looking for shortcuts' (2). Later she is surprised to learn that one can actually buy 'ready-made pierogi at Kroger—in the freezer case set' (4). Grandma's disgust is particularly aimed at Ginger, who seems to think ready-made food to be a suitable and 'easier' alternative (5), which allows time to be spent on 'other', more valuable activities than cooking. It is hinted by Pietryzk that proper food—at least as intended by Grandma Rose—should take a long time to prepare. This seems to be an important element of the way traditional cooking practices are performed within the Polish community within the book. Sutton notes that disdain for any 'time-saving device' and cooking technology can be found in many discussions of traditional cooking' with immigrant groups throughout America (132). Women, in particular, are noticeably 'suspicious' of any innovation or gadget which steers their cooking away from traditional ways (132).

It soon becomes clear that Rose's attachment to traditional, laborious ways of cooking is related to her memories of her culinary and social habits in Poland:

> When I think of those days when every meal was a struggle, when I woke with the rosters to build the fire, I do not remember wishing that food was a snap. I worked for every meal, I thanked God for every potato and every shred of cabbage. (5)

The memory of cooking—associated by Rose with a distant and clearly favoured familial past—manages to embody not only a sense of fulfilment for the individual, but also encapsulated the working philosophy of the Polish community, even in times of struggle. Kitchen labour—tacitly associated with the life of women—becomes honoured here as the exemplification of proper living, drawing attention to the social connections which transform a simple yet laborious activity into a clearly defined cultural practice.

Nonetheless, one must wonder here if Pietrzyk runs the risk of glamourising a difficult time—prior to the living modernisation of America—when women's daily life demanded a great input of physical labour. This nostalgic attachment to an idealised past seems to ignore the economic difficulties that would have forced women to 'struggle'—to use Pietrzyk's term—cook and constantly provide food for their families. Although this possibility cannot be ignored, a more positive alternative may be found. Pietrzyk, one could suggest, is attempting to find a familiar space 'amidst the frenetic over modernisation' of culinary life in America'.[121] The attention to old, Polish practices—as romanticised as they may be—aims to provide a cultural resistance to the 'conformism implicit in the replacement of all local culinary variations and techniques',[122] which defines the integration of the immigrant to the greater American scope.

In *Pears on a Willow Tree*, however, Grandma's disdain for American culinary technology does not stop at measuring systems. It is suggested here that Rose's dislike for Americanised cooking technologies is associated with a sense of social and emotional alienation brought upon the community by 'modern life'. The fact that Rose shuns the suggestions of using 'cups'—a symbol of modernised, American technology—testifies the understanding of careful culinary measurement as 'the height of antisociality'.[123] Simultaneously, the use of 'we'—necessarily contrasting a foreign sense of American 'you'—works as an alienating factor, providing a cultural and culinary divide between Rose, the Polish grandmother and Ginger, the Americanised granddaughter.

As she develops the connection between the senses—particularly touch—and the memory of the past, Pietrzyk also unveils the importance of firsthand culinary experience within a family. Grandma's culinary teaching is not based on carefully recorded recipes, but it is strictly reliant on a system of practice and oral transmission. Sutton defines this way of sharing preparation methods and recipes as a way of 'learning with the hands'.[124] Written language, it would seem, is interpreted by rose as a way of cutting corners, a desire for rules and regulations which paradoxically interrupts the immediacy of embodied practice. Susannah Hoffman suggests that while linguistic elements are not 'absent' in 'informal learning episodes, they tend to take the back seat to the combination of observation/participation'.[125] Although Hoffman draws attention to the importance of observation in cooking, the idea that oral exchanges are removed from traditional cooking experiences does not completely fulfil the idea of culinary inheritance put forward in *Pears on a Willow Tree*.

The linguistic element—or, to put it another way, the instructing element—is not completely removed from the cooking lesson, but is transformed into the life stories that accompany the culinary preparation: 'I held a duck in my hands, its heart pushing against my skin, and I knew my family would feast on its blood in *czarnina* soup [. . .] There would be moments I'd love that duck more than I could love any living creature' (6). Indeed, the cooking lesson is the ideal medium for Rose to share her experiences and vision of life with the younger female members of the family. It is possible to suggest that what is being taught in the *pierogi* session is not just a mere culinary skill. In the midst of the labour-intensive preparation of the dish, the traditional nature of the event—uniting generations of women into the kitchen—is able to recall memories of life in Poland, economic struggle and the move to America: 'This is what I did for my family, made their food with my hands. This is who I am, this is what I have—back then in the old country, when I first came to America and still now, today' (6). The oral transmission of cooking skills—together with the particular brand of embodied knowledge of 'doing with your hands'—represents the ideal chance, as Sutton puts it, for 'the older woman in the group to reflect on the good and the bad of the past and to pass on their vision to younger women'. What is being passes on to Ginger is not simply the method for preparing a Polish dish, but the history of a whole migrant family associated with it. Occupying a privileged presence in everyday life—a taste of absolute necessity—food carries with it a whole philosophy of life, testifying to the existence of a whole group of people. In this way, culinary apprenticeship becomes a medium 'for transmission in the broader sense of a woman's culture, history and everyday experience'. One can see here how Pietrzyk develops on the idea of linking culinary apprenticeship to immigrant sensibilities which is also evident through Sirine in Abu-Jaber's *Crescent*. In *Pears on a Willow Tree*, the teaching of culinary preparation could be seen as a way to include Ginger into a whole symbolic system, where traditional Polish cooking cease to be an abstract concept and finally reveals itself as the established locus for 'passing personal and collective histories'.[126]

As Grandma educates Ginger on how to assemble *pierogi*, her instructions are imprecise and leave a lot to interpretation: 'Add some dabs of sour cream, two, three, whatever you have' (7). Belonging to a broadly defined oral culture, Rose's 'traditional' recipe for *pierogi* is not a clear science; instead, it reveals itself to be a mouldable concept, open to variation. Jack Goody reminds us that that, 'since there is no fixed text from which to correct', culinary transmission in oral cultures is often a process of flexibility and innovation.[127] In encouraging personal variation, Rose entrusts upon Ginger not only the knowledge to prepare *pierogi* in the general sense, but also of the ability to shape and 'improve' the Polish dish as she wishes. *Pierogi*, in this case, becomes the exemplary embodiment of her own personal heritage. And it is precisely that heritage that is seen as the true gift, the connection of apprenticeship to an older member of the family by which 'the process of cooking is learned'.[128]

In spite of her laudable efforts to include the culinary everyday into the greater historical register, one thing must be said about Pietrzyk's treatment of food: in her desire to stress the matrilineal connections within the family and its embodied relation to not only the culinary, but the whole system of the everyday, she seems to forget the men in the story. Fathers and brothers appear rarely and, even then, their role is secondary to the lives of the women. Men seem to hover in the background, marginal figures whose only purpose seems to be to supply a frame for the female infrastructure to work. Some may want to argue that men's secondary position in *Pears on a Willow Tree* is a clear result of Pietrzyk's focus on kitchen life; as the kitchen has traditionally been (at least in the West) a domain reserved for women, it would seem natural, if not obvious, to concentrate on the lives of women. And yet, as the life stories of the women interlace with not only the culinary, but also with a whole philosophy of spirit and survival, one is left wondering if Pietrzyk is not too deliberately favouring the female condition over the male one. This is a radical way of feminising kitchen politics which Pietrzyk shares with Shange. Again, the argument could be that 'female stories' need to be told because, historically, they have been forgotten; part of this could have been due to their involvement with food, which kept them relegated to the domestic sphere as part of gender distinctions. So, in a way, Pietrzyk is showing an ironic sensibility in placing the focus on women's lives through the preparation of food, the very medium which may have played a part in their social segregation for centuries. The novel's approach to the female connection with the culinary and the domestic takes on an existentialist nuance, elevating the female experience in the face of struggle. While the praise for *Pears* and its use of culinary history is unchallenged, it would have been encouraging to see Pietrzyk making an effort to include the male sphere as well. As it is, the novel uses food to offer women an oddly privileged, almost metaphysical position into family life, constructing paradoxical stereotypes which link food to knowledge, wisdom and collective prevalence.

In the midst of Pietrzyk's construction of a distinctly female line of history, Ginger's reaction to her grandmother's dislike for modernised cooking methods is simply revelatory. She actually writes the recipe down, a practice disliked by her grandmother who claims recipe writing to be unnecessary and almost disrespectful. According to Rose, in fact, cooking skills cannot be written down or annotated and the only way for one to learn is to 'just watch' when 'everything is front of you' (2). In addition, Ginger decides to ignore Rose's lesson about measuring 'with your hands' and writes '4C flour' in 'her notebook' (2), trying to compose an adequate recipe for the traditional *pierogi*. She understands cooking as a careful, elaborate practice, reliant on accurate measurements and rules; everything is annotated with precision, from 'what was in the filling' to 'how much farmer's cheese, how much onion' (7). In order to add to the detail of the recipe, Ginger even sketches a' picture of the crimping pattern' (7). The use of the 'cookbook language' here is important on several levels. On the one hand, it could represent Ginger's inability—as suspected by her grandmother—to establish an embodied connection with the food, testifying to her inherent and forgetful modernisation. 'Past cooking techniques [. . .] involve a taken-for-granted materiality and physicality of everyday life that has been eroded by 'modernity'.[129] On the other hand, Ginger's deliberate use of modernised measurements could be seen as an act of rebellion against her family's old-fashioned, Polish ways.

In order to grasp this concept, we need to look at Ginger's overall approach to not only her grandmother's cooking, but her family's ways as well. Firstly, Ginger refuses to follow Rose's advice by turning 'her face' to 'the window' (2) when she is supposed to be watching the practice. Secondly—and perhaps most significantly—Ginger argues against Rose's slightly fatalistic approach to food, life and death in Poland. As Rose declares that 'in the old days' (4), it was a matter of 'living or dying' (4), Ginger responds with a positive yet challenging remark: 'Things are different for us . . . we have choices' (4). In this light, Ginger's dislikes of embodied measuring—in favour of cookbook language—could be viewed as a reaction towards the old ways, a way to move forward and embrace—in a metaphorical way—the conceptual freedom of choice which has established America as 'the land of freedom' in the wider imaginary. Stephen Steinberg argues that the 'loss of tradition' is a necessary part of becoming the modern Americans that the young family members in immigrant communities 'aspire to be'.[130] As Ginger modernises the cooking methods for *pierogi*, she also makes a written mark towards Americanising herself.

Ginger's Americanisation is not a solitary example in *Pears on a Willow Tree*. Nonetheless, it is through the retrieval of lost tradition and the culinary experiences of Amy (Ginger's daughter) that Pietrzyk offers a hopeful resolution to the struggle encountered by generations of 'new Americans' in the novel. Amy finds a fused stability between Polish and U.S. identities that her mother was incapable of. In a manner reminiscent of Jing-mei's embrace of the alimentary reality of China in order to 'become Chinese', Amy assimilates the culinary habits of Poland as part of her discovery of a new individual identity, a new sense of existence that fuses the old and the new in order to find an 'American' dimension. After Ginger's death, Amy finds herself in her mother's house, entrusted with her belongings. As she is left alone in her mother's empty house, she feels a deep desire to bake that she can also give in to. As Amy goes through her mother's kitchen cupboard, she finds a number of gadgets and ingredients which are the epitome of modernised living, including 'a cappuccino machine, a bread machine, a pasta maker' (255). Amy is aware that the attachment to these easy-living machines—producing such foodstuffs as 'squid ink fettuccine' (255)—was possibly part of her mother's desire to rebel against her family's traditional culinary ways. The gadgets' rebellious function is emphasised by Amy's envisioning of her grandmother Helen's scorn as she observes the fettuccine, wondering 'who would think' of that sort of 'nonsense' (255).

The presence of the food-making machines in Ginger's kitchen reinforces Amy's perception of her mother as detached from the traditional Polish foodways, rejecting the heritage and she refused to cook the food.

However, Amy's understanding of her mother's personality is challenged when she discovers, hidden in the back of a kitchen cupboard, a 'knotted produce bag' containing a 'lifetime's supply of poppy seeds' (256). The poppy seeds, we are told, are the staple ingredient for making *strucla*, a traditional cake which was consumed on a daily basis at grandma Helen's house in Detroit: 'It was what they ate with their coffee, my grandmother and her sisters sitting around the table in the kitchen' (258). The sight of the poppy seeds brings back memories of Detroit for Amy, placing food at the centre of family life:

> I never much like the cake, just as I never liked the coffee either, but I always asked for some anyway, just so I could hear my grandmother say, "This one knows good Polish food; remember how it was Ma's favourite?" (258)

Asking for the cake, although she admits to disliking it, signifies Amy's desire not only to obtain her grandmother's approval—something that only communicates a first level of conscious understanding—but also a subconscious desire to be accepted into the cultural group and come part of the ethnic system to which the family belongs. This attachment to a hidden sense of Polish identity is rendered by grandmother Helen's invocation of her own mother's presence when the cake is mentioned; the cake itself comes to signify the cultural belonging of the family, its Polish core, and brings it with it the memories of people who passed away, leaving their heritage behind. Amy's mother Ginger, on the other hand, openly rejected the poppy seed cake: 'My mother wouldn't eat the poppy seed cake [. . .] she'd take a piece but pick at it, either thinking no one noticed or not caring that they all noticed' (258).

Ginger's treatment of the cake reveals her resistance to the Polish heritage enclosed within it. Pietrzyk makes a very careful use of language here, which communicates cultural insolence: when she does not out rightly refuse to consume the food, Ginger is seen as 'picking at the cake', as if dissecting the Polish cultural system embodied in its emblematic dish. This seemingly small detail is rather revelatory, as Ginger almost ritually breaks apart the foundations of her Polish heritage. This split in signification—and difficulty of acceptance—is mirrored in Ginger's difficult relationship with her mother, as the two often clash over the importance of upholding Polish traditions and culinary ways. It is also significant that Ginger does not care about her family being aware of her constant dissection and resistance to their Polish heritage, emphasises her defiance for their traditional ways.

Although the memories of the poppy seed cake seem to re-establish Amy's ideas about her mother's approach to Polish culture, the presence of the poppy seeds themselves in Ginger's kitchen casts an aura of doubt of the woman's actual relationship with her heritage. After re-acquainting herself with the poppy seeds, Amy is overtaken by an overwhelming desire to make a poppy seed cake for herself. Panicked by the knowledge that she cannot remember how to prepare the *strucla*, Amy turns telephonically to her grandmother Helen, who slowly recounts the recipe for the cake. Remembering the recipe for the Polish poppy seed cake does not simply mean retrieving an otherwise erased culinary memory, but also signifies a yearning for social and cultural integration. For Amy, this process denotes an engagement with sensorial stimuli and levels of self-expression. Cooking, it would seem, is presented as 'not a set of rules, but images [and] experiences, techniques that can only be partially articulated through the medium of written recipes'.[131] The anxious need to remember mirrors Amy's desire for a stable subjectivity which is grounded in the cultural assimilation which hangs in the balance of on 'being Polish- American'. Her desire to retrieve her family's culinary memories can thus be understood as part of a progressive system of self-evaluation which is rooted in consumption and commensality. Helen's *strucla* recipe highlights a process of remembrance that is tied to specific elements, sensations and acquired instructions. The memories of time spent together in the kitchen return to Amy through the writing of the recipe. The usually confrontational relationship between Helen and Ginger would dissipate on the neutral ground of the kitchen, as Ginger became involved in the cooking of the cake: 'I saw my grandmother watching at the door, smiling [. . .] I'd heard them laughing [. . .] it was my mother making the cake' (263).

The distinctive significance of the poppy seeds—drawing together generations of Polish-American women within the family—emerges as Amy finally attempts to make a cake for herself, following her grandma Helen's instructions. Being affected by Alzheimer, Helen is unable to recognise her own granddaughter and the poppy seed cake recipe becomes the bridging elements between the two women. Helen claims to have learnt how to make *strucla* from her mother, following the traditional practice of 'learning with the hands' and observing the cook at work: 'I listened to her; I watched what she did' (259). It soon becomes clear that, within the Polish American family, the cake formed a symbolic connection between female members. Helen reinforces the cake's evocative power by recalling her own methods of braiding the *strucla* four-ways, a technique which she had previously learnt from her own mother. The most important element about the four-way braiding, however, is actually revealed by Amy with a special sense of emotional attachment:

> You told us how Great-Grandma used to make the four [. . .] and she called it the four-girl cake. And you said 'Here's Amy and here's Ginger, and here's me and here's Ma', and I was part of the four-girl cake'. (262)

The cake itself becomes the connective thread between the four women; four generations of Polish Americans who become symbolically connected thought the idiom of food, the symbolic matter which creates their ethnic nucleus.

As Helen recalls the methods used by her mother to make the cake, she also transmits careful instruction to Amy: 'A piece of soft butter as big as one finger folded over [. . .] Two eggs out of the icebox half an hour before you start; all you need is the yolks [. . .] Are you listening?' (259). The almost imperative question of 'are you listening' implies that what is being transmitted is not simply a list of culinary instruction, but also a social lesson about family connections, as Amy and grandmother become connected thought shared apprenticeship. Indeed, it is through listening to her grandmother's culinary recollections of baking with her family that Amy is able to recall her own memories of making the cake, when grandmother Helen actually 'showed' her how to make to 'make the braid' and put 'the poppy seeds on top' (261). It is made clear that Amy had actually forgotten how to make the cake at all—or even being involved in its preparation at any moment in time. She is only able to suddenly contextualise the event though listening to Helen's culinary recollections: 'How could I know that was what would push through [. . .] making *strucla* that one summer?'(262).

Amy's initial confession that she had forgotten about making *strucla* makes it possible to interpret its re-emergence from memory in relation to the concept of 'historical stillness'. According to Seremetakis, 'stillness is the moment when the buried, the discarded and the forgotten escape to the social surface of awareness'.[132] What had previously lapsed into oblivion suddenly becomes longed for and unbearably missed; this condition is clearly visible through Amy's desire of baking the cake, even if what she is missing is time with the deceased members of her family, rather than the cake itself. Seremetakis proposes that through culinary preparation 'the experience that embodies [. . .] emotional engagement and remembrance' is 'released, liberated at moments of stillness'.[133] Emerging from a moment of mnemonic stillness, the Polish *strucla* crystallises a system of culturally prescribed regulations, which survive only through emotional engagement. Amy's experience of 'recovered' culinary memory seems to validate Seremetakis' claim that the socio-cultural belonging 'can be effaced' by consumption and the remembrance of previous eating habits 'reanimates' specific cultural rules.[134] The conventions that dictated kitchen life in the Polish American household—including timing, ingredients and methods of preparation—are re-introduced into Amy's everyday life through the memory of a particular foodstuff which embodies them.

However, Amy does not simply 'listen' to the cooking instructions, she specifically records them and gives them permanence as she writes 'fast on the memo board', turning her grandmother's 'words into abbreviations to figure out later' (259). It is particularly interesting here how Pietrzyk uses the expression 'figure out', almost implying that recipe writing—especially between members of the same family—requires a level of decryption and almost translation. Once Amy has decoded the recipes, she is able to use them. The careful interaction between memory and recipe writing here recalls Sutton's idea that in cooking specific techniques can only be 'articulated, or memory-jogged, through the medium of written recipes'.[135] Although Sutton's contention cannot be taken to be universal—indeed, it becomes rather ineffective in instances of oral transmission, when recipes are not written down at all—it does add an extra dimension to Pietrzyk's text, showing how memory and writing (tradition and modernisation) can be utilised together in order to decipher not only culinary instructions, but also the impact of family connections on everyday activities such as food preparation.

It soon becomes obvious that as Pietrzyk exposes Amy's simultaneous s struggle and desire to unravel the recipe for *strucla*, she also unveils the daughter's hermeneutic excavation into her mother's past. Acting as the surrogate of Ginger, the *strucla*'s existence as an autobiographical document that ushers in the possibility of secrets and revelations, contradictions and concealment. As Amy begins to prepare the poppy seed cake, she does 'exactly' (263) what her grandma had said, she follows the instruction carefully, to the point of taking breaks when Helen had told her to do so. Amy re-enacts the recipe carefully, paying attention to the 'yolks whipped with salt' and 'butter' the size of her finger (263). However, once the time comes to twist the dough and create the four-way braid, she finds it an impossible task; her grandmother's instructions—which obeyed the traditional Polish method—make no sense to her: 'Right away I could see that one strand wasn't incorporated properly and was only draped over the others [. . .] I was crying, it just didn't seem possible' (264). It is important to note here how the unincorporated strands might be seen to be Ginger, the rebellious daughter who never accepted herself as part of her Polish American family. Amy's inability to prepare the braided cake becomes even more depressing for Amy as she remembers that 'women' in her family 'had been braiding bread for centuries' (265). The knowledge of letting down not only her grandma, but her entire Polish heritage is what spurs Amy to eventually attempt one last braiding of the *strucla*, which she rolls 'into four pieces' and loops 'together' (265). An amount of improvisation is involved to ensure that the poppy seed cake looks as 'traditional' as Amy can remember it. This act confirms Sutton's contention that in traditional cooking 'knowledge and procedures' are 'brought together through a combination of planning and improvisation'.[136] Indeed, the sense of tradition which emanates from the cake is only established through a mixture of grandmother's instructions and Amy's unconscious modernisation, merged together to create a product which is the fruit of both sensorial attachment and 'retrospective assessment'.[137] As the *strucla* is ready to go into the oven, Amy is satisfied with her creation and recognises its social value when she admits it is 'something you could serve to women around a kitchen table' (265).

The cake recipe in *Pears on a Willow Tree* establishes itself as a bonding element and a portal through which an exchange ensues between grandmother, mother and daughter. The etymological origin of the word 'recipe' might offer a further insight into the nature of the exchange. The word 'recipe' finds its root in the Latin word *reciperere*, meaning simultaneously 'to give and to receive'.¹³⁸ Recipes not only bear witness to the rituals, patterns and behaviour on which her life is based but, most importantly, position themselves in a process of exchange between members of the family. The evocative power of the poppy seed cake is revealed as resurrecting force as the Amy removes it from the oven. As its smells pervades the kitchen, its function completely ceases to be that of a simple biological need—food for the body—but is transformed into a resurrecting medium for the family, who also materialise in Amy's present: 'I sat at the table and ate big pieces of my warm cake, and it was almost as if they were all there with me—I honestly think I smelled the coffee, though I hadn't made any' (266).

It becomes clear that Helen's recipe for *strucla* conceals an inheritance which goes beyond material possessions. Ginger, the deceased mother, 'returns' through the cake recipe and that return, in Jodey Castricano's words, 'acts as inheritance'. Eventually, the mother's phantom and the recipes become 'inseparable'.¹³⁹ Inheritance is always passed on through a process of haunting which must be accepted in order to understand and decode the writing: 'whenever a text calls to us, we are being asked to confirm an inheritance and to respond to an injunction'.¹⁴⁰ The *strucla* recipe comes to signify an engagement with the family's 'ghosts' or, more specifically, their 'spectral signature'¹⁴¹: an intertextual relationship between Amy's present and her past can be identified, as Esther Rashkin claims, 'in narratives organised by phantoms'.¹⁴²

The mourning 'crypt' has recently proven to be fertile territory for psychoanalytic and poststructuralist theory. In their gothic revision of classical psychoanalysis, Nicolas Abraham and Maria Torok write about the trauma of loss in relation to psychic crypts. In mourning the loved one, the subject can slip into melancholia by erecting an 'inner crypt' in which the dead object can be hidden or 'devoured' perversely as a way of denying its demise. Introjection is seen as the 'normal' process through which the ego accepts the death of a loved one and slowly removes its memory from consciousness.¹⁴³ However, when this process of detachment encounters resistance a 'crypt' might be formed. In terms of psychological topography, the crypt is haunted by the memory of the dead which, paradoxically, inhabits the crypt as a 'living-dead'. In his introduction to Abraham and Torok's *The Wolf-Man's Magic Word*, Jacques Derrida argues that the crypt houses 'the ghost that comes haunting out the Unconscious of the other'.¹⁴⁴

The *strucla* recipe in *Pears on a Willow Tree* might therefore be read as a reincarnation of memory. Abraham and Torok point out that 'reconstituted from the memories of words, scenes and affects, the objective correlative of loss is buried alive in the crypt'.¹⁴⁵ The memory of both recipe and events enables Ginger to return within the writing itself; the food preparation represents a passageway through which the living-dead can return. Within the recipe, Ginger inhabits a culinary crypt. It is through her associations with food that she remains, in Derrida's words, a presence which Amy is 'perfectly willing to keep alive, but as dead [. . .] intact in any way as living'.[146] In this way, eating—seemingly the most vital and animated of activities—is disturbingly blended (in imagistic terms) with death, decomposition and the corpse. Food of course provides bodily nourishment, but the *strucla* recipe continues to feed the dead. As parental haunting is encapsulated on the page, the transcribed instructions function as a culinary crypt even after Ginger's death, as the recipe allows Amy to 'cook with ghosts'. The recipe's ghostly quality recalls Rashkin's claim that once a crypt is created, the phantom can return, 'peregrinate in several directions and inhabit [. . .] family members'.[147]

While Amy engages with her grandmother's recipe, Ginger's memory is celebrated in the act of reading, de-coding and recreating the recipes. As part of system of embodied recollection, the poppy seed cake recipe is the catalyst through which the memory of the Polish American family can be passed to the last descendant to carry on. The replication of the recipe, by Amy, is the tangible expression of this. As Derrida has argued, once one interprets a text written by another, that text 'comes back' and 'lives on'.[148] While it combines acts of self-representation with the haunting of personal and collective memory, the poppy seed cake recipe renders a culinary illustration of the past. Acting as a personal manuscript, the recipe contains a gastro-cultural knowledge which, in Theophano's words, 'transcends generations'.[149] As an anecdote of emotions and experience, the *strucla* recipe encapsulates acts of remembrance, temporal malleability and historical continuation. It is through the homely cooking instructions and its transcriptions of a particular cuisine that the voices of those who linger outside the margins of written history are given durability. The transient nature of cultural belonging is given a material appearance through the idiom of food; the homely recipe, in this way, becomes the tangible expression of domestic history.

In making the poppy seed cake, it would seem, Amy achieves more than simply correctly assembling baked goods. Not only does she remember and honour the memory of her family members who have passed on, but she also reconciliates her condition as the descendant of an immigrant family. Her poppy seed cake is the culmination of a mergence between the old and the new; she listens to her grandmother's instructions—learning with her hands—but records them in writing. As she does so, she deciphers the recipe and makes it her own, changing the preparation according to her ability and preference. Through this act, she comes to terms not only with her Polish heritage, but finds a place for her own—'American'—personality to exist. The day after preparing the cake, Amy takes a slice of it to her mother's grave. There she presents it to Ginger almost as a rituals offering: 'Four-girl cake just like Grandma's [. . .] I've got the recipe now [. . .] We know you had in you, Mom, in your veins. Just like it's in mine' (267). In showing Amy's knowledge and ownership of the *strucla* recipe, Pietrzyk suggests that the daughter also finds a way for her mother's existentialist struggle to end, solving the conflict between the traditional and the modern. Through her own 'traditionally new' poppy seed cake, Amy is able to address the delicate balance between collective and individual that Ginger was unable to discover. We can see here how Pietrzyk highlights the most coveted condition of the hyphenated American: the ability to merge the old and the new without encountering a cultural clash and the capacity to remember the memories who those who came before without losing one's sense of independence.

Although they all explore how food is perceived within immigrant contexts, it has clearly emerged in this chapter that ethnically conflicting texts offer different—even discordant—interpretations of the subject. Within any particular community, people, location, culinary artefacts and, especially, food, identify a culinary event as such. Rules concerning how to eat, what to eat and when to eat are of course the essential ingredients in defining what 'a meal' actually is. Examining the interpretation of food and cuisine in a particular cultural community offers us a way into understanding the roots of habits, beliefs and prohibitions in culinary customs. Both Truong and Tan unveil how the concept of 'tradition' can be understood as a dynamic notion which is not necessarily tied to a list of ingredients, but embodies the desire for cultural identification within a familiar community. Simultaneously, however, it emerges from the texts that the forceful notion of tradition within immigrant communities runs the risk of turning culinary practices into fabricated products. When it becomes a socio-cultural construction, culinary tradition relies prominently on the imagined vision of a particular social community rather than factual evidence.

Through different representations of culinary recollection, it also becomes apparent that the concept of 'food memory' is not straightforward. Food memories, as such, involve a variety of historicised experiences that touch on elements such as nostalgia and cultural knowledge. Taste and smell, therefore, emerge as acculturated senses; as a result, the authenticity of food memories is called into question and they become a malleable product that can be constructed and exploited. Memory is viewed as an essential part of cultural affiliation and in that framework food becomes a medium through which attachment to a particular geographical area becomes possible. However, Abu-Jaber unveils the possibility that culinary memories can be romanticised—as a result of nostalgic attachment to childhood food—and become an expression of coveted cultural belonging. A similar understanding of food, community and memory is evident in *Pears on a Willow Tree*. The memory of culinary practices, as Carolyn Korsmeyer puts it, surfaces as 'subjective but measurable, relative to culture and individual and yet shared'; culinary memories are revealed as 'transient experiences freighted by the weight of history'.[150] Although still subscribing to Abu-Jaber's romanticised sense of immigrant food practices and conflicted visions of the immigrant self, Pietrzyk uses food in order to offer a hopeful identity resolution for the hyphenated American. Culinary experience emerges as both influenced by and influencing memory. Cultural history, immigrant consciousness and individual experience are successfully synthesised through the discourse of food.[151]

Conclusion

> So it is that the narrative ... is displaced ... onto the themes of consumption, which is calculated to estrange or defamilarise our habitual perceptions and to shock us into some fresh awareness ... of our own rich commodity system ... the subliminal images of food and eating are everywhere.
> —Fredric Jameson, *Archaeologies of the Future*[1]

This study has attempted to explore a variety of culinary contexts. Perspectives on food in contemporary American fiction have emerged as bound up, explicitly or implicitly, with modes of political economy and forms of communal and national organisation. Attitudes towards food, cooking and eating have been positioned here within larger patterns of individual and cultural behaviour. Confirming that eating 'occupies an unrivalled centrality' in human lives, the texts studied have underlined the importance of food when thinking about such conceptual fields as the body, subjectivity, memory, gender, sexuality, class structures, race, ethnicity, culture and national identity.[2] A close inspection of American texts has thus confirmed and elaborated the sense of food's polysemy with which I began my discussion in the Introduction. Nonetheless, in conclusion, it is necessary to isolate several especially significant topics for review. It is also important to reflect upon some general questions raised by studies of food in literature.

Food in American fiction has emerged as inextricably linked to communication. Contemporary authors from different races and ethnicities show a desire to recover food as a communicative tool that actively constructs a path into cultural customs, pleasures and anxieties. Eating, as Fieldhouse maintains, sums up 'the attitudes, beliefs and customs and taboos affecting' the life 'of a given group'.[3] Operating as a system of communication, however, food necessarily conveys *multiple* meanings and its polysemy raises questions. In the preceding analyses, different attitudes towards, and interpretations of food have certainly been evident. From text to text, culinary significances have been shown to shift dramatically and to be contingent on very different socio-cultural contexts. Food, it would seem, can become the symbolic carrier of diverse, even opposing ideological values.

Issues of dominance have often been shown by my readings to lie at the heart of culinary practice: we have seen a considerable synchronicity between social power and control over the production, consumption and symbolic usage of food. The idea that the consumption of food itself is mediated by socio-cultural, political and economic forces has emerged as a principal concern in several, if not all, texts considered here. In Robinson's *Home*, for instance, food functions as a socially-charged signifier for in-home politics, as the preparation of beef (and its subsequent consumption) moulds into a representation of hegemonic definitions of gender. In *American Psycho*, on the other hand, we have seen how the impact of commercial economies in the yuppie era shapes patterns of consumption, as eating itself establishes a sense of personal superiority in both public and private spaces. In the novel, Ellis forms a narrative thread between horror fantasies of power and the medium of food, as an endless succession of extravagant restaurant dinner are offered an imagistic connection with slaughter, murder and even cannibalism. Ellis employs the figure of the appearance-obsessed, capitalist cannibal in order to satirise political discourses that aim to control consumers and ultimately deprive them of agency. In Flagg's fiction, however, we see yet another face of the cannibal. Flagg's interpretation is not concerned with industrial subordination so much as with racial power relations. Mobilising ethnic stereotypes connected to cannibalism, *Fried Green Tomatoes at the Whistle Stop Cafe* registers the social, political and economic exploitation of African Americans. Through the trope of cannibalism, this text unveils a relationship of interdependency between food, embodied experience and the structures of social power and political economy.

The body, it has become clear, occupies a privileged position to any representation of food in its relations to power. Nonetheless, the ways in which the consuming body interacts with hierarchical systems are multiple. Food articulates the corporeal side of existence—the body that turns food into nourishment—with distinct formations of race, class and gender. Examples of fiction have also allowed us to uncover how discourses of food and the body also extend into spiritual, ethnic and national domains. In widely differing contexts, dietary laws have been shown to operate as a means of construction of cultural hierarchies. In *The Book of Salt*, Truong connects eating to manifestations of national and racial affiliation. The text expresses the fear of racial colonisation by means of food. Eating is thereby seen to transmit ethnocentric beliefs of superiority. Expanding the idea that consumption is often bound up in struggles for socio-cultural authority, Pietrzyk similarly explores how corporeal responses to food—expressed as 'likes' and 'dislikes'—are overwritten by representational systems. In *Pears on a Willow Tree* as in other texts studied here, food preferences are shown to be the outcome of repetitive cultural practices imposed on the body.

Just as food consumption articulates the body with political cultural, and economic powers, it is also exposed as crucial to the idea of community. Given that culinary practices impose behavioural rules, the control of food intake appears in this literature as a way to regulate collective life. The concept of community, however, is a multifaceted one. Some of the contemporary writers discussed—notably Abu-Jaber, Pietrzyk, Tan and Truong—choose to highlight the importance of food rituals in the life of immigrant communities. As attachment to familiar food habits emerges as a trait in the immigrant's life, eating is portrayed as one of the most powerful expressions of cultural affiliation. Description of shared meals becomes, therefore, an ideal medium for the authors' exploration of immigrant sensibility. Food in these texts contributes decisively to what Bell and Valentine call 'defensive uses of community'.[4] Feelings surrounding food and eating evoke wider perspectives on the difficulty of integration and acceptance in a foreign country. All of these accounts of collective eating are conceptually aligned by Bell and Valentine's claim regarding the central 'role that food plays [in people's idea] of "home"'.[5]

Whilst a sense of 'food community' connects renditions of consumption in most of the examples I have examined, the culinary geographies mapped by the texts have been rich and varied. If Wells, Truong and Tan do not succumb easily to idealised descriptions of 'local' food—it is indeed hard to forget Jing-mei's disappointing first encounter with 'real' Chinese cuisine in *The Joy Luck Club*—Flagg, Pietrzyk and Abu-Jaber, by contrast, seem overly concerned with idealising familiar foods in the communities they describe. In *Crescent*, Abu-Jaber views food as a healing power for homesickness in the Arabic community. Abu-Jaber also makes this claim regarding Middle Eastern food in *The Language of Baklava*, where she describes Jordanian dishes as embodying the 'mysteries of time, loss, and grief', while 'real American' cuisine is almost always 'gummy', 'burnt' and 'flat'.[6] This idea of therapeutic consumption is also encouraged in *Fried Green Tomatoes*, where Flagg romanticises Southern food to the extent that it is able to help introverted housewife Evelyn from feeling 'old and fat and worthless' (233). In similar vein, Pietrzyk believes Polish food to have a certain degree of memory and elevates it beyond the almost 'heartless' commonality of simple, ready-made American products. In *Pears on a Willow Tree*, the contrast between the two culinary communities is pushed so far as to render Pietrzyk's claims of Polish culinary superiority unbelievable and even problematical. In her text, as in some others studied here, attributing exaggerated healing or redemptive abilities to food detracts from the rigour of culinary representation. At the same time, nostalgic, overly lyrical descriptions of food run the risk of overlaying important affirmations of communal identity with unrealistic claims of local culinary pride.

Indeed, the primary texts I have studied are very different in their diagnostic power with regard to the politics of local food communities. In particular, the texts are not equally sensitive to how food may articulate relations of cultural resistance within a community. *The Book of Salt*, for instance, *does* show an awareness of how local food regulations may express authority and ethnocentrism. The hegemonic community in this colonial setting consumes foods that are deemed appropriate only for the 'superior' race and class: Truong's privileged French minority, in Joanne Ikeda's words, is 'committed to sustaining' their narrow sense of national identity and is therefore reluctant to change its food 'beliefs and practices'.[7]

Consuming—or not consuming—the same foods creates a bond between members of the community, validating Fieldhouse's assertion that 'individuals who observe [...] food rules make a public demonstration of belonging to a group' and 'every day provide themselves with a private affirmation' of that belonging'.[8] Such 'belonging' necessarily also implies exclusion. Tan, as well as Truong, makes it clear that breaking the culinary rules of a particular group carries possible penalties of being distrusted, socially alienated, even ostracised. For these two authors, therefore, local culinary regimes are disclosed as often synonymous with social differentiation and stratification.

Other contemporary American texts, however, do not always offer such a lucid and sensitive critique of food and power within social communities. For instance, in *World of Pies* Stolz begins by registering effectively how dietary preferences are inspired by systems of social control and are inevitably connected to a particular sense of national identity and local affiliation. Yet, if the novel pushes the reader into understanding the 'American' value of certain consumable—such as hamburgers and ice cream—it is uncritical about its own modes of regional nostalgia, which feed into cycles of commodity consumption and capitalistic accumulation. In similar vein, an analysis of cooking in Flagg's novel revealed some textual insensitivity to racial division and ethnocentricity within a romantically portrayed food community. As cooking duties divide racial factions within the town in *Fried Green Tomatoes at the Whistle Stop Cafe*, so too segregation is marked in the *consumption* of particular foods. A reading of this text 'against the grain' shows how similar foodstuffs are actually consumed differently by various ethnic groupings. The meanings of food in *Fried Green Tomatoes* are therefore diverse, with foods continuously marked by enduring racial differences, tensions and traumas (including African American slavery). More broadly, my work across the thesis has sought to contest any notion of an ideologically homogenous and 'neutral' food community.

My literary discussions have also shown the foregrounding of memory in these mappings of culinary systems. Although it may seem mundane to claim that memory is the source of all culinary information, we have seen in fact that the idea of 'food memory' is powerfully charged and can be interpreted in various ways. In *World of Pies*, for instance, the memories of American war and conflict haunt the descriptions of everyday eating and specific brand consumption in late twentieth-century Texas. Memory and recipes have particularly emerged as a particular narrative coordinate in African American texts. While questions of immigration and regionality emerge as comparable issues in a number of other ethnic American literatures, the trauma of slavery still provides a singular context for African American writing. The remembrance of food connects to social, cultural and historical contexts. For Shange and Naylor, the preparation and consumption of 'soul food' makes a powerful statement towards providing a solid sense of worth and emancipation for African American communities.

Although the sense of memory which emerges from the two writers is distinctly different, the two do share a desire to recollect the suffering of ancestors and employ food as a historical coordinate to connect to the past. Echoing Shange and Naylor's treatment of memory as an important factor in the shaping of everyday activities, Tan also offers an outlook on immigrant culinary culture that is based on recollections. In *The Joy Luck Club*, memory functions implicitly to create an idea of traditional Chinese cuisine. The representation of memory in Tan's text seems to validate Fieldhouse's claim that food maintains 'continuity' by a set of 'culture-specific' protocols, which include 'characteristic flavourings and preparation methods'.[9]

As contemporary American fiction engages with representation of local dishes, tastes and people, the concept regionality becomes entangled with issues of memory and recollection. The region, however, comes into view as multi-faceted concept. In *Fried Green Tomatoes,* food generates memories of past times in Alabama that are characterised by both affection—sustaining emotional attachments among people—and trauma. Wells' conception of regional food in *Divine Secrets*, on the other hand, places a greater emphasis on taste and experience, linking the experience of food to previous culinary knowledge which is, in turn, connected to an idealised vision of people, communities and geographical locations. Appreciation and craving of regional foods do not simply rely on an autonomous model of senses, but that taste itself is dramatically influenced by memory. Overall, my readings of the primary texts have highlighted the *variability* of food memories: culinary recollections can be both traumatic and benignly nostalgic, both progressive and reactionary.

Throughout this study, I have endeavoured to contribute towards the necessary integration of the culinary 'everyday' into literary scholarship. With its familiar routines, frequently domestic settings, and convivial atmosphere, eating is liable to join other everyday activities mapped in texts that are often overlooked and taken for granted within contemporary Western society. This is unfortunate, and I want to conclude by arguing more generally that literary criticism should be alert to the significance of food in all the materials it studies. Sensitivity to literary representations of food preparation and consumption will, for example, extend our analysis of gender politics. It has been implicit within this study that women tend to write about food in literary texts more than men do. The reasons for female authors' interest in food may appear obvious—given cooking's traditional associations with women—but are in reality complex and ambiguous. Sally Cline, for example, argues that in a patriarchal society, 'women control food' in literature 'because they cannot control their lives' more broadly.[10] Sceats develops this claim by suggesting that the turn of female writers towards a concern with food is animated by a change in social patterns of work and consumption: as 'women's roles as cooks and carers [. . .] are threatened', they channel a desire to shape and influence lives into the genre of food writing.[11] Feminist interest in the motivations underlying women's production—and consumption—of food fiction will be of use to analysis of gendering more broadly in contemporary American society.

Literary food studies seem urgent for a second reason, too. The emphasis on transnational culinary assimilation in many of the examples I have analysed allows authors to voice general anxieties about globalised geographies of consumption. In *Pears on Willow Tree*, the arousal of Americanised consumer appetites is signalled by the seemingly unappetising 'frozen *pierogi*' and tv dinners. In Abu-Jaber's novel, American cooking is accused of just 'dumping salt into the pot' (221) and fails miserably in comparison to the taste of 'perfect' Middle Eastern baklava, stuffed squashes and grape leaves. In *Divine Secrets of the Ya-Ya Sisterhood*, Wells expresses a desire to maintain examples from French Creole cuisine, such as *boudin* and crayfish *étouffée*, alive in the face of a commercial threat from more broadly Americanised (and distinctly un-regional) dishes. For Tan, 'creamed corn' and 'peanut butter sandwiches' (153) are deeply unsatisfying when compared to traditional Chinese cuisine, like 'wonton soup' and 'sweet barbecued pork' (31). One cannot fail to spot a clear resistance in contemporary food fiction to globalised food preferences. Maintaining a sense of the 'traditional' in food writing is often intended to expel political and economic forces that threaten to destroy regional identities. At the cost sometimes of nostalgia and a dubious ethnic 'purity', the commodification of the culinary is resisted through a celebration of dishes which, as my readings have shown, aim to preserve a sense of cultural distinctiveness. In contemporary American fiction, one can perceive a kind of mission to 'save' culinary traditions from globalisation.

As issues of culinary homogeny become prominent, one must also bear in mind the capitalist forces in contemporary American society feeding over-consumption and what Fredric Jameson fittingly calls 'commodity bulimia'.[12] My discussion has inevitably drawn attention to the dangers of contemporary food literature succumbing to a questionable, but highly marketable nostalgia. It is important to consider the extent to which culinary melancholia can be transformed into a saleable feature of food literature as a genre. I here suggest that some examples of contemporary American fiction might, on occasions, be bracketed with other technologies of 'gastro-porn'—what I like to refer to as 'the foodie phenomenon'—bringing food representations and gratifications to the reader.[13] In providing the reader with 'consumable' descriptions of ethnic, regional and traditional dishes, some of the texts I considered in this book similarly make culinary experiences and histories attractive to the would-be purchaser. This idea is reinforced by the presence of specific recipes and cooking instructions which are left as an enticing accompaniment at the end of the narrative, like in the case of *Fried Green Tomatoes* and *Crescent*; these texts do not shy away from strengthening the commercial value of the food novel, whetting the reader's cultural appetite and transforming fiction into a fully purchasable recipe book. Evidence such as this exposes how food fiction itself forms, in

Bell and Valentine's words, an 'inherent part of consumer culture'.[14] Contemporary literary studies, therefore, must maintain a critical awareness of the manners of ethnocentricity, nostalgia and commodity fetishism that often underline representations of food in American fiction.

Nonetheless, I do not intend to conclude with a pessimistic assessment of culinary politics in contemporary writing. Sensitivity to the diversities of food consumption, preparation and traditions in contemporary American fiction now offers an unmissable opportunity to identify forms of political resistance within an era of globalised economies. The critical interest in 'the fiction of food' lies precisely in its ability to adapt to shifting cultural and ethnic contexts and its refusal to be tied to a single discursive or representational form. Attention to how American writers represent food in fiction allows us to expose and to critique 'the tacit assumptions and unspoken rules' that govern everyday experience 'within the social order'.[15]

Notes

NOTES TO THE INTRODUCTION

1. Marjorie DeVault, *Feeding the Family: The Social Organization of Caring as Gendered Work* (Chicago and London: University of Chicago Press, 1991), p. 35.
2. Wendy Leeds-Hurwitz, *Semiotics and Communication: Signs, Codes, Cultures* (Hillsdale: Erlbaum, 1993), p. 90.
3. The list of works within the field of 'food studies' is long. Other notable examples of the past fifteen years include: Geoff Tansey and Tony Worsley, *The Food System* (London: Earthscan, 1995); Alan Beardsworth and Teresa Keil, *Sociology on the Menu: An Invitation to the Study of Food and Society* (London: Routledge, 1996); Margaret Visser, *The Rituals of Dinner: The Origins, Evolutions, Eccentricities and the Meaning of Table Manners* (London: Penguin, 1996); Helen Macbeth, *Food Preferences and Taste: Continuity and Change* (Oxford: Berghahn, 1997); Carole Counihan, *The Anthropology of Food and Body: Gender, Meaning and Power* (London: Routledge, 1999); J.L. Flandrin, *Food: A Culinary History from Antiquity to the Present* (Irvington: Columbia University Press, 1999); Mark Conner and Christopher Armitage, *The Social Psychology of Food* (Maidenhead: Open University Press, 2002); Eric Schlosser, *Fast Food Nation: What the All-American Meal is Doing to the World* (London: Penguin, 2002); Tim Lang and Michael Heasman, *Food Wars: The Battle for Mouths, Minds and Markets* (London: Earthscan, 2003); Bob Ashley, Joanne Hollows, Steve Jones and Ben Taylor, *Food and Cultural Studies* (London: Routledge, 2004); Alexandra Woods Logue, *The Psychology of Eating and Drinking* (London: Routledge, 2004); James Watson and Melissa Caldwell, eds., *The Cultural Politics of Food and Eating: A Reader* (London: Wiley Blackwell, 2004); E.N. Anderson, *Everyone Eats: Understanding Food and Culture* (New York: New York University Press, 2005); Massimo Montanari, *Food is Culture* (Irvington: Columbia University Press, 2006); Joan Thirsk, *Food in Early Modern England: Phases, Fads, Fashions* (London: Hambledon Continuum, 2007); Marion Nestle, *Food Politics: How the Food Industry Influences Nutrition and Health* (Berkeley: University of California Press, 2007); Erik Millstones, *The Atlas of Food: Who Eats What, Where and Why* (London: Earthscan, 2008); Carolyn Steel, *Hungry City: How Food Shapes Our Lives* (London: Chatto & Windus, 2008); Michael Pollan, *In Defence of Food: The Myth of Nutrition and the Pleasures of Eating* (London: Allen Lane, 2008).
4. It is still essential to remember the importance of the 'genetic melting pot', whose existence was vehemently denied by the neo-ethnicity movement of the Seventies. Theodore P. Wright points out that, for many ethnic groups

in America, marrying outside their ethnic circle is now an accepted practice. Wright, however, also reminds us that this genetic intermixing only applies (on a general scale) not only to particular ethnic groups (Jews, for example), but is also a distinct phenomenon of the growing and established city. Equally, a desire to maintain a certain ethnic 'distinction' can still be identified among other groups in America, such as Hindus and Muslims. See 'The Identity and Changing Status of Former Elite Minorities: Contrasting Cases of North Indian Muslims and American WASPs' in *Rethinking Ethnicity*, ed. by Eric P. Kauffmann (London and New York: Routledge, 2004), p. 34.
5. Tamar Jacoby, 'Defining Assimilation for the 21st Century' in *Reinventing the Melting Pot*, ed. by Tamar Jacoby (New York: Basic, 2004), p. 5.
6. Ibid.
7. Significant examples of studies in food and literature include: David Bevan, ed., *Literary Gastronomy* (Amsterdam: Rodolphi, 1988); Mary Anne Schofield, ed., *Cooking by the Book: Food in Literature and Culture* (Madison: Popular Press, 1989); Gian-Paolo Biasin, *The Flavors of Modernity: Food and the Novel* (Princeton: Princeton University Press, 1993); Maud Ellmann, *The Hunger Artists: Starving, Writing and Imprisonment* (London: Virago, 1993); Gail Turley Houston, *Consuming Fictions: Gender, Class and Hunger in Dickens's Novels* (Carbondale: Southern Illinois Press, 1994); Anna Shapiro, *A Feast of Words: For Lovers of Food and Fiction* (New York: Norton, 1996); Emily Gowers, *The Loaded Table: Representations of Food in Roman Literature* (New York: Oxford University Press, 1997); Susannah Skubal, *Word of Mouth: Food and Fiction After Freud* (London: Routledge, 2002); Robert Appelbaum, *Aguecheek's Beef, Belch's Hiccup, and Other Gastronomic Interjections: Literature, Culture, and Food Among the Early Moderns* (Chicago: University of Chicago Press, 2006); Carolyn Daniels, *Voracious Children: Who Eats Whom in Children's Literature* (New York: Routledge, 2006); Joan Fitzpatrick, *Food and Shakespeare* (Aldershot: Ashgate, 2007); Tomoko Aoyama, *Reading Food in Modern Japanese Literature* (Honolulu: University of Hawaii Press, 2008); Sarah Keeling and Scott Pollard, eds., *Critical Approaches to Food in Children's Literature* (New York: Routledge, 2008); Maggie Lane, *Jane Austen and Food* (Hambledon: London, 2007); Nathaniel McDonald, *Not Bread Alone: The Uses of Food in the Old Testament* (Oxford: Open University Press, 2008).
8. There are of course journal articles and anthologised essays that discuss food in recent and contemporary literature. These include: Cecil Beach, 'A Table: The Power of Food in French Women's Theatre', *Theatre Research International*, 23 (1998), 233–41; Minrose Gwin, 'Mentioning the Tamales: Food and Drink in Katherine Anne Porter's *Flowering Judas and Other Stories*', *Mississippi Quarterly*, 38 (1984–85), 44–57; Pi-Li Hsiao, 'Food Imagery in Amy Tan's *The Joy Luck Club* and The *Kitchen God's Wife*', *Journal of Humanities and Social Sciences*, 1 (2000), 205–227.
9. Lynn Marie Houston, 'Hunger' in *The Toni Morrison Encyclopaedia*, ed. by Elizabeth Ann Beaulieu (Westport: Greenwood, 2003), p. 165.
10. Doris Witt, 'From Fiction to Foodways: Working at the Intersections of African American Literary and Cultural Studies' in *African American Foodways: Explorations of History and Culture*, ed. by Anne L. Bower (Urbana: University of Illinois Press, 2009), p. 117.
11. Ibid.
12. Robert Lee, *Multicultural American Literature* (Edinburgh: Edinburgh University Press, 2003), p. 1.
13. Ibid., p. 2.

14. Ibid.
15. Terry Eagleton, 'Edible Écriture' in *Consuming Passions: Food in the Age of Anxiety*, ed. by Sian Griffiths and Jennifer Wallace (Manchester: Manchester University Press, 1998), p. 207.
16. Sarah Sceats, *Food, Consumption and the Body in Contemporary Women's Fiction* (Cambridge: Cambridge University Press, 2004), p. 126.
17. Elizabeth Grosz, *Volatile Bodies: Toward a Corporeal Feminism* (Bloomington: Indiana University Press, 1994), p. 87.
18. Maurice Merleau-Ponty, *Phenomenology of Perception* (London: Routledge, 2005), p. 216.
19. Ibid, p. 57.
20. Maurice Merleau-Ponty, *The Visible and the Invisible* (Evanston: Northwestern University Press, 1968), p. 133.
21. Eric Matthews, *The Philosophy of Merleau-Ponty* (Chesham: Acumen, 2002), p. 49.
22. See Carolyn Korsmeyer, *Making Sense of Taste: Food and Philosophy* (Ithaca: Cornell University Press, 2002), p. 21.
23. Robert Jütte, *A History of the Senses: From Antiquity to Cyberspace* (Cambridge: Polity, 2004), p. 61.
24. Dabney Townsend and Carolyn Korsmeyer, 'Taste: Modern and Recent History', in *Encyclopaedia of Aesthetics*, Volume IV, ed. by Michaela Kelly (Oxford: Oxford University Press, 1998), p. 361.
25. Merleau-Ponty, *Phenomenology of Perception*, p. 26.
26. Grosz, *Volatile Bodies*, p. 91.
27. Merleau-Ponty, *Phenomenology of Perception*, p. xiv.
28. Sigmund Freud, 'The Ego and the Id', in *The Pelican Freud*, Vol. 11 (Harmondsworth: Penguin, 1984), p. 365.
29. Ibid.
30. Sigmund Freud, *Three Essays on Sexuality* (New York: Basic Books, 1961), p. 88.
31. Sigmund Freud, *Civilisation and its Discontents* (New York: Norton, 1961), p. 15.
32. Julia Kristeva, *Revolution in Poetic Language* (New York: Columbia University Press, 1984), p. 26.
33. Grosz, *Volatile Bodies*, p. 92.
34. DeVault, *Feeding the Family*, p. 118.
35. Ibid. See also Piatti-Farnell, 'The Delicious Side of the Story' in *The Richard and Judy Book Club Reader*, ed. Helen Cousins and Jenni Ramone (Aldershot: Ashgate, 2011).
36. Stephen Mennell, Anne Murcott and Annake van Otterloo, *The Sociology of Food* (London: Sage, 1993), p. 96.
37. Nickie Charles and Melanie Kerr, *Women, Food and Families* (Manchester: Manchester University Press, 1988), p. 46.
38. Carol Adams, *The Sexual Politics of Meat: A Feminist-Vegetarian Critical Theory*, (Cambridge: Polity, 1990), p. 25.
39. Jack Goody, *Cooking, Cuisine and Class: A Study in Comparative Sociology* (Cambridge: Cambridge University Press, 1982), p. 71.
40. Adams, *The Sexual Politics of Meat*, p. 33.
41. See Sigmund Freud, *Totem and Taboo* (London: Routledge, 1991).
42. Paul Atkinson, 'Eating Virtue', in *The Sociology of Food and Eating: Essays on the Sociological Significance of Food*, ed. by Anne Murcott (Aldershot: Gower, 1983), p. 11.
43. Claude Lévi-Strauss, 'The Culinary Triangle', in *Food and Culture: A Reader*, ed. by Carole Counihan and Penny Van Esterik (London: Routledge, 1997),

p. 29; see also Lévi-Strauss, *Introduction to a Science of Mythology/The Raw and The Cooked* (London: Cape, 1970).
44. Lévi-Strauss, 'The Culinary Triangle', p. 28.
45. Ibid., p. 29.
46. Ibid.
47. Ibid.
48. Deborah Lupton, *Food, the Body and the Self* (London: Sage, 1996), p. 25.
49. Nick Fiddes, *Meat: A Natural Symbol* (London: Routledge, 1991), p. 33.
50. Although, of course, the concepts of 'diet' and 'health' have become instrumental in shaping eating habits in Western societies during the last decade.
51. What interests Barthes is the possibility of applying a methodology derived from Saussurean linguistics to the domain of culture defined in its broadest and most inclusive sense.
52. Roland Barthes, 'Toward a Psychology of Contemporary Food Consumption' in *Food and Culture: A Reader*, p. 23.
53. Lupton, *Food, the Body and the Self*, p. 9.
54. Ibid., p. 94.
55. Ibid., p. 95.
56. Pierre Bourdieu, *Distinction: A Social Critique of the Judgement of Taste* (London: Routledge & Kegan Paul, 1984), p. 190.
57. Ibid.
58. Sydney Mintz, *Tasting Food, Tasting Freedom: Excursions into Eating, Culture, and the Past* (Boston: Beacon Press, 1996), p. 7.
59. Alan Warde, *Consumption, Food and Taste: Culinary Antinomies and Commodity Culture* (London: Sage, 1997), p. 62.
60. See Piatti-Farnell, 'The Delicious Side of the Story' in *The Richard and Judy Book Club Reader*, ed. Helen Cousins and Jenni Ramone (Aldershot: Ashgate, 2011).
61. Warde, *Consumption, Food and Taste*, p. 64.
62. Ibid., p. 64.
63. See Piatti-Farnell, 'The Delicious Side of the Story'.
64. Lupton, *Food, the Body and the Self*, p. 22.
65. Mary Douglas and Baron Isherwood, *The World of Goods* (London: Routledge, 1996), pp. 51 and 66.
66. Jean Baudrillard, *Selected Writings* (Cambridge: Polity, 1988), p. 24.
67. Martyn J. Lee, *Consumer Culture Reborn: The Cultural Politics of Consumption* (London: Routledge, 1993), p. 23.
68. Grant McCracken, *Culture and Consumption: New Approaches to the Symbolic Character of Consumer Goods and Activities* (Bloomington: Indiana University Press, 1991), p. 85.
69. Ibid.
70. Lupton, *Food, the Body and the Self*, p. 22.
71. Ibid., p. 23.
72. Michel de Certeau, 'The Practice of Everyday Life' in *Cultural Theory and Popular Culture: A Reader*, ed. by John Storey (New York: Harvester Wheatsheaf, 1994), pp. 474–75.
73. Ibid., p. 475.
74. Ibid., p. 480.
75. Lupton, *Food, the Body and the Self*, p. 98.
76. Ibid.
77. Ibid.
78. Joanne Finkelstein, *Dining Out* (Cambridge: Polity, 1989), p. 130.
79. Ibid.
80. Lupton, *Food, the Body and the Self*, p. 99.

81. Ibid., p.1.

NOTES TO CHAPTER 1

1. Tom Wolfe, *The Bonfire of the Vanities* (1987; London: Vintage; 2010), p. 556.
2. Bob Ashley, Joanne Hollows, Steve Jones and Ben Taylor, *Food and Cultural Studies* (London: Routledge, 2004), p. 124.
3. Marilynne Robinson, *Home* (2008; London: Virago, 2010), p. 164. Additional page numbers are given in the text in parentheses.
4. Julia Twigg, 'Vegetarianism and the Meaning of Meat' in *The Sociology of Food and Eating: Essays on the Sociological Significance of Food*, ed. by Anne Murcott (Aldershot: Gower, 1983), pp. 21–22.
5. Nicki Charles and Marion Kerr, *Women, Food and Families* (Manchester: Manchester University Press, 1988), pp. 19 and 1.7
6. Brett Silverstein, *Cost of Competence: Why Inequality Causes Depression, Eating Disorders and Illness in Women* (New York: Oxford University Press, 1995), p. 85.
7. Ibid.
8. Peter Blos, *The Adolescent Personality: A Study of Individual Behaviour* (New York: Appleton-Century, 1941), p. 57.
9. Marjorie DeVault, *Feeding the Family The Social Organization of Caring as Gendered Work* (Chicago and London: University of Chicago Press, 1991), p. 118.
10. Karen Stolz, *World of Pies* (New York: Hyperion, 2000), p. 6. Additional page numbers are given in the text in parentheses.
11. David Bell and Gill Valentine, *Consuming Geographies: We Are Where We Eat* (London: Routledge, 1997), pp. 63 and 64.
12. Ibid., p. 73.
13. Ibid.
14. DeVault, *Feeding the Family*, p. 17.
15. Ibid., p. 17.
16. Bob Ashley, *Food and Cultural Studies*, p. 124.
17. Rosalind Coward, *Female Desire* (London: Paladin, 1984), p. 103.
18. Ashley, *Food and Cultural Studies*, p. 124.
19. Nickie Charles and Mariobn Kerr, *Women, Food and Families* (Manchester: Manchester University Press, 1988), p. 18.
20. Ashley, *Food and Cultural Studies*, p. 128.
21. DeVault, *Feeding the Family*, p. 118.
22. Bell and Valentine, *Consuming Geographies*, p. 65.
23. Barbara Sewell, *The Lost Art of Pie Making Made Easy* (Asheville: Native Ground, 2004), p. 4.
24. Janet Clarkson, *Pie: A Global History* (London: Reaktion, 2009), p. 25.
25. Ibid., pp. 91 and 92.
26. Sewell, *The Lost Art of Pie*, p. 4. It is really no surprise that Sewell's already overly nostalgic vision of femininity and pie-baking proceeds to spurn and antagonise the achievements of female emancipation, an act which denies any desire to escape gender-defined kitchen politics: 'Then along came the 1960s and 70s. Stampedes of liberated housewives traded in their aprons and rolling pins for psychedelic coloured muu-muus and jobs outside the home. And what did these women leave in their wake?'(p. 4).
27. Anne Funderburg, *Chocolate, Strawberry and Vanilla: A History of American Ice Cream* (Madison: Bowling Green State University Press, 1995), p. 141.
28. Ibid.

29. Alan Davidson, *Oxford Companion to Food* (Oxford University Press: Oxford, 1999), pp. 392—393.
30. Funderburg, *Chocolate, Strawberry and Vanilla*, p. 2.
31. Davidson, *Oxford Companion to Food*, p. 393.
32. Funderburg, *Chocolate, Strawberry and Vanilla*, p. 2.
33. Ibid., p. 161.
34. Harry A. Ploski and James Williams, *The Negro Almanac: A Reference Work on the African American* Gale Research: Detroit, 1989), p. 1077.
35. Wayne Hopkins, 'Social Worker Cites Contributions of Negro to Philadelphia's Progress' in *The Philadelphia Tribune*, June 2, 1932; p. 9.
36. Lester A. Walton, 'Philly Citizen Was First Maker of Ice Cream', in *The Pittsburgh Courier*, May 19, 1928; p. 12.
37. Fundenburg, *Chocolate, Strawberry and Vanilla*, p. 161.
38. Ibid., p. 142.
39. Ibid., pp. 142 and 161.
40. Josh Ozerzsky, *Hamburger: A History* (New Haven: Yale University Press, 2008), p. 2.
41. Ibid., pp. 3 and 1.
42. Ibid., p. 1.
43. Ibid., p. 2.
44. Mark Pendergrast, *For God, Country and Coca-Cola* (New York: Basic Books, 2000), p. 9.
45. Ibid., p. 7.
46. Ibid., pp. 8 and 9.
47. Constance Hays, *The Real Thing: Truth and Power at the Coca-Cola Company* (New York: Random House, 2004), x.
48. Ibid., p. ix.
49. Ibid., p. x.
50. Pendergrast, *For God, Country and Coca-Cola*, 9.
51. Hays, *The Real Thing*, p. ix.
52. Ibid., xi.
53. Ibid., xi.
54. See Howard L. Applegate, *Coca-Cola: A History in Photographs, 1930–1969* (Hudson: Iconografix, 1996).
55. Colin Campbell, *The Romantic Ethic and the Spirit of Modern Consumerism* (Oxford: Basil Blackwell, 1987), p. 92.
56. Consumer society was developing concomitantly with an interest in Freudian theory, which became a principal device in marketing strategies. Advertising campaigns were saturated with symbols and configurations which were intended to affect daily acts of consumption. These included bright colours and shapes which were designed to influence contemporary ideals of behaviour and social value.
57. Vance Packard, *The Hidden Persuaders* (Harmondsworth: Penguin, 1960), p. 11.
58. Many of these 'technological' inventions were inspired by military science from the Second World War. Looking for ways to transport and preserve large quantities of food more efficiently—shipping and flying it in bulk to different theatres of operation—the American government funded the development of advanced freezing techniques. After the war was over, the surplus of frozen goods was placed in the domestic market.
59. David Potter, *People of Plenty: Economic Abundance and the American Character* (Chicago: University of Chicago Press, 1954), p. 188.
60. Sylvia Plath, *Letters Home: Correspondence 1950–1963* (London: Faber and Faber,1975), p. 433.

61. Brett Easton Ellis, *American Psycho* (Basingstoke: Picador, 1991), p. 11. Additional page numbers are given in the text in parentheses.
62. Deborah Lupton, *Food, The Body and the Self* (London: Sage, 1996), p. 47.
63. Frank Arthur, 'For a Sociology of the Body: An Analytical Review' in *The Body: Social Process and Cultural Theory*, ed. by Mike Featherstone, Mike Hepworth and Bryan Turner (London: Sage, 1991), p. 63.
64. Roland Barthes, 'Ornamental Cookery' in *Mythologies* (London: Grant & Cutler, 1994), p. 78.
65. Ibid., p. 79.
66. Bell and Valentine, *Consuming Geographies*, p. 31.
67. E.N. Todhunter, 'Food Habits, Food Faddism and Nutrition' in *Food, Nutrition and Health: World Review of Nutrition and Dietetics*, 16, ed. by M. Rechcigl (Basel: Karger, 1973), p. 301.
68. Lupton, *Food, The Body and the Self*, p. 98
69. Peter Saunders, 'The Meaning of "Home" in Contemporary English Culture', *Housing Studies* 4 (1989): 184.
70. Bell and Valentine, *Consuming Geographies*, p. 125.
71. Ibid., p. 125.
72. Alan Beardsworth and Teresea Keil, 'Putting Menu on the Agenda', *Sociology* 24 (1990): 143.
73. Ibid., 143.
74. In *Discipline and Punish: The Birth of the Prison* (London: Penguin, 1991), Michel Foucault discusses shifting punishment regimes in which prisoners were to be most effectively controlled by constant *visibility*—in contrast to previous restraint methods, such as dungeons, that preferred prisoner *invisibility*. In this system, each imprisoned individual is kept under the constant gaze of guards and wardens.
75. Foucault, *Discipline and Punish*, p. 27. Foucault, of course, discusses panopticism in relation to the prison. However, his references to other locations in which panoptic control can be employed—such as school and hospitals—make it possible to extend the idea model of panoptic surveillance to a commercial context.
76. Ibid., p. 205.
77. Indeed, Foucault stresses how in contemporary society, surveillance is a central mechanism of social control. Towards the end of the twentieth century, particularly, panoptic control of the market extended to the idea of closely observing customers and orchestrating their purchase preferences.
78. David Lyon, *Surveillance Society: Monitoring Everyday Life* (Maidenhead: Open University Press, 2001), p. 64.
79. Bell and Valentine, *Consuming Geographies*, p. 30.
80. Ibid., p. 124.
81. Wolfe, *The Bonfire of the Vanities*, p. 590.
82. Carol Adams, *The Sexual Politics of Meat* (Cambridge: Polity, 1990), p. 48.
83. Ibid., p. 40.
84. Roger Haden, 'Taste in an Age of Convenience: From Frozen Food to Meals in The Matrix' in *The Taste Culture Reader: Experiencing Food and Drink*, ed. by Carolyn Korsmeyer (Oxford: Berg, 2005), p. 344.
85. Jean Baudrillard, 'The Pseudo-event and Neo-reality' in *Revenge of the Crystal: Selected Writings on the Modern Object and its Destiny, 1968–1983* (Sydney: Pluto Press/Power Institute of Fine Arts, 1990), p. 92.
86. Guy Debord, *Society of Spectacle* (New York: Zone Books, 1994), p. 12.
87. Ibid., p. 44.
88. Haden, 'Taste in an Age of Convenience', p. 351.
89. Lewis Hyde, *The Gift: Imagination and the Erotic Life of Property* (New York: Vintage, 1983), p.10

90. Rowan Jacobsen, *Chocolate Unwrapped: The Surprising Health Benefits of America's Favourite Passion* (Montpelier: Invisible Cities Press, 2003), p. 9.
91. Ibid.
92. Ibid., p. 13.
93. Crystal Bartolovich, 'Consumerism or The Cultural Logic of Late Cannibalism' in *Cannibalism and the Colonial World*, ed. by Francis Barker, Peter Hulme and Margaret Iversen (Cambridge: Cambridge University Press, 1998), p. 210.
94. Ashley, *Food and Cultural Studies*, p. 124.
95. June Crawford, *Emotion and Gender: Constructing Meaning from Memory* (London: Sage, 1992), p. 126.
96. Alan Warde and Lydia Martens, *Eating Out: Social Differentiation, Consumption and Pleasure* (Cambridge: Cambridge University Press, 2000), p. 16.

NOTES TO CHAPTER 2

1. Craig Claiborne, *Southern Cooking* (Chapel Hill: University of Georgia Press, 2007), p. 4.
2. David Bell and Gill Valentine, *Consuming Geographies We Are Where We Eat* (London: Routledge, 1997), p. 150.
3. Ibid., pp. 150 and 158.
4. Phil Crang, 'The World on a Plate', quoted in Bell and Valentine, *Consuming Geographies*, p. 13.
5. Bell and Valentine, *Consuming Geographies*, p. 151.
6. R.J. Johnston, 'Region, Place and Locale: An Introduction to Different Concepts of Regional Geography' in *Regional Geography: Currents Developments and Future Prospects*, ed. by R.J. Johnston, J. Hauer and G. Hoekveld (London: Routledge, 1990), p. 130.
7. Bell and Valentine, *Consuming Geographies*, p. 4.
8. Paul Fieldhouse, *Food and Nutrition: Customs and Culture* (London: Chapman & Hall, 1995), p. 76.
9. Note that the word 'cafe' in the novel's title and quotations is consistent with Flagg's spelling.
10. Joanne Hawks and Sheila Skemp, 'Introduction' in *Sex, Race, and the Role of Women in the South: Essays*, ed. by Joanne Hawks and Sheila Skemp (Jackson: University Press of Mississippi, 1983), p. xiii. The imbrications of food and identity are extravagantly conspicuous in Southern literature and a large number of examples can be found from nineteenth-century slave narratives to the present day.
11. Fannie Flagg, *Fried Green Tomatoes at the Whistle Stop Cafe* (1987; London: Vintage, 1992), p. 123. Additional page numbers are given in the text in parentheses.
12. Alice A. Deck, '"Now Then—Who Said Biscuits?" The Black Woman Cook as Fetish in American Advertising, 1905–1953', in *Kitchen Culture in America: Popular Representations of Food, Gender and Race*, ed. by Sherrie A. Inness (Philadelphia: University of Pennsylvania Press, 2001), p. 80.
13. Ibid.
14. Jessamyn Neuhaus, *Manly Meals and Mom's Home Cooking: Cookbooks and Gender in Modern America* (Baltimore: John Hopkins University Press, 2003), p. 130.
15. Deborah Lupton, *Food, the Body and the Self* (London: SAGE, 1996), p. 25.

16. Nickie Charles and Marion Kerr, *Women, Food and Families* (Manchester: Manchester University Press, 1988), p. 2.
17. Elizabeth Hallam and Jenny Hockey, *Death, Memory and Material Culture* (Oxford: Berg, 2001) p. 204. This idea is of course not new; one should also consider the work of Marx Benjamin and Adorno in this regard.
18. Karl Marx, *Economic and Philosophic Manuscripts of 1844* (London: Lawrence & Wishart, 1970), p. 141.
19. Susan Stuart, 'From the Museum of Touch', in *Material Memories: Design and Evocation*, ed. by Marius Kwint, Christopher Breward and Jeremy Aynsley (Oxford: Berg, 1999) p. 23.
20. Deck, '"Now Then—Who Said Biscuits?"', p. 90.
21. Ibid., p. 70.
22. Patricia Turner, *Ceramic Uncles and Celluloid Mammies: Black Images and Their Influence on Culture* (New York: Anchor Books, 1994), p. 49. The owners of the David Milling Company did more than just invent an 'image', they actually gave Aunt Jemima a history. According to advertising folklore, before the Civil War Aunt Jemima was a worker—obviously a euphemism for 'slave'—at the house of Colonel Higbee, with whom she remained until his death, preparing for him and his family her wholesome pancakes. After the Colonel's death, and the end of the Civil War, Aunt Jemima is said to have revealed her pancake recipe to soldiers from the North so that everyone could enjoy them and remember the Higbee family she had so loved.
23. Catherine Clinton, The *Plantation Mistress: Woman's World in the Old South* (New York: Pantheon, 1982), p. 201. Although records do acknowledge the occasional presence of female slaves in the main plantation household, this remained a very sporadic occurrence. Clinton reminds us that slaves represented significant expense and very few plantation owners could afford to use them in the house rather than in the fields. The presence of black women as workers in white households, Clinton specifies, is, ironically, not documented in detail until the Emancipation that followed the Civil War (p. 202).
24. Ibid.
25. Sally Cline, *Just Desserts: Women and Food* (London: Deutsch, 1990), p. 2.
26. Deck, '"Now Then—Who Said Biscuits?"', p. 70.
27. Ibid.
28. Hope Norman and Louise Simon, 'Preface' in *Louisiana Entertains: Official Cookbook*, ed. by Hope Norman and Louise Simon (Memphis: Wimmer Brothers, 1984), vii.
29. Donald Bogle, *Toms, Coons, Mulattoes, Mammies, and Bucks: An Interpretive History of Blacks in American Films* (New York: Continuum, 1989), pp. 35–36.
30. Ibid., p. 36.
31. Lisa Anderson, *Mammies No More: The Changing Image of Black Women on Stage and Screen* (Oxford: Rowman & Littlefield, 1997), p. 10.
32. Marvalene Hughes, 'Soul, Black Women and Food', in *Food and Culture: A Reader*, ed. by Carole Counihan and Penny Van Esterik (London: Routledge, 1997), p. 276.
33. Carole Counihan, *Food in the USA* (New York: Routledge, 2002), p. 92.
34. Ibid.
35. Glenda R. Carpio, 'Conjuring Up the Mystery of Slavery', *American Literature*, 77 (2005) 563.
36. Ibid.
37. Maggie Kilgour, 'The Function of Cannibalism at the Present Time', in *Cannibalism and the Colonial World*, ed. by Francis Barker, Peter Hulme and Margaret Iversen (Cambridge: Cambridge University Press, 1998), p. 239.

38. Frantz Fanon, *Black Skins, White Masks* (New York: Grove Weidenfeld, 1991), p. 225.
39. Rebecca Wells, *Divine Secrets of the Ya-Ya Sisterhood*, (New York: Harper Collins, 1996), pp. 443, 424 and 457. Additional page numbers are given in the text in parentheses.
40. Paige Gutierrez, 'The Social and Symbolic Uses of Ethnic/Regional Foodways: Cajun and Crawfish in South Louisiana' in *Ethnic and Regional Foodways of the Unites States*, ed. by Lind Keller Brown and Kay Mussell (Knoxville: University of Tennessee Press, 1984), p. 169.
41. Ibid., p. 171.
42. Ibid., p. 172.
43. Ibid., p. 173.
44. Brown and Mussell, 'Introduction' in *Ethnic and Regional Foodways in the Unites States*, p. 5.
45. Howard Wight Marshall, 'Meat Preservation on the Farm in Missouri's "Little Dixie"', *The Journal of American Folklore* 92 (1979): 408.
46. Brown and Mussell, 'Introduction', p. 5.
47. Gutierrez, 'The Social and Symbolic Uses of Ethnic/Regional Foodways: Cajun and Crawfish in South Louisiana', p. 171.
48. Ibid., p. 172.
49. Ibid., p. 172.
50. Ibid., p. 169.
51. Maurice Merleau-Ponty, *Phenomenology of Perception* (London: Routledge, 2005), p. 17. In his methodology, Merleau-Ponty evokes the Saussurian model of language by applying a system of substitution to ideas of memory and visual recollection.
52. David Sutton, 'Synaesthesia, Memory and the Taste of Home' in *The Taste Culture Reader: Experiencing Food and Drink*, ed. by Carolyn Korsmeyer (Oxford: Berg, 2005), p. 310.
53. Ibid.
54. Ibid.
55. Hallam and Hockey, *Death, Memory and Material Culture*, p. 3.
56. Amy Trubek, 'Place Matters' in *The Taste Culture Reader*, p. 269.
57. Ibid., p. 265.
58. Ibid., p. 260.
59. Ibid., p. 263.
60. Ibid., p. 261.
61. Ibid., p. 268.
62. Barry Jean Ancelet, Jay Edwards, and Glen Pitre, *Cajun Country* (Jackson: University Press of Mississippi, 1991), p. 140.
63. Paige Gutierrez, *Cajun Foodways* (Jackson: University Press of Mississippi, 1992), p. 35.
64. Ibid., p. 35.
65. Ibid., pp. 48 and 49.
66. Ibid, p. 49.
67. Bell and Valentine, *Consuming Geographies*, p. 150.
68. Ibid., p. 151.
69. Ibid., p. 153.
70. Barbara Allen, 'The Genealogical Landscape and the Southern Sense of Place' in *Sense of Place: American Regional Cultures*, ed. by Barbara Allen and Thomas j. Schlereth (Lexington: University Press of Kentucky, 1990), p. 152.
71. Ibid.

NOTES TO CHAPTER 3

1. Ntozake Shange, *If I Can Cook You Know God Can* (Boston: Beacon Press, 1998), p. 2.
2. Psyche A. Williams-Forson, *Building Houses Out of Chicken Legs: Black Women, Food and Power* (Chapel Hill: The University of Carolina Press, 2006) p. 2.
3. Ibid.
4. William Frank Mitchell, *African American Food Culture* (Westport: Greenwood, 2009), p. 19.
5. Ibid.
6. Doris Witt, 'From Fiction to Foodways: Working at the Intersections of African American Literary and Cultural Studies' in *African American Foodways: Explorations of History and Culture*, ed. by Anne L. Bower (Urbana: University of Illinois Press, 2009), p. 117.
7. Ibid.
8. Ibid.
9. Bebe Moore Campbell, *Brothers and Sisters* (New York, Putnam, 2009), p. 337.
10. Doris Witt, 'From Fiction to Foodways', p. 117.
11. Ibid.
12. Ibid.
13. Williams-Forson, *Building Houses Out of Chicken Legs*, p. 2.
14. Emma Parker, 'Apple Pie Ideology and the Politics of Appetite in the Novels of Toni Morrison', *Contemporary Literature* 39.1 (1998): 622.
15. Lynn Marie Houston, 'Hunger' in *The Toni Morrison Encyclopaedia*, ed. by Elizabeth Ann Beaulieu (Westport: Greenwood, 2003), p. 165.
16. Ibid.
17. Ibid., p. 167.
18. Toni Morrison, *Jazz* (1992; New York; Alfred A. Knopf, 2002), p. 119.
19. Toni Morrison, *Sula* (1973: New York: Plume, 1982), p. 46.
20. Richard Follett, *The Sugar Masters: Planters and Slaves in Louisiana's Cane World, 1820–1860* (Baton Rouge: Louisiana University Press, 2005), pp. 78, 93, 104. Also see Andrew Dix and Lorna Piatti, 'Bonbons in Abundance: The Politics of Sweetness in Kate Chopin's Fiction' in *Culinary Aesthetics and Practices in 19th-Century American Literature*, ed. by Monika Elbert and Marie Drews (New York: Palgrave McMillan, 2009).
21. George W. Cable, *The Creoles of Louisiana* (1884; Gretna, LA: Pelican, 2000), 11.
22. Karl Marx, *Selected Writings* (Oxford: Oxford University Press, 1977), p. 320.
23. Elizabeth House, 'The "Sweet Life" in Toni Morrison's Fiction', *American Literature* 56.2 (1984): 190.
24. Toni Morrison, *The Bluest Eyes* (New York: Harper Collins, 1996), p. 121. Additional page numbers are given in the text in parentheses.
25. Parker, 'Apple Pie Ideology and the Politics of Appetite in the Novels of Toni Morrison', 619.
26. Audre Lorde, 'Age, Race, Class and Sex: Women Redefining Difference' in *Out There: Marginalisation and Contemporary Cultures*, ed. by Russell Freguson, Martha Gever, Tring Minh-ha and Cornel West, p. 281. Also see Parker, 'Apple Pie Ideology and the Politics of Appetite in the Novels of Toni Morrison'.
27. Edward P. Jones, *The Known World* (2003; Hammersmith: Harper, 2004), pp. 1–2. Additional page numbers are given in the text in parentheses.

28. Wayne Flynt, *Dixie's Forgotten People* (Bloomington: Indiana University Press, 2004), p. 40.
29. See 'Three Essays on Sexuality' in *The Essentials of Psychoanalysis*, ed. by Anna Freud (London: Penguin, 1991), pp. 277–375.
30. Sigmund Freud, *The Complete Introductory Lectures on Psychoanalysis*, Vol. 1 (London: Allen and Unwin, 1971), p. 192.
31. See Robert Root-Bernestein and Michele, *Honey Mud Maggots and Other Medical Marvels* (London: Macmillan, 1999)
32. Herbert Covey and Wayne Einsach, *What The Slaves Ate: Recollections of African American Foods and Foodways from the Slaves Narratives* (Santa Barbara: Greenwood, 2009), p. 17.
33. Ibid
34. Dorothy Schneider and Carl Schneider, *Slavery in America: From Colonial Times to the Civil War* (New York: Facts on File, 2000), p. 83.
35. Ibid.
36. Ntozake Shange, *Sassafrass, Cypress and Indigo* , (1982; New York; St. Martin's Griffin, 2010) p. 4. Additional page numbers are given in the text in parentheses.
37. Doris Grumbach, '*Sassafrass, Cypress and Indigo* by Ntozake Shange', *The Washington Post*, 22 August 1982.
38. See Marialisa Calta, 'The Art of the Novel as Cookbook', *The New York Times*, 17 February 1993.
39. Ibid.
40. Patricia Clark, 'Archiving Epistemologies and the Narrativity of Recepies in Ntozake Shange's *Sassfrass, Cypress, and Indigo*', *Callaloo* 30.1 (2007): 150.
41. Judith Ann Carney, *Black Rice: The African Origins of Rice Cultivation in America* (Cambridge: Harvard University Press, 2001), p. 2.
42. Clark, 'Archiving Epistemologies and the Narrativity of Recepies in Ntozake Shange's *Sassfrass, Cypress, and Indigo*', p. 151.
43. Arlene Elder, 'Sassafrass, Cypresss and Indigo: Ntozake Shange's Neo-Slaves/Blues Narrative', *African American Review* 26.1 (1992): 99.
44. Ibid.
45. Carney, *Black Rice*, p. 1.
46. Ibid. p. 2.
47. Ibid., p. 4.
48. Quoted in Carney, *Black Rice*, p. 3.
49. Ibid., p. 3.
50. Ibid., p. 6.
51. Janet Theophano, *Eat My Words: Reading Women's Lives Through The Cookbooks They Wrote* (New York: Palgrave, 2002), p. 122.
52. Traci Marie Kelly, '"If I Were a Voodoo Priestess": Women's Culinary Autobiographies', in *Kitchen Culture in America: Popular Representations of Food, Gender and Race*, ed. by Sherrie A. Inness (Philadelphia: University of Pennsylvania Press, 2001), p. 252.
53. Ibid., p. 258.
54. Ibid.
55. Kelly, '"If I Were a Voodoo Priestess"', p. 253.
56. Janet Floyd and Laurel Forster, *The Recipe Reader: Narratives—Contexts—Traditions* (Aldershot: Ashgate, 2003), p. 1.
57. Margaret Randall, *Hunger's Table: Women, Food and Politics* (Watsonville: Papier-Mache Press, 1997), p. 7.
58. Theophano, *Eat My Words*, p. 49.
59. Janet Todd, *Feminist Literary History: A Defence* (Cambridge: Polity, 1988), p. 63. Todd also stresses the importance of not creating a female history

separate from 'male history': 'Civic events, economic changes and religious controversy are profoundly relevant. Balance is needed. Menstruation is not the whole female experience' (63).
60. Jessahym Neuhaus, *Manly Meals and Mom's Home Cooking: Cookbooks and Gender in Modern America* (Baltimore: Johns Hopkins University Press, 2003), p. 1.
61. Marcel Mauss, *The Gift: The Form and Reason for Exchange in Archaic Societies* (London: Routledge, 1990), p. 10.
62. Martyn J. Lee, *Consumer Culture Reborn: The Cultural Politics of Consumption* (London: Routledge, 1993), p. 27.
63. Ursula King, 'Goddesses, Witches, Androgyny and Beyond?' in *Women in the World's Religions: Past and Present*, ed. by Ursula King (New York: Paragon House, 1986), p. 207.
64. Floyd and Forster, *The Recipe Reader*, p. 2.
65. Ron Scapp and Brian Seitz, 'Introduction' in *Eating Culture*, (Albany: State University of New York Press, 1998), p. 1.
66. Barbara Cooper, *Magical Realism in West African Fiction: Seeing with a Third Eye* (London: Routledge, 1998), p. 1.
67. Meinrad Craighead, "Immanent Mother" in *The Feminist Mystic and other Essays on Women and Spirituality*, ed. by Mary Giles (New York: Crossroad, 1982), p.78—79.
68. Sigmund Freud, *Totem and Taboo* (London: Routledge, 1991), p. 91.
69. Joanne Harris, *Chocolat* (1999; Maidenhead: Black Swan, 2000), p. 62.
70. Freud, *Totem and Taboo* (London: Routledge,1 991), p. 97.
71. Ronald Hutton, *The Pagan Religions of the Ancient British Isles: Their Nature and Legacy* (Oxford: Blackwell, 1993), p. 290.
72. Catherine C. Ward, 'Gloria Naylor's *Linden Hills*: A Modern Inferno', *Contemporary Literature* 28 (1987): 67.
73. Gloria Naylor, *Linden Hills* (1985; London; Penguin, 1986) p. 140. Additional page numbers are given in the text in parentheses.
74. Hilde Bruch, *Eating Disorders: Obesity, Anorexia Nervosa and the Person Within*, (New York, Basic Books, 1979) p. 222. Also see Richard Gordon, *Eating Disorders: Anatomy of a Social Epidemic* (Oxford: Blackwell, 2000).
75. Susie Orbach, *Fat is a Feminist Issue* (London: Arrow, 1989), p. 26. It must be said, however, that feminist scholarship often tends to overlook the impact of eating disorders on males. Although present in smaller percentages, eating disorders can be found amongst men as well. Food loathing or over-eating is often related to issues with bodily representation and gender-roles, posing questions regarding the effects that bodily culture and female emancipation have had on representations of conventional masculinity. As Richard Gordon argues, in eating disorder patients, issues with food 'revolve around the nearly universal concerns with . . . autonomy, self-esteem, achievement, and control' (*Eating Disorders: Anatomy of a Social Epidemic*, p. 95).
76. Sigmund Freud, 'Repression' in *The Essentials of Psychoanalysis*, ed. by Anna Freud (London: Penguin, 1991), p. 523.
77. Ibid.
78. Ibid.
79. Gloria Naylor, *Bailey's Café* (1992; London: Minerva, 1993), p. 119. Additional page numbers are given in the text in parentheses.
80. Cavey and Einsach, *What the Slaves Ate*, p. 81.
81. Andrew Warnes, *Savage Barbecue: Race, Culture and the Invention of America's First Food* (Athens: University of Georgia Press, 2008), p. 21.
82. Ibid., p. 89.
83. Ibid.

84. Sydney Mintz, *Tasting Food, Tasting Freedom Excursions into Eating, Culture, and the Past* (Boston: Beacon Press, 1996), pp. 97–98.
85. Elizabeth Pleck, 'The Making of the Domestic Occasion: The History of Thanksgiving in the United States', *Journal of Social History* 32.4 (1999): 774.
86. Warnes, *Savage Barbecue*, p. 89.
87. Eric Hobsbawn, 'Mass-Producing Traditions: Europe, 1870–1914 ' in *The Invention of Tradition*, ed. by Eric Hobsbawn and Terence Ranger (London: Cambridge University Press, 2005), p. 268.
88. Warnes, *Savage Barbecue*, p. 90.
89. Maxine Lavon Montgomery, 'Authority, Multivocality, and the New World Order in Gloria Naylor's *Bailey's Café*' *African American Review* 29.1 (1995): 27.
90. Ibid.
91. Mary Ellen Snodgrass, *Encyclopaedia of Feminist Literature* (New York: Facts on File, 2006), p. 486.
92. Ibid., p. 392.

NOTES TO CHAPTER 4

1. Diana Abu-Jaber, *The Language of Baklava: A Memoir* (2005; Peterborough: Anchor Books, 2006), pp. 6 and 26.
2. Tina De Rosa, *Paper Fish* (1989; New York: Feminist Press, 2003), p. 10.
3. Wenying Xu, *Eating Identities: Reading Food in Asian American Literature* (Honolulu: University of Hawaii Press, 2008), p. 3.
4. Deborah Lupton, *Food, the Body and the Self*, p. 26.
5. Xu, *Eating Identities:*, p. 13. Examples of Asian American literature with an emphasis on food include Frank Chin, *Donald Duk* (Minneapolis: Coffee House Press, 1991), Joy Kogawa, *Obasan* (Peterborough: Anchor, 1993) and David Won Louie, *The Barbarians Are Coming* (New York: Putnam, 2000).
6. Ibid.
7. Ibid.
8. Mark Kurlansky, *Salt: A World History* (London: Vintage, 2003), p. 3.
9. Monique Truong, *The Book of Salt* (2003; London: Vintage, 2004), p. 177. Additional page numbers are given in the text in parentheses.
10. Genesis, in *The Holy Bible*, 19: 23–26.
11. For the Christian tradition, salt is polysemic: not only does it betoken punishment but it also signifies permanence. Kurlansky notes that the culinary functions of salt as a preservative and a purifying agent have been extended metaphorically so that the substance 'is associated not only with longevity [. . .] but by extension with truth and wisdom' (*Salt*, p. 7).
12. Xu, *Eating Identities*, p. 135.
13. See Kurlansky, *Salt*, p. 72.
14. Ibid., p. 228.
15. Ibid., p. 226.
16. Ibid., p. 233.
17. Matthias Jakob Schleiden, *Das Salz* (1875), quoted in Kurlansky, *Salt*, p. 225.
18. Paul Fieldhouse, *Food and Nutrition: Customs and Culture* (London: Chapman and Hall, 1995), p. 52.
19. Lupton, *Food, the Body and the Self* (London: Sage, 1996), p. 29.
20. Joanne Finkelstein, *Dining Out: A Sociology of Modern Manners* (Cambridge: Polity, 1989), p. 3.

21. See Roy Wood, *The Sociology of the Meal* (Edinburgh: Edinburgh University Press, 1995), p. 105.
22. Ibid.
23. Pasi Falk, 'Homo Culinarius: Towards a Historical Anthropology of Taste', *Social Science Information*, 30.4 (1991): 774.
24. Paul Fieldhouse, *Food and Nutrition Customs and Culture* (London: Chapman and Hall, 1995), p. 32.
25. Alan Warde, *Consumption, Food and Taste: Culinary Antinomies and Commodity Culture* (London: Sage, 1997), p. 9.
26. Ibid.
27. Pierre Bourdieu, *Distinction A Social Critique of the Judgement of Taste* (London: Routledge & Kegan Paul, 1984), p. 170. Bourdieu discusses taste in relation to twentieth century French class division systems; nonetheless, his observations on the value of culinary taste as a class marker can be productively applied to the wider French colonial context of *The Book of Salt*.
28. Ibid., p. 175.
29. Ibid., p. 56.
30. Julia Kristeva, *Powers of Horror: An Essay on Abjection* (New York: Columbia University Press, 1982), p. 4.
31. Ibid.
32. Ibid.
33. Edward Said, *Orientalism* (London: Penguin, 2003), p. 204.
34. Iris Marion Young, *Justice and the Politics of Difference* (Princeton: Princeton University Press, 1990), p. 42.
35. Judith Butler, *Bodies That Matter: On the Discursive Limits of 'Sex'* (New York and London: Routledge, 1993), p. 3.
36. Lupton, *Food, the Body and the Self*, p. 16.
37. Ibid., p. 17.
38. As Mikhail Bakhtin insists, it is through the act of ingesting food into the body that we take in the world. *Rabelais and his World* (Bloomington: Indiana University Press, 1984), p. 281.
39. Claude Fischler, 'Food, Self and Identity', *Social Science Information*, 27 (1988) p. 281.
40. Kristeva, *Powers of Horror*, pp. 65–69.
41. Janet Price and Margrit Shildrick, 'Mapping the Colonial Body: Sexual Economies and the State of Colonial India', in *Gender and Colonialism*, ed. by Timothy Foley, Lionel Pilkington, Sean Ryder and Elizabeth Tilley (Galway: Galway University Press, 1995), p. 87. See also, Michel Foucault, *Discipline and Punish: The Birth of the Prison* (London: Penguin, 1991), p. 28.
42. Price and Shildrick, 'Mapping the Colonial Body', p. 87.
43. According to patriarchal mythology, the ideal 'closed' body is male whilst the female body is demonised as 'open' and 'weak'. In similar fashion, the East has been stereotypically represented as 'female', waiting to be 'penetrated' by Western male imperialism. It would seem, however, that Truong proposes an interpretation of the female colonist's body not as 'open' but as a sealed container of Western occupation.
44. Gilles Deleuze and Félix Guattari, *Anti-Oedipus: Capitalism and Schizophrenia* (London: Continuum, 2004), p. 95.
45. Thomas Hobbes, *Leviathan* (Oxford: Oxford University Press, 1998), p. 8; see also Simon King, *Insect Nations: Visions of the Ant World from Kropotkin to Bergson* (Ashby-de-la Zouch: InkerMen, 2006), p. 32.
46. Xu, *Eating Identities*, p. 136.
47. Ibid., p. 140.

48. John Paul Zronik, *Salt* (New York: Crabtree, 2004), p. 32.
49. Ibid., p. 21.
50. Thomas L. Purvis, *A Dictionary of American History* (Oxford: Blackwells, 1999), p. 387.
51. Xu, *Eating Identities*, p.13. One must be aware of the fact that, in a literary context, commercial success can be achieved by scattering, in Xu's words, 'exotic cultural details, among which food practices are most popular'(p. 13). Therefore, the use of culinary tropes is not necessarily polemical but informed, at least in part, by its likely exoticism for a possible readership.
52. Warde, *Consumption, Food and Taste*, p. 61.
53. David Leiwei Li, *Imagining the Nation: Asian American Literature and Cultural Consent* (Stanford: Stanford University Press, 1998), p. 112.
54. Xu, *Eating Identities*, p. 10. The racial laws of the time prohibited the Chinese from working in new mines, so the food industry represented one of the few alternative sources of employment available. In 1882, the United States Government passed the 'Chinese Exclusion Act', which prevented Chinese immigrants from becoming naturalised citizens. This exclusion was revoked only after World War II in recognition of China's role as a military ally. It is significant that the Chinese mothers of Tan's novel go to the United States in this later period, when they can actually become 'proper' American citizens.
55. Xu, *Eating Identities*, p. 10.
56. Ibid., p. 10.
57. Per Otnes, 'What Do Meals Do?', in *Palatable Worlds: Sociocultural Food Studies*, ed. by Elisabeth L. Fürst (Oslo: Solum, 1991), p. 105.
58. Wood, *The Sociology of the Meal*, p. 48.
59. Amy Tan, *The Joy Luck Club* (1989; London: Vintage, 1991), p. 176. Additional page numbers are given in the text in parentheses.
60. Wood, *The Sociology of Food and Eating*, p. 47.
61. Lisa Heldke, 'But is it Authentic? Culinary Travel and the Search for the "Genuine Article"', in *The Taste Culture Reader: Experiencing Food and Drink*, ed. by Carolyn Korsmeyer (Oxford: Berg, 2005), p. 390.
62. Warde, *Consumption, Food and Taste*, p. 61.
63. Wood, *The Sociology of the Meal*, p. 47.
64. We might recall Lisa Heldke's caution that 'even if we could agree that a dish was prepared authentically, there is no guarantee whatsoever that the eater will be equipped to experience it as authentic' ('But is it Authentic?', p. 388).
65. This summary of Dewey's remarks appears in Heldke, 'But is it Authentic?, p. 38.
66. John Dewey, *Art as Experience*, Vol. 10 of *John Dewey, The Later Works, 1925–1953* (Carbondale: Southern Illinois Press, 1987), p. 113.
67. Warde, *Consumption, Food and Taste*, p. 66.
68. Xu, *Eating Identities*, p. 3.
69. Leiwei Li, *Imagining the Nation*, pp. 25–26.
70. Xu, *Eating Identities*, p. 8.
71. Xu sums up 'derogatory Orientalist' views of Chinese culinary habits: '"They eat rats." "They eat dogs and cats." "They eat monkey brains." "They eat snakes and grasshoppers"'. However, Xu also points out that there is probably 'a certain degree of truth in these accusations' (*Eating Identities*, p. 8).
72. Frank Chin and Jeffrey Chan, 'Racist Love', in *Seeing Through Shuck*, ed. by Richard Kostellanz (New York: Ballantine Books, 1972), pp. 66–67.
73. Leiwei Li, *Imagining the Nation*, p. 25.
74. Trinh T. Minh-ha, *Woman, Native, Other: Writing, Postcoloniality and Feminism* (Indianapolis: Indiana University Press, 1989), p. 89.

75. Yuan Yuan, 'The Semiotics of "China Narrative" in the Con/Texts of Kingston and Tan', in *Ideas of Home*, ed. by Geoffrey Kain (East Lansing: Michigan State University Press, 1997), p. 159.
76. Edward Said, *Orientalism*, p. 273.
77. Joanne Mäkelä, 'Defining a Meal' in *Palatable Worlds*, p. 92. Mäkelä's claim seems to be inspired by a common sociological approach to eating that perceives only communal meals as an appropriate form of eating. In this framework, one cannot consume a 'real meal' if eating alone.
78. Warde, *Consumption, Food and Taste*, p. 64.
79. David Bell and Gill Valentine, *Consuming Geographies* (London: Routledge, 1997), p. 66. Also see Piatti-Farnell, 'The Delicious Side of the Story' in *The Richard and Judy Book Club Reader*, ed. by Helen Cousins and Jenni Ramone (Aldershot: Ashgate, 2011).
80. H.D. Renner, *The Origin of Food Habits* (London: Faber, 1944), pp. 53 and 55.
81. Ibid., p. 58.
82. Abu-Jaber, *The Language of Baklava*, pp. 4–20.
83. Diana Abu-Jaber, *Crescent* (2003; New York; Norton, 2004), p. 218. Additional page numbers are given in the text in parentheses.
84. David Sutton, 'Synaesthesia, Memory and the Taste of Home' in *The Taste Culture Reader: Experiencing Food and Drink*, ed. by Carolyn Korsmeyer (Oxford: Berg, 2005), p. 305.
85. Ibid., p. 308.
86. Abu-Jaber, *The Language of Baklava*, p. 6
87. Arjun Appadurai, 'Consumption, Duration and History', *Stanford Literary Review*, 10 (1993): 12.
88. Appadurai reminds us that 'the small habits of consumption can have a great impact in the organisation of large scale consumption patterns, which may be contrived of much more complex orders of repetition' ('Consumption, Duration and History', 13). This concept is significant when thinking of immigrant contexts, in which the large-scale cultural consumption patterns from the original country have been shifted to a new country by the individual (and shape the developing of everyday eating habits).
89. Andreea Deciu Ritivoi, *Yesterday's Self: Nostalgia and the Immigrant Identity*, (Oxford: Rowman & Littlefield, 2002), p. 19.
90. Natalie Davis and Randolph Starn 'Introduction', *Representations*, 26 (1989): 3.
91. Elizabeth Hallam and Jenny Hockey, *Death, Memory and Material Culture* (Oxford: Berg, 2001), p. 7.
92. Nadia Seremetakis, *The Senses Still: Perception and Memory as Material Culture in Modernity* (Chicago: University of Chicago Press, 1996) p. 37.
93. Elisabeth Bronfen, *The Knotted Subject: Hysteria and its Discontents* (Princeton: Princeton University Press, 1998), p. 273.
94. Luce Giard, Michel de Certeau, Pierre Mayol and S.F. Rendall, *The Practice of Everyday Life, Vol. 2, Living and Cooking* (Berkeley: University of California Press, 1985), p. 157.
95. Ritivoi, *Yesterday's Self*, p. 32.
96. Nadia Seremetakis, 'The Breast of Aphrodite' in *The Taste Culture Reader*, p. 300.
97. Ibid.
98. James Fernandez, *Bwiti: An Ethnography of the Religious Imagination of Africa* (Princeton: Princeton University Press, 1982), p. 203.
99. Sutton, 'Synaesthesia, Memory and the Taste of Home', p. 307.
100. Boym also analyses the possible etymological origins of the English word 'nostalgia' and its relationship to the Greek terms '*nostos*' and '*alghia*'.

101. Svetlana Boym, *The Future of Nostalgia* (New York: Basic Books, 2001), p. 41.
102. Ibid.
103. Ritivoi, *Yesterday's Self*, p. 32
104. Ibid.
105. Abu-Jaber seems to suggest that eating with one's hands differs greatly from, for instance, eating a take-away burger from a US fast food restaurant. This suggestion appears to be justified by attributing a sense of 'history' to the practice of hand-feeding that is difficult to find in a commercialised American meal.
106. Roger Haden, 'Taste in an Age of Convenience: From Frozen Food to Meals in *The Matrix*', in *The Taste Culture Reader*, p. 349.
107. Sadly, however, Abu-Jaber does not illustrate how the tactile Arabic meal is a more authentic, memory-laden experience than, for instance, eating a burger and fries in a fast food restaurant (where, similarly, cutlery is not supplied).
108. Susan Bordo, *Unbearable Weight: Feminism, Western Culture, and the Body* (Berkeley: University of California Press, 1993), p. 16.
109. David Morgan, *Family Connections: An Introduction to Family Studies* (Cambridge: Polity, 1996), p. 166.
110. Janet Theophano, *Eat My Words: Reading Women's Lives through the Cookbooks They Wrote* (New York: Palgrave, 2002), p. 8.
111. Leslie Pietrzyk, *Pears on a Willow Tree* (1998; New York: Perennial, 2002), p. 5. Additional page numbers are given in the text in parentheses.
112. David Sutton, *Remembrance of Repasts* (Oxford: Berg, 2006), p. 129.
113. Luce Giard, *The Practice of Everyday Life, Vol. 2, Living and Cooking* (Berkeley: University of California Press, 1985), p. 212.
114. Ibid., p. 269.
115. Steven Connor, *The Book of Skin* (London: Reaktion, 2004), p. 259.
116. Pasi Falk, *The Consuming Body* (London: Sage, 1994), p. 45.
117. Sutton, *Remembrance of Repasts*, p. 127.
118. Ibid., pp. 134–135.
119. Seremetakis, *The Senses Still*, p. 11.
120. Sutton, *Remembrance of Repasts*, p. 133.
121. Ibid., p 132.
122. Ibid.
123. Ibid., p. 133.
124. Ibid., p. 138.
125. Susannah Hoffman, paraphrased in Sutton, *Remembrance of Repasts*, p. 137.
126. Sutton, *Remembrance of Repasts*, p. 137.
127. Jack Goody, *The Power of the Written Tradition* (Cambridge: Cambridge University Press, 2000), p. 40.
128. Giard, *Practice of Everyday Life, Vol. 2, Living and Cooking*, p. 221.
129. Sutton, *Remembrance of Repasts*, p. 133.
130. Stephen Steinberg, 'Bubbie's Challah' in *Eating Culture*, ed. by Ron Scapp and Brian Seitz (Albany, State University of New York Press, 1998), p. 296.
131. Sutton, *Remembrance of Repasts*, p. 135.
132. Seremetakis, *The Senses Still*, p. 12.
133. Ibid., p. 14.
134. Ibid., p. 11.
135. Sutton, *Remembrance of Repasts*, p. 135.
136. Ibid., p. 129.
137. Ibid., p. 129.

138. Janet Floyd and Laurel Forster, *The Recipe Reader: Narratives—Contexts—Traditions* (Aldershot: Ashgate, 2003), p. 6.
139. Jodey Castricano, *Cryptomimesis: The Gothic and Jacques Derrida's Ghost Writing* (London: McGill-Queen's University Press, 2003), p. 29.
140. Ibid., p. 17.
141. Ibid.
142. Esther Rashkin, *Family Secrets and the Psychoanalysis of Narrative* (Princeton: Princeton University Press, 1992), p. 45.
143. See Nicolas Abraham and Maria Torok, *The Shell and the Kernel: Renewals of Psychoanalysis* (Chicago: University of Chicago Press, 1994).
144. Jacques Derrida, 'Fors', 'Introduction' in Nicholas Abraham and Maria Torok, *The Wolf Man's Magic Word: A Cryptonomy* (Minneapolis: University of Minnesota Press, 1986), xxi.
   Rashkin, *Family Secrets*, p. 119.
145. Nicholas Abraham and Maria Torok, 'Mourning or Melancholia: Introjection *versus* Incorporation' in *The Shell and the Kernel*, p. 130.
146. Derrida, 'Fors', xxi.
147. Rashkin, *Family Secrets*, p. 10.
148. Jacques Derrida, 'Roundtable on Translation' in *The Ear of the Other: Otobiography, Transference, Translation* (London: University of Nebraska Press, 1985), p. 158.
149. Theophano, *Eat My Words*, p. 49.
150. Carolyn Korsmeyer, 'Introduction: Perspectives on Taste' in *The Taste Culture Reader*, p. 8.
151. See Piatti-Farnell, 'The Delicious Side of the Story' in *The Richard and Judy Book Club Reader*, ed. by Helen Cousins and Jenni Ramone (Aldershot: Ashgate, 2011).

NOTES TO THE CONCLUSION

1. Fredric Jameson, *Archaeologies of the Future: The Desire Called Utopia and Other Science Fictions* (Cambridge: Cambridge University Press, 2004), p. 156.
2. David Bell and Gill Valentine, *Consuming Geographies: We Are Where We Eat* (London: Routledge, 1997), p. 3.
3. Paul Fieldhouse, *Food and Nutrition: Customs and Culture* (London: Chapman and Hall, 1995), p. 30. Also see Piatti-Farnell, 'The Delicious Side of the Story' in *The Richard and Judy Book Club Reader*, ed. by Helen Cousins and Jenni Ramone (Aldershot: Ashgate, 2011).
4. Bell and Valentine, *Consuming Geographies*, p. 204.
5. Ibid., p. 65.
6. Diana Abu-Jaber, *The Language of Baklava: A Memoir* (2005; Peterborough: Anchor Books, 2006), pp. 191, 73 and 38.
7. Joanne Ikeda, 'Culture, Food and Nutrition in Increasingly Culturally Diverse Societies' in *A Sociology of Food and Nutrition: The Social Appetite*, ed. by John Germov and Lauren Williams (Oxford: Oxford University Press, 1999), p. 151.
8. Fieldhouse, *Food and Nutrition*, p. 122.
9. Ibid., p. 76.
10. Sally Cline, *Just Desserts: Women and Food* (London: Deutsch, 1990), p. 2.
11. Sarah Sceats, *Food, Consumption and the Body in Contemporary Women's Fiction*, p. 185.
12. Jameson, *Archaeologies of the Future*, p. 390.

13. David Bell and Gill Valentine, *Consuming Geographies: We Are Where We Eat* (London: Routledge, 1997), p. 203. Also see Lorna Piatti-Farnell, 'The Delicious Side of the Story' in *The Richard and Judy Book Club Reader*.
14. Ibid., pp. 202–203.
15. Keya Ganguly, *States of Exception: Everyday Life and Postcolonial Identity* (Minneapolis: University of Minnesota Press, 2001), p. 119.

Bibliography

PRIMARY TEXTS

Abu-Jaber, Diana, *Crescent* (2003; New York; Norton, 2004)
Campbell, Bebe Moore, *Brothers and Sisters* (New York, Putnam, 2009)
De Rosa, Tina, *Paper Fish* (1989; New York: Feminist Press, 2003)
Ellis, Brett Easton, *American Psycho* (Basingstoke: Picador, 1991)
Flagg, Fannie, *Fried Green Tomatoes at the Whistle Stop Cafe* (1987; London: Vintage, 1992)
Franzen, Jonathan, *The Corrections* (2001; New York: Picador, 2002)
Jones, Edward P., *The Known World* (2003; Hammersmith: Harper, 2004)
Morrison, Toni, *Beloved* (1987; New York: Alfred A. Knopf, 2006)
———. *Jazz* (1992; New York: Alfred A. Knopf, 2002)
———. *Song of Solomon* (1977; New York; Vintage, 2004)
———. *Sula* (1973; New York: Plume,1982)
———. *The Bluest Eyes* (1970; New York; Vintage, 2007)
Naylor Gloria, *Bailey's Café* (1992; London: Minerva, 1993)
———. *Linden Hills* (1985; London: Penguin, 1986)
Pietrzyk, Leslie, *Pears on a Willow Tree* (1998; New York: Perennial, 2002)
Robinson, Marilynne, *Home* (2008; London: Virago, 2010)
Shange, Ntozake, *Sassafrass, Cypress and Indigo* (1982; New York; St. Martin's Griffin, 2010)
Stolz, Karen, *World of Pies* (New York: Hyperion, 2000)
Tan, Amy, *The Joy Luck Club* (1989; London: Vintage, 1991)
Truong, Monique, *The Book of Salt* (2003; London: Vintage, 2004)
Wells, Rebecca, *Divine Secrets of the Ya-Ya Sisterhood* (New York: Harper Collins, 1996)
Wolfe, Tom, *The Bonfire of the Vanities* (1987; London: Vintage, 2010)

SECONDARY TEXTS

Abraham, Nicholas and Maria Torok, *The Shell and the Kernel: Renewals of Psychoanalysis* (Chicago: University of Chicago Press, 1994)
———. *The Wolf Man's Magic Word: A Cryptonomy* (Minneapolis: University of Minnesota Press, 1986)
Abu-Jaber, Diana, *The Language of Baklava: A Memoir* (2005; Peterborough: Anchor Books, 2006)
Adams, Carol, *The Sexual Politics of Meat: A Feminist-Vegetarian Critical Theory* (Cambridge: Polity, 1990)

Allen, Barbara, 'The Genealogical Landscape and the Southern Sense of Place' in *Sense of Place: American Regional Cultures*, ed. by Barbara Allen and Thomas J. Schlereth (Lexington: University Press of Kentucky, 1990), pp. 1–13

Ancelet, Barry Jean, Jay Edwards and Glen Pitre, *Cajun Country* (Jackson: University Press of Mississippi, 1991)

Anderson, E.N., *Everyone Eats: Understanding Food and Culture* (New York: New York University Press, 2005)

Anderson, Lisa, *Mammies No More: The Changing Image of Black Women on Stage and Screen* (Oxford: Rowman & Littlefield, 1997)

Aoyama, Tomoko, *Reading Food in Modern Japanese Literature* (Honolulu: University of Hawaii Press, 2008)

Appadurai, Arjun, 'Consumption, Duration and History', *Stanford Literary Review*, 10 (1993), 11–23

Appelbaum, Robert, *Aguecheek's Beef, Belch's Hiccup, and Other Gastronomic Interjections: Literature, Culture, and Food among the Early Moderns* (Chicago: University of Chicago Press, 2006)

Applegate, Howard L., *Coca-Cola: A History in Photographs, 1930–1969* (Hudson: Iconografix, 1996)

Ashley, Bob, Joanne Hollows, Steve Jones and Ben Taylor, *Food and Cultural Studies* (London: Routledge, 2004)

Atkinson, Paul, 'Eating Virtue' in *The Sociology of Food and Eating: Essays on the Sociological Significance of Food*, ed. by Anne Murcott (Aldershot: Gower, 1983), pp. 9–17

Bakhtin, Mikhail, *Rabelais and His World* (Bloomington: Indiana University Press, 1984)

Barthes, Roland, 'Toward a Psychology of Contemporary Food Consumption' in *Food and Culture: A Reader*, ed. by Carole Counihan and Penny Van Esterik (London: Routledge, 1997), pp. 20–27

———. *Mythologies* (London: Grant & Cutler, 1994)

Bartolovich, Crystal, 'Consumerism or the Cultural Logic of Late Cannibalism' in *Cannibalism and the Colonial World*, ed. by Francis Barker, Peter Hulme and Margaret Iversen (Cambridge: Cambridge University Press, 1998), pp. 204–237

Baudrillard, Jean, *Revenge of the Crystal: Selected Writings on the Modern Object and its Destiny* (Sydney: Pluto Press/Power Institute of Fine Arts, 1990)

———. *Selected Writings* (Cambridge: Polity, 1988)

Beach, Cecil, 'A Table: The Power of Food in French Women's Theatre', *Theatre Research International*, 23 (1998), 233–241

Beardsworth, Alan and Teresa Keil, 'Putting Menu on the Agenda', *Sociology*, 24, 1990: 143–168

———. *Sociology on the Menu: An Invitation to the Study of Food and Society* (London: Routledge, 1996)

Beit-Hallami, Benjamin and Michael Argyle, *The Psychology of Religious Behaviour* (London: Routledge, 1997)

Bell, David and Gill Valentine, *Consuming Geographies: We Are Where We Eat* (London: Routledge, 1997)

Bevan, David, ed., *Literary Gastronomy* (Amsterdam: Rodolphi, 1988)

Biasin, Gian-Paolo, *The Flavors of Modernity: Food and the Novel* (Princeton: Princeton University Press, 1993)

Blos, Peter, *The Adolescent Personality: A Study of Individual Behaviour* (New York: Appleton-Century, 1941)

Bogle, Donald, *Toms, Coons, Mulattoes, Mammies, and Bucks: An Interpretive History of Blacks in American Films* (New York: Continuum, 1989)

Bordo, Susan, *Unbearable Weight: Feminism, Western Culture, and the Body* (Berkeley: University of California Press, 1993)
Bourdieu, Pierre, *Distinction: A Social Critique of the Judgement of Taste* (London: Routledge & Kegan Paul, 1984)
Boym, Svetlana, *The Future of Nostalgia* (New York: Basic Books, 2001)
Bronfen, Elisabeth, *The Knotted Subject: Hysteria and its Discontents* (Princeton: Princeton University Press, 1998)
Brown, Linda Keller and Kay Mussell (eds.) *Ethnic and Regional Foodways of the Unites States* (Knoxville: University of Tennessee Press, 1984)
Bruch, Hilde, *Eating Disorders: Obesity, Anorexia Nervosa and the Person Within* (New York, Basic Books, 1979)
Butler, Judith, *Bodies That Matter: On the Discursive Limits of 'Sex'* (New York and London: Routledge, 1993)
Calta, Marialisa, 'The Art of the Novel as Cookbook', *The New York Times*, 17 February 1993
Campbell, Colin, *The Romantic Ethic and the Spirit of Modern Consumerism* (Oxford: Basil Blackwell, 1987)
Carney, Judith Ann, *Black Rice: The African origins of Rice Cultivation in America* (Cambridge: Harvard University Press, 2001)
Carpio, Glenda, 'Conjuring Up the Mystery of Slavery', *American Literature*, 77 (2005), 563–589
Castricano, Jodey, *Cryptomimesis: The Gothic and Jacques Derrida's Ghost Writing* (London: McGill-Queen's University Press, 2003)
Charles, Nickie and Marion Kerr, *Women, Food and Families* (Manchester: Manchester University Press, 1988)
Chin, Frank, *Donald Duk* (Minneapolis: Coffee House Press, 1991)
Chin, Frank and Jeffrey Chan, 'Racist Love' in *Seeing through Shuck*, ed. by Richard Kostelanetz (New York: Ballantine Books, 1972), pp. 65–79
Claiborne, Craig, *Southern Cooking* (Chapel Hill: University of Georgia Press, 2007)
Clark, Patricia, 'Archiving Epistemologies and the Narrativity of Recepies in Ntozake Shange's Sassfrass, Cypress, & Indigo', *Callaloo* 30.1 (2007): 150–162
Clarkson, Janet, *Pie: A Global History* (London: Reaktion, 2009)
Cline, Sally, *Just Desserts: Women and Food* (London: Deutsch, 1990)
Clinton, Catherine, *The Plantation Mistress: Woman's World in the Old South* (New York: Pantheon, 1982)
Conner, Mark and Christopher Armitage, *The Social Psychology of Food* (Maidenhead: Open University Press, 2002)
Connor, Steven, *The Book of Skin* (London: Reaktion, 2004)
Counihan, Carole, *Food in the USA* (New York: Routledge, 2002)
———. *The Anthropology of Food and Body: Gender, Meaning and Power* (London: Routledge, 1999)
Covey, Herbert and Wayne Einsach, *What The Slaves Ate: Recollections of African American Foods and Foodways from the Slaves Narratives* (Santa Barbara: Greenwood, 2009)
Coward, Rosalind, *Female Desire* (London: Paladin, 1984)
Crawford, June, *Emotion and Gender: Constructing Meaning from Memory* (London: Sage, 1992)
Daniels, Carolyn, *Voracious Children: Who Eats Whom in Children's Literature* (New York: Routledge, 2006)
Davidson, Alan, *Oxford Companion to Food* (Oxford University Press: Oxford, 1999)
Davis, Natalie and Randolph Starn, 'Introduction', *Representations*, 26 (1989), 1–6

Debord, Guy, *Society of Spectacle* (New York: Zone Books, 1994)

De Certeau, Michel, 'The Practice of Everyday Life' in *Cultural Theory and Popular Culture: A Reader*, ed. by John Storey (New York: Harvester Wheatsheaf, 1994), pp. 474–485

Deck, Alice A., '"Now Then—Who Said Biscuits?": The Black Woman Cook as Fetish in American Advertising, 1905–1953', in *Kitchen Culture in America: Popular Representations of Food, Gender and Race*, ed. by Sherrie A. Inness (Philadelphia: University of Pennsylvania Press, 2001), pp. 69–94

Deleuze, Gilles and Félix Guattari, *Anti-Oedipus: Capitalism and Schizophrenia* (London: Continuum, 2004)

Derrida, Jacques, 'Roundtable on Translation" in *The Ear of the Other: Otobiography, Transference, Translation* (London: University of Nebraska Press, 1985), pp. 93–161

DeVault, Marjorie, *Feeding the Family: The Social Organization of Caring as Gendered Work* (Chicago and London: University of Chicago Press, 1991)

Dewey, John, *Art as Experience*, Vol. 10 of *John Dewey: The Later Works, 1925–1953* (Carbondale: Southern Illinois Press, 1987)

Dix, Andrew and Lorna Piatti, 'Bonbons in Abundance: The Politics of Sweetness in Kate Chopin's Fiction' in *Culinary Aesthetics and Practices in 19th Century American Literature* ed. Monika Elbert and Marie Drews (New York: Palgrave McMillan, 2009), pp. 53–74

Douglas, Mary and Baron Isherwood, *The World of Goods: Towards an Anthropology of Consumption* (London: Routledge, 1996)

Eagleton, Terry, 'Edible Écriture', in *Consuming Passions: Food in the Age of Anxiety*, ed. by Sian Griffiths and Jennifer Wallace (Manchester: Manchester University Press, 1998), pp. 203–208

Elder, Arlene, 'Sassafrass, Cypresss and Indigo: Ntozake Shange's Neo-Slaves/ Blues Narrative', *African American Review* 26.1 (1992): 99–112

Ellmann, Maud, *The Hunger Artists: Starving, Writing and Imprisonment* (London: Virago, 1993)

Falk, Pasi, 'Homo Culinarius: Towards a Historical Anthropology of Taste' *Social Science Information*, 30 (1991), 757–790

———. *The Consuming Body* (London: Sage, 1994)

Fanon, Frantz, *Black Skins, White Masks* (New York: Grove Weidenfeld, 1991)

Featherstone, Mike, *The Body: Social Process and Cultural Theory* (London: Sage, 1991)

Fernandez, James, *Bwiti: An Ethnography of the Religious Imagination of Africa* (Princeton: Princeton University Press, 1982)

Fiddes, Nick, *Meat: A Natural Symbol* (London: Routledge, 1991)

Fieldhouse, Paul, *Food and Nutrition: Customs and Culture* (London: Chapman & Hall, 1995)

Finkelstein, Joanne, *Dining Out: A Sociology of Modern Manners* (Cambridge: Polity, 1989)

Fischler, Claude 'Food, Self and Identity', *Social Science Information*, 27 (1988), 275–292

Fitzpatrick, Joan, *Food and Shakespeare* (Aldershot: Ashgate, 2007)

Flandrin, J.L., *Food: A Culinary History from Antiquity to the Present* (Irvington: Columbia University Press, 1999)

Floyd, Janet and Laurel Foster, *The Recipe Reader: Narratives—Contexts—Traditions* (Aldershot: Ashgate, 2003)

Flynt, Wayne, *Dixie's Forgotten People* (Bloomington: Indiana University Press, 2004)

Follett, Richard, *The Sugar Masters: Planters and Slaves in Louisiana's Cane World, 1820–1860* (Baton Rouge: Louisiana State University Press, 2005)

Foucault, Michel, *Discipline and Punish: The Birth of the Prison* (London: Penguin, 1991)
Frank, Arthur, 'For a Sociology of the Body: An Analytical Review' in *The Body: Social Process and Cultural Theory*, ed. by Michael Featherstone, Mike Hepworth and Bryan Turner (London: Sage, 1991), pp. 36–102
Freud, Sigmund, *Civilisation and its Discontents* (New York: Norton, 1961)
———. *The Essentials of Psychoanalysis*, ed. by Anna Freud (London: Penguin, 1991)
———. *The Complete Introductory Lectures on Psychoanalysis*, Vol. 1 (London: Allen and Unwin, 1971)
———. *The Pelican Freud*, Vol. 11 (Harmondsworth: Penguin, 1984)
———. *Three Essays on Sexuality* (New York: Basic Books, 1961)
———. *Totem and Taboo* (London: Routledge, 1991)
Funderburg, Anne, *Chocolate, Strawberry and Vanilla: A History of American Ice Cream* (Madison: Bowling Green State University Press, 1995)
Ganguly, Keya, *States of Exception: Everyday Life and Postcolonial Identity* (Minneapolis: University of Minnesota Press, 2001)
Giard, Luce, Michel de Certeau, Pierre Mayol and S.F. Rendall, *The Practice of Everyday Life, Vol. 2, Living and Cooking* (Berkeley: University of California Press, 1985)
Goody, Jack, *Cooking, Cuisine and Class: A Study in Comparative Sociology* (Cambridge: Cambridge University Press, 1982)
———. *The Power of the Written Tradition* (Cambridge: Cambridge University Press, 2000)
Gordon, Richard, *Eating Disorders: Anatomy of a Social Epidemic* (Oxford: Blackwell, 2000)
Gowers, Emily, *The Loaded Table: Representations of Food in Roman Literature* (New York: Oxford University Press, 1997)
Grosz, Elizabeth, *Volatile Bodies: Toward a Corporeal Feminism* (Bloomington: Indiana University Press, 1994)
Grumbach, Doris, '*Sassafrass, Cypress and Indigo* by Ntozake Shange', *The Washington Post*, 22 August 1982
Gutierrez, Paige, *Cajun Foodways* (Jackson: University Press of Mississippi, 1992)
———'The Social and Symbolic Uses of Ethnic/Regional Foodways: Cajun and Crawfish in South Louisiana' in *Ethnic and Regional Foodways of the Unites States*, ed. by Linda Keller Brown and Kay Mussell (Knoxville: University of Tennessee Press, 1984), pp.169–183
Gwin, Minrose, 'Mentioning the Tamales: Food and Drink in Katherine Anne Porter's *Flowering Judas and Other Stories*', *Mississippi Quarterly*, 38 (1984–1985), 44–57
Haden, Roger, 'Taste in an Age of Convenience: From Frozen Food to Meals in The Matrix' in *The Taste Culture Reader: Experiencing Food and Drink*, ed. by Carolyn Korsmeyer (Oxford: Berg, 2005), pp. 344–358
Hallam, Elizabeth and Jenny Hockey, *Death, Memory and Material Culture* (Oxford: Berg, 2001)
Harris, Joanne, *Chocolat* (1999; Maidenhead: Black Swan, 2000)
Hawks, Joanne and Sheila Skemp, eds., *Sex, Race, and the Role of Women in the South: Essays* (Jackson: University Press of Mississippi, 1983)
Hays, Constance, *The Real Thing: Truth and Power at the Coca-Cola Company* (New York: Random House, 2004)
Heldke, Lisa, 'But is it Authentic? Culinary Travel and the Search for the "Genuine Article"', in *The Taste Culture Reader: Experiencing Food and Drink*, ed. by Carolyn Korsmeyer (Oxford: Berg, 2005), pp. 385–394

Hobbes, Thomas, *Leviathan* (Oxford: Oxford University Press, 1998)

Hobsbawn, Eric 'Mass-Producing Traditions: Europe, 1870–1914' in *The Invention of Tradition*, ed. by Eric Hobsbawn and Terence Ranger (London: Cambridge University Press, 2005), pp. 263–307

Hopkins, Wayne 'Social Worker Cites Contributions of Negro to Philadelphia's Progress' in *The Philadelphia Tribune*; 2 June 1932

House, Elizabeth, 'The "Sweet Life" in Toni Morrison's Fiction', *American Literature* 56.2 (1984): 181–202

Houston, Gail Turley, *Consuming Fictions: Gender, Class and Hunger in Dickens's Novels* (Carbondale: Southern Illinois Press, 1994)

Houston, Lynn Marie, 'Hunger' in *The Toni Morrison Encyclopaedia*, ed. by Elizabeth Ann Beaulieu (Westport: Greenwood, 2003), pp. 165–167

Hsiao, Pi-Li, 'Food Imagery in Amy Tan's *The Joy Luck Club* and *The Kitchen God's Wife*', *Journal of Humanities and Social Sciences*, 1 (2000), 205–227

Hughes, Marvalene, 'Soul, Black Women and Food', in *Food and Culture: A Reader*, ed. by Carole Counihan and Penny Van Esterik (London: Routledge, 1997), pp. 272–280

Hutton, Ronald, *The Pagan Religions of the Ancient British Isles: Their Nature and Legacy* (Oxford: Blackwell, 1993)

Hyde, Lewis, *The Gift: Imagination and the Erotic Life of Property* (New York: Vintage, 1983)

Ikeda, Joanne, 'Culture, Food and Nutrition in Increasingly Culturally Diverse Societies', in *A Sociology of Food and Nutrition: The Social Appetite*, ed. by John Germov and Lauren Williams (Oxford: Oxford University Press, 1999), pp. 149–168

Jacobsen, Rowan, *Chocolate Unwrapped: The Surprising Health Benefits of America's Favorite Passion* (Montpelier: Invisible Cities Press, 2003)

Jacoby, Tamar, 'Defining Assimilation for the 21st Century', in *Reinventing the Melting Pot*, ed. by Tamar Jacoby (New York: Basic, 2004), pp. 3–16

Jameson, Fredric, *Archaeologies of the Future: The Desire Called Utopia and Other Science Fictions* (London: Verso 2005)

Johnston, R.J., J. Hauer and G. Hoekveld (eds.) *Regional Geography: Currents Developments and Future Prospects* (London: Routledge, 1990)

Jütte, Robert, *A History of the Senses: From Antiquity to Cyberspace* (Cambridge: Polity, 2005)

Keeling, Sarah and Scott Pollard, eds., *Critical Approaches to Food in Children's Literature* (New York: Routledge, 2008)

Kelly, Traci Marie, '"If I Were a Voodoo Priestess": Women's Culinary Autobiographies' in *Kitchen Culture in America: Popular Representations of Food, Gender and Race*, ed. by Sherrie A. Inness (Philadelphia: University of Pennsylvania Press, 2001), pp. 251–270

Kilgour, Maggie, 'The Function of Cannibalism at the Present Time' in *Cannibalism and the Colonial World*, ed. by Francis Barker, Peter Hulme and Margaret Iversen (Cambridge: Cambridge University Press, 1998), pp. 238–259

King, Simon, *Insect Nations: Visions of the Ant World from Kropotkin to Bergson* (Ashby-de-la Zouch: InkerMen, 2006)

King, Ursula, 'Goddesses, Witches, Androgyny and Beyond?', in *Women in the World's Religions: Past and Present*, ed. by Ursula King (New York: Paragon House, 1986), pp. 201–218

Kogawa, Joy, *Obasan* (Peterborough: Anchor, 1993)

Korsmeyer, Carolyn, 'Introduction: Perspectives on Taste', in *The Taste Culture Reader: Experiencing Food and Drink*, ed. by Carolyn Korsmeyer (Oxford: Berg, 2005), pp. 1–9

———. *Making Sense of Taste: Food and Philosophy* (Ithaca: Cornell University Press, 2002)
Kristeva, Julia, *Powers of Horror: An Essay on Abjection* (New York: Columbia University Press, 1982)
———. *Revolution in Poetic Language* (New York: Columbia University Press, 1984)
Kurlansky, Mark, *Salt: A World History* (London: Vintage, 2003)
Lane, Maggie, *Jane Austen and Food* (London: Hambledon, 2007)
Lang, Tim and Michael Heasman, *Food Wars: The Battle for Mouths, Minds and Markets* (London: Earthscan, 2003)
Lee, Martyn J., *Consumer Culture Reborn: The Cultural Politics of Consumption* (London: Routledge, 1993)
Leeds-Hurwitz, Wendy, *Semiotics and Communication: Signs, Codes and Cultures* (Hillsdale: Erlbaum, 1993)
Leiwei Li, David, *Imagining the Nation: Asian American Literature and Cultural Consent* (Stanford: Stanford University Press, 1998)
Lévi-Strauss, Claude, *Introduction to a Science of Mythology/The Raw and The Cooked* (London: Cape, 1970)
———.'The Culinary Triangle', in *Food and Culture: A Reader*, ed. by Carole Counihan and Penny Van Esterik (London: Routledge, 1997), pp. 28–35
Lorde, Audre, 'Age, Race, Class and Sex: Women Redefining Difference' in *Out There: Marginalisation and Contemporary Cultures*, ed. by Russell Freguson, Martha Gever, Tring Minh-ha and Cornel West, pp. 261–288
Louie, David Won, *The Barbarians Are Coming* (New York: Putnam, 2000)
Lupton, Deborah, *Food, the Body and the Self* (London: Sage, 1996)
Lyon, David, *Surveillance Society: Monitoring Everyday Life* (Maidenhead: Open University Press, 2001)
Mäkelä, Joanne, 'Defining a Meal' in *Palatable Worlds: Sociocultural Food Studies*, ed. by Elisabeth L. Fürst (Oslo: Solum, 1991), pp. 87–96
Marshall, Howard Wight 'Meat Preservation on the Farm in Missouri's "Little Dixie"', *The Journal of American Folklore* 92 (1979): 408–410
Marx, Karl, *Economic and Philosophic Manuscripts of 1844* (London: Lawrence & Wishart, 1970)
———. *Selected Writings* (Oxford: Oxford University Press, 1977)
Matthews, Eric, *The Philosophy of Merleau-Ponty* (Chesham: Acumen, 2002)
Mauss, Marcel, *The Gift: The Form and Reason for Exchange in Archaic Societies* (London: Routledge, 1990)
Macbeth, Helen, *Food Preferences and Taste: Continuity and Change* (Oxford: Berghahn, 1997)
McCracken, Grant, *Culture and Consumption: New Approaches to the Symbolic Character of Consumer Goods and Activities* (Bloomington: Indiana University Press, 1991)
McDonald, Nathaniel, *Not Bread Alone: The Uses of Food in the Old Testament* (Oxford: Open University Press, 2008)
Mennell, Stephen, Anne Murcott and Annake Van Otterloo, *The Sociology of Food: Eating, Diet and Culture* (London: Sage, 1993)
Merleau-Ponty, Maurice, *Phenomenology of Perception* (London: Routledge, 2005)
———. *The Visible and the Invisible* (Evaston: Northwestern University Press, 1968)
Millstones, Erik, *The Atlas of Food: Who Eats What, Where and Why* (London: Earthscan, 2008)
Minh-ha, Trinh T., *Woman, Native, Other: Writing, Postcoloniality and Feminism* (Indianapolis: Indiana University Press, 1989)

Mintz, Sydney, *Tasting Food, Tasting Freedom: Excursions into Eating, Culture, and the Past* (Boston: Beacon Press, 1996)

Mitchell, William Frank, *African American Food Culture* (Westport: Greenwood, 2009)

Montanari, Massimo *Food is Culture* (Irvington: Columbia University Press, 2006)

Montgomery, Maxine Lavon 'Authority, Multivocality, and the New World Order in Gloria Naylor's *Bailey's Café.*' *African American Review* 29.1 (1995): 27–33

Morgan, David, *Family Connections: An Introduction to Family Studies* (Cambridge: Polity, 1996)

Nestle, Marion, *Food Politics: How the Food Industry Influences Nutrition and Health* (Berkeley: University of California Press, 2007)

Neuhaus, Jessamyn, *Manly Meals and Mom's Home Cooking: Cookbooks and Gender in Modern America* (Baltimore: John Hopkins University Press, 2003)

Norman, Hope and Louise Simon, eds., *Louisiana Entertains: Official Cookbook* (Memphis: Wimmer Brothers, 1984)

Orbach, Susie, *Fat is a Feminist Issue* (London: Arrow, 1989)

Otnes, Per, 'What Do Meals Do?', in *Palatable Worlds: Sociocultural Food Studies*, ed. by Elisabeth L. Fürst (Oslo: Solum, 1991), pp. 97–110

Ozerszky, Josh, *Hamburger: A History* (New Haven: Yale University Press, 2008)

Packard, Vance, *The Hidden Persuaders* (Harmondsworth: Penguin, 1960)

Parker, Emma, '"Apple Pie" Ideology and the Politics of Appetite in the Novels of Toni Morrison', *Contemporary Literature* 39.1 (1998): 614–643

Pendergrast, Mark, *For God, Country and Coca-Cola*, 2nd Ed. (New York: Basic Books, 2000)

Piatti-Farnell, Lorna, 'The Delicious Side of the Story' in *The Richard and Judy Book Club Reader*, ed. by Helen Cousins and Jenni Ramone (Aldershot: Ashgate, 2011).

Plath, Sylvia, *Letters Home: Correspondence 1950–1963* (London: Faber and Faber, 1975)

Pleck, Elizabeth, 'The Making of the Domestic Occasion: The History of Thanksgiving in the United States', *Journal of Social History* 32.4 (1999):773–789

Ploski, Harry A., and James Williams, *The Negro Almanac: A Reference Work on the African American* 5th Ed. (Gale Research: Detroit, 1989)

Pollan, Michael, *In Defence of Food: The Myth of Nutrition and the Pleasures of Eating* (London: Allen Lane, 2008)

Potter, David, *People of Plenty: Economic Abundance and the American Character* (Chicago: University of Chicago Press, 1954)

Price, Janet and Margrit Shildrick, 'Mapping the Colonial Body: Sexual Economies and the State of Colonial India' in *Gender and Colonialism*, ed. by Timothy Foley, Lionel Pilkington, Sean Ryder and Elizabeth Tilley (Galway: Galway University Press, 1995), pp. 86–102

Purvis, Thomas L., *A Dictionary of American History* (Oxford: Blackwell, 1999)

Randall, Margaret, *Hunger's Table: Women, Food and Politics* (Watsonville: Papier-Mache Press, 1997)

Rashkin, Esther, *Family Secrets and the Psychoanalysis of Narrative* (Princeton: Princeton University Press, 1992)

Renner, H.D., *The Origin of Food Habits* (London: Faber, 1944)

Ritivoi, Andreea Deciu, *Yesterday's Self: Nostalgia and the Immigrant Identity* (Oxford: Rowman & Littlefield, 2002)

Ritzer, George, *The McDonaldization of Society* (London: Pine Forge Press, 2004)

Root-Bernstein, Robert and Michele, *Honey Mud Maggots and Other Medical Marvels* (London: Macmillan, 1999)

Said, Edward, *Orientalism* (London: Penguin, 2003)
Sanday, Peggy Reeves, *Cannibalism as a Cultural System* (Cambridge: Cambridge University Press, 1986)
Saunders, Peter 'The Meaning of "Home" in Contemporary English Culture', *Housing Studies* 4.3 (1989): 177–192
Sceats, Sarah, *Food, Consumption and the Body in Contemporary Women's Fiction* (Cambridge: Cambridge University Press, 2004)
Schlosser, Eric, *Fast Food Nation: What the All-American Meal is Doing to the World* (London: Penguin, 2002)
Schofield, Mary Anne, ed., *Cooking by the Book: Food in Literature and Culture* (Madison: Popular Press, 1989)
Seremetakis, Nadia, 'The Breast of Aphrodite' in *The Taste Culture Reader: Experiencing Food and Drink*, ed. by Carolyn Korsmeyer, (Oxford: Berg, 2005), pp. 297–303
———. ed., *The Senses Still: Perception and Memory as Material Culture in Modernity* (Chicago: University of Chicago Press, 1996)
Sewell, Barbara, *The Lost Art of Pie Making Made Easy* (Asheville: Native Ground, 2004)
Schneider, Dorothy and Carl Schneider, *Slavery in America: From Colonial Times to the Civil War*, (New York: Facts on File, 2000)
Shange, Ntozake, *If I Can Cook You Know God Can* (Boston: Beacon Press, 1998)
Shapiro, Anna, *A Feast of Words: For Lovers of Food and Fiction* (New York: Norton, 1996)
Silverstein, Brett, *Cost of Competence: Why Inequality Causes Depression, Eating Disorders and Illness in Women* (New York: Oxford University Press, 1995)
Skubal, Susannah, *Word of Mouth: Food and Fiction after Freud* (London: Routledge, 2002)
Snodgrass, Mary Ellen, *Encyclopaedia of Feminist Literature* (New York: Facts on File, 2006)
Steel, Carolyn, *Hungry City: How Food Shapes our Lives* (London: Chatto & Windus, 2008)
Steinberg, Stephen, 'Bubbie's Challah' in *Eating Culture*, ed. by Ron Scapp and Brian Seitz (Albany, State University of New York Press, 1998), pp. 295–297
Stuart, Susan, 'From the Museum of Touch' in *Material Memories: Design and Evocation*, ed. by Marius Kwint, Christopher Breward and Jeremy Aynsley (Oxford: Berg,1999), pp. 17–36
Sutton, David, *Remembrance of Repasts: An Anthropology of Food and Memory* (Oxford; Berg, 2006)
———. 'Synaesthesia, Memory, and the Taste of Home' in *The Taste Culture Reader: Experiencing Food and Drink*, ed. by Carolyn Korsmeyer (Oxford: Berg, 2005), pp. 304–316
Tannahill, Reay, *Food in History* (London: Penguin, 1988)
Tansey, Geoff and Tony Worsley, The *Food System* (London: Earthscan, 1995)
The Holy Bible, Modern Version
Theophano, Janet, *Eat My Words: Reading Women's Lives Through The Cookbooks They Wrote* (New York: Palgrave, 2002)
Thirsk, Joan, *Food in Early Modern England: Phases, Fads, Fashions* (London: Hambledon Continuum, 2007)
Todd, Janet, *Feminist Literary History: A Defence* (Cambridge: Polity, 1988)
Todhunter, E.N., 'Food Habits, Food Faddism and Nutrition', in *Food, Nutrition and Health: World Review of Nutrition and Dietetics*, 16, ed. by M. Rechcigl (Basel: Karger, 1973), pp. 186–317
Toklas, Alice B., *The Alice B. Toklas Cook Book* (New York: Perennial, 1984)

Townsend, Dabney and Carolyn Korsmeyer, 'Taste: Modern and Recent History', in *Encyclopaedia of Aesthetics*, Vol. IV, ed. by Michael Kelly (Oxford: Oxford University Press, 1998), pp. 355–362

Trubek, Amy, 'Place Matters', in *The Taste Culture Reader: Experiencing Food and Drink*, ed. by Carolyn Korsmeyer (Oxford: Berg, 2005), pp. 260–271

Turner, Patricia, *Ceramic Uncles and Celluloid Mammies: Black Images and Their Influence on Culture* (New York: Anchor Books, 1994)

Twigg, Julia, 'Vegetarianism and the Meaning of Meat', in *The Sociology of Food and Eating: Essays on the Sociological Significance of Food*, ed. by Anne Murcott (Aldershot: Gower, 1983), pp. 18–30

Visser, Margaret, *The Rituals of Dinner: The Origins, Evolutions, Eccentricities and the Meaning of Table Manners* (London: Penguin, 1996)

Walton, Lester A., 'Philly Citizen Was First Maker of Ice Cream' in *The Pittsburgh Courier*; 19 May 1928

Ward, Catherine C., 'Gloria Naylor's *Linden Hills*: A Modern Inferno', *Contemporary Literature* 28 (1987): 67–81

Warde, Alan, *Consumption, Food and Taste: Culinary Antinomies and Commodity Culture* (London: Sage, 1997)

Warde, Alan and Lydia Martens, *Eating Out: Social Differentiation, Consumption and Pleasure* (Cambridge: Cambridge University Press, 2000)

Warnes, Andrew, *Savage Barbecue: Race, Culture and the Invention of America's First Food* (Athens: University of Georgia Press, 2008)

Watson, James and Melissa Caldwell, eds., *The Cultural Politics of Food and Eating: A Reader* (London: Wiley Blackwell, 2004)

Williams-Forson, Psyche A., (Chapel Hill: The University of North Carolina Press, 2006)

Witt, Doris, 'From Fiction to Foodways: Working at the Intersections of African American Literary and Cultural Studies' in *African American Foodways: Explorations of History and Culture*, ed. by Anne L. Bower (Urbana: University of Illinois Press, 2009), pp. 101–125

Wood, Roy, *The Sociology of the Meal* (Edinburgh: Edinburgh University Press, 1995)

Woods Logue, Alexandra, *The Psychology of Eating and Drinking* (London: Routledge, 2004)

Wright, Theodore P., 'The Identity and Changing Status of Former Elite Minorities: Contrasting Cases of North Indian Muslims and American WASPs' in *Rethinking Ethnicity*, ed. by Eric P. Kauffmann (London and New York: Routledge, 2004), pp. 31–39

Xu, Wenying, *Eating Identities: Reading Food in Asian American Literature* (Honolulu: University of Hawaii Press, 2008)

Young, Iris Marion, *Justice and the Politics of Difference* (Princeton: Princeton University Press, 1990)

Yuan, Yuan, 'The Semiotics of "China Narrative" in the Con/Texts of Kingston and Tan' in *Ideas of Home*, ed. by Geoffrey Kain (East Lansing: Michigan State University Press, 1997), pp. 157–170

Zronik, John Paul, *Salt* (New York: Crabtree, 2004)

Index

A
abjection 6, 110; and race 111–112
Abu-Jaber, Diana 6, 125; *Crescent* 126–132, 132, 151; *The Language of Baklava* 105, 125, 127, 151
advertising 7, 15, 28; and Coca-Cola 37–40; and Western ideology 40, 57; and racial politics 60
African American: 57, 64, 152; fiction trends 4, 5–6; ice cream history 30–31; Southern assumptions of 58–62; food 78–104
African traditions 84, 87, 88, 89
Alabama 55, 56, 58, 63, 153
American culinary, The 2–3, 154–155
'American food' 82, 97, 99; and culinary distinction 106, 107, 109, 110, 114, 151
ante-bellum 82, 101
anthropology 1, 7, 10, 11, 11–15, 93, 133
appetite: consumer appetites 47, 154; cultural appetite and food books 154
apprenticeship: and culinary memory 129, 135–138, 143
Arab-American 126, 130; see also Iraqi-American
Asian American: fiction and food 105–106, 116
Aunt Jemima 59, 60, 64
authenticity: and traditional foods 5, 14, 71, 116, 118–120, 123–126

B
barbecue 11, 33, 154; and African Americans 97–102
Barthes, Roland 12, 41
Baudrillard, Jean 15, 47

beef 19–21, 33–34, 100, 131, 150
Bell, David and Gill Valentine, 22, 25, 41, 43, 53, 54, 74, 125, 151, 155
body 1, 7, 8, 9, 13, 15, 41, 57, 63, 64, 96; and pollution 112–114; techniques of the body 127; and culinary knowledge 134–136, 149, 150
Bourdieu, Pierre 13, 110
Boym, Svetlana 130

C
café 55–63, 102–104
Cajun 65, 67, 73; history 65–66; cuisine 66, 68, 70–72, 74–75; coffee 72–73; French patois 67; class 68
Campbell, Bebe Moore, *Brothers and Sisters* 78
candy 28, 79, 81
cannibalism/cannibal 10, 40, 48, 63–64, 150
capitalism/capitalist 15, 16, 37, 38, 39, 40, 41, 44, 50, 57, 78, 80, 150, 152, 154
Carney, Judith 87, 88, 89
Charles, Nicky and Marion Kerr 11, 20, 57
China (country) 116, 119, 122–123, 140
china (crockery) 20, 22, 86, 101
Chinatown (San Francisco) 121
Chinese-American 4, 116–117, 120–121
Chinese food 117–118, 121–124, 151
chocolate 11, 48–50, 79
Christianity 107
Civil Rights Movement 27, 76–77

clay-eating, see geophagy
Coca-Cola 5, 35–40
coffee 72–73, 126, 141, 145
colonialism: Spanish conquest 49; and cannibalism 64; and the barbecue 100–101; and French food politics 106–114, 118, 151
collard greens 53, 62, 76, 77, 98
commodity 13–14, 109, 149; and race 78, 80–82 commodity culture15, 38, 41, 46–47, 57, 152; 'commodity bulimia' 154–155
community 12, 14, 25, 35, 55–57, 60, 65–67, 74, 77, 79, 81, 84, 91, 102, 105, 108, 110, 116, 121, 123, 126, 133, 136–137, 147, 150–151
consumerism 5, 14–16, 33, 37–39, 41, 44, 47–50, 57, 60, 110, 150
cooking 4, 7, 11–12, 17, 66; and gender 10–11, 19–25; and display 40–41; and racial divisions 27, 58–62, 82, 150
corn/corn products 53, 63, 74, 77, 83, 84, 98
crayfish/crawfish 66–72
crypt 145–146
cuisine 2, 3, 5, 6, 12, 14, 41, 47, 147; and region 53–55, 59, 65, 66, 70–72, 77; African American: 77–78, 86, 88, 89, 98, 100; and immigrant identity 105, 106, 108, 109, 113, 131, 133; and tradition 116, 118, 120, 123–124, 146
cultural assimilation 2, 3, 6, 54, 89, 125–126, 131, 142, 154
cultural materialism 7, 15–17, 38
cake 11, 23; ash cakes 83, 84, 98; *strucla* 141–146

D
De Certeau, Michel 15, 16
Debord, Guy 47
Depression era 55–56, 60, 61
De Rosa, Tina, *Paper Fish* 105
DeVault, Marjorie 1, 21, 23, 25
dinner 18, 22–24, 112, 117, 123, 150; Sunday dinner 19–21; and display 40–42, 46, 48
display: and food 40–44, 47, 50, 110
Douglas, Mary 13; and Baron Isherwood 14, 15

E
eating disorders 95–96
eating habits 2, 3, 6, 12, 14, 15–16, 22, 53–54, 66, 71, 74, 77, 83, 84, 88, 97–98, 105
Eighties, The 40, 42, 46, 48, 50, 52, 92, 104
Ellis, Brett Easton 5; *American Psycho* 40–51, 52, 150
ethnicity 1, 2–4, 6, 12, 14, 15, 21, 27, 30, 56, 62–68, 72, 75, 76–78, 87–89, 94, 97, 99, 101–106, 121–123, 125, 130, 141–142, 147, 149, 150, 152
Europe/European 26, 28, 29, 30, 49, 50, 87, 98, 100

F
family 6, 11, 16, 74, 117–118, 127–128, 133–134; and kitchen politics 19–25, 28, 32, 42, 51–52; and culinary traditions 137–39, 142–146
Flagg, Fannie 5, 65; *Fried Green Tomatoes at the Whistle Stop Cafe* 55–64, 82, 103, 150, 151, 152, 153, 154
fortune cookies 122–123
Foucault, Michel 44
Freud, Sigmund 9, 10, 11, 39, 83, 93, 94, 96
Franzen, Jonathan, *The Corrections* 18
fruit salad 50–52
Funderburg, Anne 29, 32

G
gender roles 11, 19, 21–25
geophagy 83–84
gift 91, 138
globalisation/global 1, 3, 4, 54, 77, 102, 154, 155
Grosz, Elizabeth 7, 9, 10
Gutierrez, Paige 65, 66, 68, 72

H
hands: eating with 131–132; cooking with one's 134–136
hamburger 4, 33–35, 124, 152
Harris, Joanne 93
history: American 2–5, 26, 27; of ice cream 30–31, 33; of hamburgers 33; a sense of the past 36–37, 50, 71; Southern 57, 62, 63, 67;

African American 6, 64, 76–104; of salt 108, 114–115; and culinary habits 134–135, 138–139, 146–148
Hobbes, Thomas 113
home 4, 16, 18–42, 50–51, 70, 73–75, 126–127, 129, 130, 132, 151
homosexuality 107
hunger 6, 7, 127; and African Americans 79, 81–82
hyphenated American 6, 147–148

I

ice cream 18, 20, 27–33, 35, 56, 59, 152,
immigration/immigrant: and American history 2–3, 4, 147; and literature 4, 6, 105, 115; and food practices 112, 116, 121, 122–123, 125–130, 138, 146; and culinary Americanisation 137, 140
Indochina 109, 112
introjection (Freudian)11, 81, 83, 145
Iraq: memory of 127–128, 130–131; Iraqi recipes 128–129
Iraqi-American 126, 127–129, 131–132
Italian-American writers, 4, 105

J

Jameson, Fredric 149, 154
Jones, Edward P. 6, 82; *The Known World* 82–85

K

kitchen 11, 92, 95; kitchen philosophy in the Sixties 24; and domestic labour 23, 24; as a racialised site of labour 58, 60–62, 64, 82, 96; associations with motherhood 69; and colonial politics 108, 109, 115; as familiar space 128, 129; as female domain 132–133, 136, 138, 139, 141
Kristeva, Julia 10, 110, 112
Ku Klux Klan 56, 57

L

lamb 90, 131
Lévi-Strauss, Claude 12
Lorde, Audre 82
Louisiana 53, 65–75, 80
Lupton, Deborah 12, 13, 14, 15, 16, 17, 41, 42, 56, 105, 108, 112

M

mammy 58–61, 64
magic: and consumer experiences 41; and recipes 85–94
magical realism 93
Marx, Karl 47, 57, 80
masturbation 83
Mauss, Marcel 91
McCracken, Grant 15
Merleau-Ponty, Maurice 7, 8, 9, 69
meal 18; as structure 13; home meals 19–25, 33, 40–42; restaurant meals 16, 42–47, 50–52
meat 5, 19–21, 24, 26, 34, 41, 46, 98, 100, 126; and men 11, 20
melting pot, the (metaphor) 2–3
memory 14, 40, 54, 56–57, 62, 64, 149, 151–153; and the senses 69–71; and history 87, 91, 104; and culinary experience 125–130, 134, 136–137, 142–148
men 11–12, 138–139
middle-class 94
Mintz, Sydney 14, 88, 100
Morrison, Toni , 6, 78–79; *Beloved* 79; *Jazz* 79; *Sula* 79; *Song of Solomon* 79; *The Bluest Eyes* 81–82
mothers: and love 11, 117–118; and cooking duties 21–26; and daughters 68–75, 120, 123–124, 129, 140–147; motherland 112–113;
multiculturalism 2–4
mysticism 70, 72, 73, 89–90, 92, 93–94, 96, 103

N

Naylor, Gloria 6, 78, 152, 153; *Linden Hills* 94–97; *Bailey's Café* 97–104
New York 18, 40, 53, 90
Nineties, The 46, 50, 52, 104
nostalgia 6, 147, 152, 154; and American food icons 28, 31, 35, 38, 39, 52; and the post-bellum period 59; and immigrant culinary identity 125–132; restorative nostalgia 130; reflective nostalgia 131
nurturing 21, 23, 59, 79, 81

O

oral stage 83
Orientalism 111, 121–124

Index

overeating 59, 95

P

pancakes 4, 59, 122
phenomenology 7–9, 69
phobias 96
pie 4, 25–27, 29, 53, 79, 82
Pietrzyk, Leslie 6; *Pears on a Willow Tree* 132–148, 150, 151, 154
Plath, Sylvia 39
Polish-American 132–133, 135–139, 140–144, 146, 151
poppy seeds 141, 142
post-bellum 31, 36, 98
psychoanalysis 9–10, 39, 83, 145

R

race 58, 64, 77, 90, 97–102
recipes 14, 26, 45, 58, 60, 78, 85–103, 128, 129, 130, 133, 137, 142–146, 152, 154
region 1, 26, 31, 53–75
restaurant 5, 16, 18, 33, 42–48, 50–52, 77, 78, 109, 120–122, 150
repression 96
rice 24; and African Americans 76, 84, 88, 90
Ritivoi, Andreea Deciu 127, 129, 131
Robinson, Marylinne 5; *Gilead* 19; *Home* 19–21, 52, 150

S

Said, Edward 111, 123
salad bowl, the (metaphor) 2, 3
salt 103, 106, 114, 115; in Judeo-Christian symbolism 107; and Vietnamese/French history 107–108
San Francisco 116, 118, 120, 121
self, the 8–9, 15–17, 42–44, 48, 52, 59, 78, 79–82, 85–86, 87, 89, 90–91, 95–96, 106, 109, 111–112, 117, 129, 132, 142
Seremetakis, Nadia 129, 130, 136, 143
sexuality 83, 84, 149
Shange, Ntozake 6, 78, 85, 152, 153; *Sassafrass, Cypress and Indigo* 86–94, 103, 104; *for coloured girls who have considered suicide/when the rainbow is enuf* 85; *If I Can Cook/ You Know God Can* 76
sisterhood: and culinary heritage 91–92

slavery 59, 62, 63, 64, 76, 78, 82, 88, 89, 98, 101, 152
smell (senses) 8–9, 19, 20, 69- 72, 88, 100, 105, 107, 129, 145, 147
social class 1, 5, 105, 149; and taste 13; and the body 15; and ideal meals 24; and the history of ice cream 29, 30, 33; and African Americans 97–99
soil-eating, see geophagy
soul food 6, 62, 76–77, 86–88, 97, 152
Southern: literature 5, 55, 58, 59; history 56–57, 84; cuisine 58–59, 60, 62, 76, 98, 100, 151
starvation 95
stereotypes 18, 27, 29, 59, 64, 76, 81–82, 84, 103, 121–122, 139, 150
Stolz, Karen, 5; *World of Pies* 21–40, 50–52, 55, 152
sugar: and ice cream 29, 30; and African Americans 79–82
surveillance society 42, 44–45, 48, 50
sushi 40–41

T

Tan, Amy 6; *The Joy Luck Club* 116–125, 151, 153
taste (gustatory) 8–10, 13, 16, 34, 38, 57, 69–72, 98, 100, 105, 115, 127, 132, 147, 153
taste (social) 13, 30, 42, 45, 102, 106, 109, 110, 119
technology 14, 30, 39, 47, 132; and food preparation 134, 135–137
terroir, goût du 71
Texas 21, 53, 152
tradition 68, 72, 86; culinary 4, 5, 6, 14, 21, 26, 29, 54, 57, 60, 67, 76, 78, 84, 85, 87, 89, 98, 100, 101, 102, 116–125, 126, 133, 135–144, 147, 153, 154, 155
touch (senses) 8, 46, 105, 127; and eating 131–132; and cooking 134–138
Truong, Monique 6, 116, 118, 131; *The Book of Salt* 105–116, 147

V

Vietnam War 28, 31, 32, 114–115
Vietnamese food: and French colonialism 108 -111, 113; and salt, 107–108
voodoo 63, 64

W

Warde, Alan 14, 51, 110, 116, 119, 121, 124
Wells, Rebecca, 5, 151; *Divine Secrets of the Ya-Ya Sisterhood* 65–75, 153, 154
Witt, Doris 4, 77, 78
Wolfe, Tom, *Bonfire of the Vanities* 18; and *American Psycho* 46
women 56–57, and cooking 10–11, 20–23, 25, 136–139; and African American typecasting 59, 62–63, 82; and African American food 85–87, 104; and domestic history 91, 93–95, 117, 133; and eating disorders 95–96; and colonial politics 112–113; and family connections 142–144; as food writers 153–154
working-class 24, 82, 97

Y

yuppie 18, 40, 52, 150

Printed in Great Britain
by Amazon